STUDIES IN LAW, POLITICS, AND SOCIETY

STUDIES IN LAW, POLITICS, AND SOCIETY

Series Editor: Austin Sarat

Volumes 1–2:   Edited by Rita J. Simon

Volume 3:   Edited by Steven Spitzer

Volumes 4–9:   Edited by Steven Spitzer and Andrew S. Scull

Volumes 10–16:   Edited by Susan S. Sibey and Austin Sarat

Volumes 17–33:   Edited by Austin Sarat and Patricia Ewick

Volumes 34–44:   Edited by Austin Sarat

STUDIES IN LAW, POLITICS, AND SOCIETY

EDITED BY

AUSTIN SARAT

Department of Law, Jurisprudence & Social Thought and Political Science, Amherst College, USA

Emerald

JAI

United Kingdom – North America – Japan
India – Malaysia – China

JAI Press is an imprint of Emerald Group Publishing Limited
Howard House, Wagon Lane, Bingley BD16 1WA, UK

First edition 2008

Copyright © 2008 Emerald Group Publishing Limited

Reprints and permission service
Contact: booksandseries@emeraldinsight.com

British Library Cataloguing in Publication Data
A catalogue record for this book is available from the British Library

ISBN: 978-1-84855-090-2
ISSN: 1059-4337 (Series)

Awarded in recognition of
Emerald's production
department's adherence to
quality systems and processes
when preparing scholarly
journals for print

INVESTOR IN PEOPLE

CONTENTS

LIST OF CONTRIBUTORS

Scott W. Barclay	Political Science, University at Albany, SUNY
Katherine Beckett	Department of Sociology and Law, Societies and Justice Program
Angelina Godoy	Law, Societies, and Justice, University of Washington
M. Catherine Gruber	Linguistics, University of Chicago
Ruthy Lazar	Osgoode Hall Law School, York University
Randy Lippert	Department of Sociology, University of Windsor
Jody Lyneé Madeira	Law, Indiana University
Grace Park	Osgoode Hall Law School, York University
William J. Phelan, IV	Law, American Bar Association
Gerald Turkel	Department of Sociology and Criminal Justice University of Delaware
Gabriela Wasileski	Department of Sociology and Criminal Justice University of Delaware
Patricia J. Woods	Political Science, University of Florida

EDITORIAL BOARD

ix

PART I:
ON SENTENCING AND PUNISHMENT

RECONCEPTUALIZING VICTIMIZATION AND AGENCY IN THE DISCOURSE OF BATTERED WOMEN WHO KILL

Ruthy Lazar

ABSTRACT

The ways in which battered women respond to domestic violence, and the ways the legal system constructs those responses, constitute the framework of this chapter. The analysis focuses on mitigation in sentences of battered women who killed their abusers and examines the manifestation of agency and victimization in the mitigation structure. My thesis is that these women are perceived by courts solely as victims who lack agency and autonomy. Three main themes emerge from the analysis: first, the courts focus on the mental state of the defendants, stressing their psychological deficiencies as the primary mitigating factors. Secondly, many cases are categorized by courts as unique cases. Thirdly, in several cases the courts portray the women as "victims of circumstances". An alternative analysis to that offered by the courts, one that seeks to reframe the mitigation process, is introduced in this chapter. According to this analysis, the narrative used in cases of battered women who kill should be changed to reflect dimensions of agency and resistance. In the suggested discourse, the abuse these women suffer is acknowledged, but is

Studies in Law, Politics, and Society, Volume 45, 3–45
ISSN: 1059-4337/doi:10.1016/S1059-4337(08)45001-9

used to explain the women's urge to self-preservation and thus, the rationality and reasonableness of their acts.

INTRODUCTION

'Gender-based violence is perhaps the most widespread and socially tolerated of human rights violations' (United Nation Population Fund, 2005). Violence directed at women by their intimate partners is an acute social problem in our society. It has been estimated that nearly three in ten Canadian women who have ever been married or lived in a common-law relationship have been physically or sexually assaulted by a marital partner at some point during the relationship (Chewter, 2003).[1]

The ways in which women respond to domestic violence, and the ways the legal system constructs those responses, constitute the framework of this chapter. The discussion will focus on the unique situation within the criminal justice system of battered women who kill their violent male partners,[2] and how the justice system perceives these women and deals with their acts of killing.

The analysis will focus on sentencing of battered women who killed their abusers or other men and were convicted of manslaughter. More specifically, mitigating factors that affect the sentences of these women, such as the abuse they suffered, will be examined. The goal of the analysis is to examine the way these mitigating factors are placed with respect to different conceptions of women's agency.

The main thesis is that these women are perceived by courts solely as victims who lack agency and autonomy. The common narrative in the mitigation of the sentences is the mental state of the women, which is perceived as a product of the abuse they suffered at the hands of their abusers. Although considering the abuse as a factor in the sentencing decisions is a positive step within the criminal justice system towards achieving equality for battered women who kill, associating it solely with women's psychological deficiencies, and describing it using notions of victimization, creates serious difficulties for battered women.

One of the implications of such a paradigm may be the formation of a rigid dichotomy between women who 'deserve' the sympathy of the courts (women who are perceived as victims) and women who do not deserve it (women who are perceived as agents). Another is the reinforcement of the stereotypical image of battered women as passive, submissive and psychologically defective. In depicting the women as victims, the approach of the courts obscures any aspects of resistance and choice these women may have demonstrated in their acts and further creates a superficial distinction between victimization and agency and between oppression and resistance.

The Impetus for Doing the Research

Several feminist commentators have argued that the introduction of the Battered Woman Syndrome (hereinafter referred to as BWS) in the case of *R. v. Lavalle* (1990) did not generate a 'a rash of acquittals' as expected (Sheehy, 2001, p. 533), but rather created greater willingness on the part of the judiciary and the courts in such cases to facilitate guilty pleas to manslaughter and impose lenient sentences (Shaffer, 1997, p. 18).

In light of this observation, the 'sentencing phase' in cases of battered women who kill merits further exploration. Additionally, there has been limited academic attention aimed at studying the sentencing of battered women who kill in Canada. This chapter is aimed at further closing this gap in research.

By exploring this topic, two goals can be achieved. First, analysis of sentencing decisions can serve as a tool for developing a consistent sentencing model that responds to the characteristics of battered women who kill and to their legal needs. Secondly, the sentencing phase is an essential component to be explored in order to achieve equality within the legal system for these women.

As a background to the analysis, I provide a three-part preface, beginning with an examination of the doctrine of self-defence and the constraints it created for battered women who killed their abusers. I then look at the development of BWS while describing its nature and the goals it aimed to achieve. I conclude the preface by briefly presenting the case of *Lavallee*, in which the Supreme Court of Canada acknowledged, for the first time, the admissibility of expert evidence on BWS. The various distortions of the testimony on BWS and the feminist critique of the way it is used in courts are discussed in the second part of the chapter.

Questions of agency and victimization in the discourse of battered women who kill constitute part three of the chapter. Here, I will use feminist' theories of agency and victimization and look at the legal image of battered women and its relation to the dichotomy of victimization and agency.

In the fourth part of the chapter, I analyze sentencing decisions handed out to battered women who killed their abusers or other men and were convicted of manslaughter, while examining how the sentences were mitigated and how this fits with different conceptions of women's agency. As an introduction to this section, I briefly present the sentencing framework of the offence of manslaughter, along with a general discussion of sentencing, in Canada.

SELF-DEFENCE AND THE EVOLUTION OF BWS

The Doctrine of Self-Defence and its Implications for Battered Women Who Kill Their Abusers

Studies have revealed that when a woman kills a man, the most common precursor to the event is the abuse the woman experienced by this man. Prior to the introduction of BWS in the case of *Lavallee*, battered women who killed used several defences, among them provocation, insanity and self-defence. The doctrine of self-defence operates as a justification for the act and, as such, can secure an acquittal. An examination of this defence constitutes the main focus of this part of the chapter.

Although the law of self-defence is argued to be universally applicable and is perceived as being neutral and objective, it is widely recognized that the doctrine was developed solely in the context of male reaction to violence and was shaped by male social conceptions of justification (Stubbs & Tolmie, 1994, pp. 192–193, 195). Consequently, before the introduction of BWS, women who were on trial for killing their abusers faced substantial hurdles when pleading self-defence in their cases.

The law of self-defence in Canada imposes two requirements in *s.34* of the *Criminal Code*. First, the accused must act under a reasonable apprehension of suffering imminent death or bodily harm at the hands of the assailant. Secondly, the accused must believe, on reasonable grounds, that she, or he, cannot otherwise escape the danger. These requirements pose serious difficulties for battered women who kill their violent male partners. A battered woman's concept of imminence may be different from that of a man or a woman who have not been subjected to a life of abuse. The requirement of imminent danger, as interpreted by courts throughout the years, cannot reflect the complex realities of battered women, who, in the context of ongoing battering and constant abuse, may be able to anticipate the next violent act. A battered woman's perception of threat and danger is a reflection of her reality of abuse and battering and, thus, is different from that of other people. Many battered women feel they are in imminent danger and kill their abusers while the latter are sleeping, for instance, or walking away from them. According to the legal interpretation of imminent danger, these women would most probably lose their right to claim self-defence (Sheehy, Stubbs, & Tolmie, 1992, pp. 373–374).

The second element of the law of self-defence is the reasonableness of the act. This requirement presents particular problems for battered women who kill their violent partners, as these defendants find it extremely difficult to convey to a jury or a judge that their acts were reasonable. Juries often fail to comprehend the nature of abusive relationships. They cannot capture the full picture of the abuse and the terror and may, furthermore, deny the extent of it. Thus, they are often reluctant to sympathize with, or have difficulties understanding, the responses of battered women to the violence (Schneider, 1996, p. 503).

The doctrine of self-defence has traditionally looked at what an 'ordinary man' would do in such circumstances. Consequently, it did not account for differing experiences of violence and could not reflect or capture the reality of battered women. The unique characteristics of the lives of battered women – the difficulties in escaping abusive relationships; the power dynamic between the two parties; the extent of the abuse; and the constant fear of being beaten and tortured, for example – are often ignored by courts and, thus, cannot serve to explain the reasonableness of the act of killing.

Feminist scholars indicate that the failure of the law to accommodate battered women who kill their violent male partners is not based solely on the legal construction of the doctrine of self-defence. It has been argued that a systemic gender bias in the criminal justice system, and prevailing stereotypes of battered women, are also factors that explain the failure of the system to recognize women's self-defence claims (Schneider, 1996, pp. 483–485). Gender stereotypes that view women as subjective, emotional, passive and weak make it hard for battered women to be viewed as rational and reasonable actors and to claim that their resort to killing was reasonable given the circumstances of their lives.

The broader social and cultural context is also an important component in analyzing the reaction of battered women to violence. The failure of the police, the criminal justice system and other social services to provide adequate protection to battered women and to respond to their particular needs makes them particularly vulnerable to violence, and can also serve to explain the reasonableness of their act. Julie Stubbs and Julia Tolmie put it as follows:

> Their [battered women's] vulnerability to violence within an intimate relationship stems
> from well-documented social realities such as failure by police and the criminal justice

system to provide them with adequate protection, separation assault, economic
dependence or financial hardship, a crisis in refuge accommodation, a shortage of safe
and affordable housing, social isolation, a reluctance to leave children in the custody of a
violent partner and cultural constraints and pressures. (1994, p. 194)

The failure of the doctrine of self-defence to provide a proper defence to
battered women who kill their abusers in self-defence, and the reluctance of
the criminal justice system to acknowledge these acts as self-defence, led to
the introduction of BWS.

The Battered Woman Syndrome

BWS is introduced in court in the form of expert testimony seeking to
contextualize women's acts of killing. The effect, in each case, is to ensure
that the realities of battered women are heard and seen in courts and thus to
provide battered women who kill their violent male partners with equal
access to the claim of self-defence.

The testimony on BWS is based on two theoretical structures as
developed by American psychologist Lenore Walker: the cycle theory of
violence,[3] and the theory of learned helplessness[4] (Walker, 2000).

According to the cycle theory of violence, the continued nature of
domestic violence affects a woman's ability to leave a relationship or to act
against the abuser and, thus, can provide the court with the means of
understanding why some battered women do not leave abusive relationships. It depicts a woman's decision to stay with the abuser as understandable and reasonable in view of her having a psychological state induced
by repetitive abuse. BWS aims to dispute prevailing misconceptions about
domestic violence, such as the characterization of violence within the
relationship as rare; the assumption that battered women can always leave;
and the view that battered women are either exaggerating when describing
the violence or even enjoying it. By explaining the harmful effects of
continuous abuse on a woman, BWS also seeks to eliminate stereotypes of
battered women as masochistic and unreasonable actors.

Proponents of BWS perceived this evidence to be a tool that could
provide a forum for educating judges, lawyers and jurors about the
experiences of abused women and the way women are affected by this abuse.
It was aimed to provide the court with the unique circumstances and the
particular characteristics of the lives of battered women and thus, to
challenge the structure of the legal rule of self-defence; to contextualize the
experiences of battered women; to provide the jurors with the perspectives

of abused women, and consequently to achieve equality for battered women within the justice system.

The Case of Lavallee

In 1990, the Supreme Court of Canada, for the first time, acknowledged the legal relevance of evidence of BWS to the defence of self-defence in the case of a battered woman who killed her abuser.

Angelique Lyn Lavallee was charged with the second-degree murder of her common-law husband, Kevin Rust, after shooting him in the back of the head while he was leaving her bedroom. According to the evidence at trial, Rust had abused Lavallee during their relationship. Lavallee claimed to act in self-defence while relying on *s.34(2)* of the *Criminal Code*. The section specifies the criteria, as discussed earlier, for the application of the defence. At trial, the defence introduced expert evidence on BWS. Lavallee was acquitted by a jury, but the verdict was overturned by a majority of the Manitoba Court of Appeal, which sent the case back for retrial.[5] The Supreme Court of Canada upheld the trial judge's decision, arguing that the judge was right in admitting expert evidence on BWS in order to explain the reasonableness of Lavallee's act, that is, to determine whether or not she reasonably apprehended "imminent danger" and if she reasonably believed that she did not have any alternative but to use deadly force against her husband.

This was the first time that the Supreme Court acknowledged the importance of evidence on BWS, but the decision was also groundbreaking on several other accounts. Madame Justice Wilson not only accepted the role of BWS in exposing the difference between battered women who kill in self-defence and other defendants who act in self-defence, but also included the broader societal, cultural and economic context in her analysis.[6]

In spite of the feminist, comprehensive analysis introduced in *Lavallee* by the Supreme Court, feminists dealing with issues of domestic violence were concerned that the use of BWS would pose hurdles for battered women who kill (Stubbs & Tolmie, 1994, p. 388). The next section of the chapter discusses the difficulties created by the use of BWS, which support the various concerns raised by feminists.

LIMITATIONS OF BWS

Notwithstanding its contribution to the legal status of battered women who kill, BWS is not without its critics. Feminist scholars have recognized the problematic implications of relying on a syndrome to explain women's behaviour and to convey their realities in court.

The first weakness of BWS is the medicalization of violence against women and the stigmatization of battered women as ill and dysfunctional persons. On this point, it is argued that the medical terminology – that is, referring to a battered woman's situation as a 'syndrome' – is suggestive of an illness or clinical disorder. Thus, instead of normalizing the battered woman's action and constructing it as a rational reaction to the violence, BWS pathologizes women (Crocker, 1985; Schneider, 1996; Shaffer, 1997; Sheehy, 1994).[7]

An additional limitation of BWS emerges from the content of the testimony in court cases. Use of the testimony has focused on the helplessness theory, which represents the passivity of the woman. Battered women have been described as passive, as unable to respond adequately to the circumstances and, more importantly, as having no control of their actions. Thus, 'in suggesting that women's perceptions that they could not escape the violence were irrational and imaginary, battered woman syndrome implied that women remained in abusive relationships because they were too emotionally damaged to react in a "normal" way" (Shaffer, 1997, p. 11).[8] By portraying battered women as dysfunctional and irrational, and by stressing the elements of passivity and loss of control, BWS conveys the message that battered women are not reasonable actors. This image of battered women thereby undermines the actual purpose of BWS in providing such defendants with a self-defence claim that reflects the situation in which they live and act.

Another weakness of BWS is its association with victimization. Emphasizing a woman's passivity and loss of control, and focusing on her weakness and helplessness, creates a rigid dichotomy between victimization and agency, and thus structures victimization and agency as two contradictory elements. The realities of battered women, however, tell us a much more complicated story, in which oppression and resistance, and victimization and agency, coexist. Thus, 'neither victimization nor agency should be glorified, understood as static, viewed in isolation, or perceived as an individual or personal issue' (Schneider, 2000, p. 74).

Various scholars have challenged the association of battered women solely with the notion of victimization, and have described their acts as representing both agency and victimization. For these scholars, agency represents much more than the act of leaving the abuser and terminating the relationship and, thus, it is a multifaceted notion consisting of many other forms of reactions to intimate violence (Schuller, 2003, p. 233).[9]

By stressing helplessness and passivity, BWS fails to capture the complexities of the lives of battered women, and the differences between battered women. Portraying all battered women as victims, BWS reinforces uniformity when there are diverse abusive relationships; it strengthens similarity where there are different women experiencing different realities and reacting to the abuse in different ways.[10]

The rigidity of BWS, and its use to emphasize one element of a battered women's behaviour, that is, her helplessness, creates a stereotypical image of battered women and, as a result, excludes other women's stories and experiences. The exclusion of battered women who do not fit the model created by BWS is strongly exemplified in the case of marginalized groups of women, such as Black women or Aboriginal women. Because the syndrome implies that there is a typical battered woman, who is required to be helpless, passive, gentle and weak, women who are stereotypically viewed as strong, assertive and tough face hurdles convincing a jury that they acted in self-defence.[11]

A major limitation of BWS is that it overlooks the societal and cultural framework within which battered women live and act. Emphasizing the psychological characteristics of battered women shifts the focus from the objective hurdles of leaving abusive relationships to the mental 'problems' of the women. By focusing on a woman's mental condition, BWS ignores the batterer's acts, the availability of social services, economic opportunities accessible to women, lack of shelters, availability of child care arrangements, response of the police and the criminal justice system, social perceptions of family and motherhood, and so on.

A related issue is the existence of gender bias in the criminal justice system. Dominance of male-oriented legal doctrines, historic discrimination and marginalization of women in the legal arena, and stereotypes of women and of victims are all factors to be considered in cases of battered women defendants.[12]

To sum up, when BWS was first introduced, it attempted to explicate the resort of many battered women to killing their abusers by conveying their realities and experiences to the courts. An additional importance of this doctrine was the educational message it sent to society regarding domestic violence. However, as demonstrated, BWS was transformed into a stereotypical depiction of battered women, explaining their behaviour by using notions of passivity and victimization rather than contextualizing their responses and situating the reactions within a social and cultural framework. The following excerpt demonstrates this point.

The campaign to allow battered woman syndrome into court may well have begun with
the best of intentions, then, but the theory now seems to be fast becoming a straitjacket
which tries to confine the realities of battered women and domestic violence within rigid
parameters which do little to challenge society's, or the law's, understanding of spousal
abuse, women's violence, female agency and femininity itself. (Morrissey, 2003, p. 78)

Thus, as long as old norms and prejudicial perceptions of women continue to
dominate the social and legal discourse of domestic violence, the BWS will
remain a limited tool in changing the legal reality of battered women who kill.

QUESTIONS OF AGENCY AND VICTIMIZATION IN THE DISCOURSE OF BATTERED WOMEN WHO KILL

The feminist discourse of autonomy and agency has occupied various
feminist scholars from different disciplines and has resulted in a range of
scholarly works, a detailed discussion of which is beyond the scope of this
section. My purpose in introducing highlights of this discourse is to
contextualize my own analysis of cases of battered women and to situate it
within a broader theoretical framework that, hopefully, will illuminate
certain ideas and notions.

In mainstream liberal theories, societal and cultural contexts, socializa-
tion and social relations, gender aspects, and other sociological elements are
not central to the formation of the notion of autonomy and so, do not
occupy an important part of the liberal discourse of this concept.[13]

The liberal notion of autonomy was heavily criticized by feminist
philosophers and feminist political and social theorists, who have recognized
the impact of the broader societal framework on the construction of the
concept of autonomy and on the ability of individuals to make autonomous
decisions. They have challenged the rigid definition of autonomy as
developed by liberal theories, stressing the need to go beyond the traditional
liberal elements of autonomy to include social context, which for many
women is one in which oppression, racism and marginalization occur. For
feminist scholars, the societal framework in which women are socialized and
raised is an important feature to consider when structuring autonomy, since
societal values and norms, relationships and societal interactions, inequality
and racism are all factors that influence the way women act and behave.
Autonomy, for feminist scholars, is a complex idea that is influenced and
shaped by societal aspects, such as gender roles, perceptions of femininity
and masculinity, power relations, and social interaction to name some.[14]

The concept of "relational autonomy" illustrates this approach. In contrast with the traditional perspectives on autonomy, informed by liberal thinking, which focus on the individual, "relational" or "contextual" autonomy is related to a broader (oppressive) context. Relational autonomy is premised on the belief that individuals' identities, choices, decisions, feelings, and acts are reflective of social relationships and are shaped by a set of intersectional factors such as gender, race, ethnicity, religion, sexual orientation, social status, and more. Relational autonomy thus seeks to emphasize the development of autonomy as part of individuals' relationships, both intimate relationships and broader social ones.

The concept of relational autonomy is also employed by Caroline McLeod and Susan Sherwin (Sherwin, 1998). These scholars seek to explore an individual's social and economic location in order to assess the decisions made by this individual. By adopting the paradigm of relational autonomy, for McLeod and Sherwin, society will not just seek to offer more rights to women but will rather seek to change their social situations. Understanding autonomy in such a way will assist in viewing the broader framework within which decisions are made, and not only focusing on the individual state of mind.

The use of the concept of agency in this feminist discourse coincides with that of autonomy. However, some feminist scholars have made a distinction between these two concepts. Although the distinction is discussed within a discourse of health care for women, it is valuable and applicable to the discourse of violence against women. For these scholars, agency can exist where autonomy is not present. Individuals who lack autonomy due to oppression do not necessarily lack agency since they act, react and respond within oppressive conditions. Bell and Mosher, for example, in their discussion of medicine's response to wife abuse, argue that abused women are not autonomous, since they are oppressed; however they make choices between the limited available options they have and thus express agency (Bell & Mosher, 1998).

Themes of victimization and agency are central in the discussion of domestic violence in general, and of battered women in particular. As was discussed earlier, the dichotomy between agent and victim is manifested heavily in the discussion of abused women and their responses to violence.

The issue of 'exit', that is, the question of why a battered woman stays in an abusive relationship, 'colours almost every legal and social inquiry about battering' (Mahoney, 1994, p. 79). Staying in abusive relationships is perceived, and further associated by society, with victimization, with lack of agency and with incapacity to act against the abuser. Leaving, on the other hand, is viewed as an act against the violence, and thus as a product of an agent and autonomous person. On this point, Elizabeth Schneider contends: 'Women's victimization and agency are each understood to exist as the absence of the other – as if one must be either a pure victim or pure agent, when in fact they are profoundly interrelated' (2000, p. 76). Battered women's experiences have proven to be complex and, thus, the assumption that battered women can always leave overlooks the broader social framework, in which unequal power between men and women still exists. The objective difficulties in leaving abusive relationships demonstrate the above-mentioned complexity. Lack of economic opportunities, shortage of shelters and child care arrangements, lack of available social services, concern for one's children, and societal beliefs about family and marriage are elements of these difficulties and are present and alive in the lives of many battered women.

Emphasizing exit is based on a notion of agency that requires battered women to leave abusive relationships in order to demonstrate resistance. This notion thus fails to acknowledge women's varied experiences and the social contexts within which they act. A 'failure' to leave portrays the woman as a victim who does not act – who is not an agent. Martha Mahoney further explains this concept of agency.

> In our society agency and victimization are each known by the absence of the other: you are an agent if you are not a victim, and you are a victim if you are in no way an agent. In this concept, agency does not mean acting for oneself under conditions of oppression it means *being without oppression*, either having ended oppression or never having experienced it at all. (1994, p. 60)

The social expectations imposed upon battered women to leave abusive relationships, and the association of the leaving with agency, conceal the many other forms of resistance performed by battered women. To regard separation from the abuser as the only form of agency is to fail to acknowledge that battered women act in various ways against the violence, and are making choices within the context of oppression and abuse[15] (Dutton, 1993, pp. 1227–1228). Mahoney also contends that to compartmentalize battered women's acts into 'staying' and 'leaving' conceals many acts of self-assertion, such as telling the abuser to stop, seeking counselling, or making him promise not to do it again (1994, p. 84).

Although battered women cope with domestic violence through various means of resistance, these forms of action are not categorized or perceived as forms of agency as long as the women stay in the abusive relationship – as long as they 'fail' to leave. Kathy Abrams (1999) contends that the ways battered women react and cope with battering and abuse 'do not always involve explicit confrontation; therefore, they are not always recognized as forms of resistance or as manifestation of agency' (p. 883). For Abrams, however, these acts should be recognized as forms of agency or, as she terms them, forms of 'self-direction'[16] (1999, p. 834).

According to the notions of autonomy and agency as constructed by liberal theories, acts such as gathering information, funds and support from family and friends, protecting the children from the abuser, going to counselling, or trying to work on the relationship will not be recognized by society as forms of agency. However, these responses should be contextualized and understood as part of a broader system of social and political inequality. Here, employing the analysis that distinguishes autonomy from agency, as discussed by Sherwin, Mosher and Bell, may serve to dismantle the false dichotomy between agency and victimization that prevents battered women from being perceived as agents who are making reasonable and rational choices. By doing so, a more inclusive account of women's agency will be conveyed and more forms of behaviour will be encompassed by this notion.

Equating exit from abusive relationships with agency also ignores the fact that many battered women do leave the abuser. In a study on women's help-seeking behaviours, it was found that more than 70% of the battered women had left home at some time in response to violence (Mahoney, 1991, p. 61). However, as mentioned earlier, lack of external help, such as availability of shelters or child care arrangements, prevents many women from successfully separating from the abuser and escaping the violence. Thus, as long as the efforts of battered women to leave their relationships are not 'successful', these efforts are not recognized by society as forms of resistance or struggle, and the women are still viewed as helpless and passive.

The association of victimization with staying with the abuser implies that women can always leave. Furthermore, it ignores the important fact that battered women who leave, or have decided to leave their abusers, are being exposed to greater danger to their lives. 'Separation assault' is a term coined by Martha Mahoney to describe the escalation in the violence inflicted on an abused woman who leaves or attempts to leave her abuser. According to this notion, when a battered woman leaves or decides to leave an abusive relationship, the quest of the abuser for control over the woman is at risk. Mahoney puts it as follows: '[The attack on the woman] is an attempt to gain, retain, or regain power in a relationship, or to punish the woman for ending the relationship. Thus, the abuser's violence becomes more severe, more dangerous and often lethal' (1991, p. 68).

Stereotypes of battered women as pathological, passive, dependent and helpless also help conceal their resistance and strength and, consequently, weaken their agency. The fiction that domestic violence is rare plays a crucial role in the construction of these stereotypical images of battered women. If domestic violence is exceptional, these women are the 'others' and, thus, they are not ordinary women. They are not like 'us'.

Expert testimony on battered women, as discussed earlier, also works to strengthen these negative images. Its use in court to explain a battered woman's 'failure' to leave the relationship, and its focus on the psychological elements of the woman's behaviour – her incapacity to escape the abuser, and her passivity and helplessness – portrays the woman solely as victim and overshadows other forms of resistance this woman may have shown in the course of the relationship.

Studies on the way battered women defendants are perceived by the judiciary suggest that these women are not viewed as actors or agents, but solely as victims. Martha Shaffer, for example, analyzed the post-*Lavallee* cases in Canada in which women who were charged with a criminal offence had raised BWS as part of their defence or as a mitigating factor in sentencing (Shaffer, 1997). Although not representative, her analysis suggests that battered women are expected to show a passive behaviour and 'to be devoid of autonomy, and thus, incapable of taking any independent action' (Shaffer, 1997, pp. 19, 33).

Notions of agency and autonomy are also discussed in a PhD work on the legal treatment within the Australian Criminal Justice System of battered women who kill (Bradfield, 2002, unpublished). As part of her research, the author analyzes sentencing decisions in cases of battered women convicted of killing their violent partners. Describing the analysis and findings is beyond the scope of this chapter; however, several important themes that are introduced in the research are relevant to my discussion and can illuminate some of the notions presented in this chapter.

Bradfield asserts that in the exercise of sentencing discretion in cases where women kill their violent partners, the court's approach to these women was based on notions of 'mercy' and 'sympathy'. This approach, although empathic to the situation of battered women who kill, raises serious difficulties for these women.

First, by constructing lenient sentencing in cases of battered women in terms of mercy, the courts characterize these cases as exceptional cases, which do not (and cannot) fit the usual mitigatory framework. That means that rather than accepting the legitimacy of the women's actions by recognizing that their acts of killing were justified under the rules of self-defence or provocation, the courts treat them as 'different' cases that require a 'different' treatment (Bradfield, 2002, p. 384). As a result, 'mercy is only offered to women who conform to the stereotype of the appropriate victim – pathological, domestic and irrational' (Bradfield, 2002, p. 344). Thus, the focus in these cases is not the problem of domestic violence and the acts battered women take to protect themselves from the batterers, but the psychological deficiencies of the women. Offering mercy and sympathy only to women who can conform to the stereotype of 'the passive helpless woman', this approach helps to obscure or undermine battered women's forms of agency (Bradfield, 2002, p. 344).

Secondly, battered women's actions are perceived by courts as part of the 'domestic violence' problem; that is, the court does not distinguish between acts of violence that represent the abuser's quest for power and control and acts of violence that are (justified) responses to abuse and battering – acts that are responses to this quest. Thus, the courts view the women's actions as being as serious and severe as all acts of violence, and this 'enables the court to make strong statements about the sanctity of human life and the seriousness of the accused's actions and then impose a non-custodial sentence in cases deemed to be "exceptional"' (Bradfield, 2002, p. 384). Using a merciful and compassionate approach to sentencing in these cases, the courts do not acknowledge the seriousness of domestic violence but instead 'compensate' the women for the abuse and the battering they have been through. Consequently, the legitimacy of their actions is not even part of the legal discussion.

The third concern about the merciful approach that Bradfield raises is that the existence of a history of violence is not treated consistently by courts. Rather than recognizing the existence of domestic violence as a mitigating factor, the conformity of the accused with the stereotypical image of a 'good' victim (pathological, unreasonable and irrational) is at the core of the judicial analysis. Thus, the woman's personality and mental problems are the key concerns of the sentencing process, rather than the seriousness of the violence (Bradfield, 2002, p. 385).

To sum up Bradfield's main contentions, it may be argued that within the merciful approach adopted by the Australian courts in sentencing battered women who kill their violent partners, the courts stress the unique and unusual circumstances of the cases in which lenient sentences are imposed. This means that every case is examined through a narrow lens, without considering the broader societal framework and the societal nature of the problem of domestic violence. The sentencing in each case, thus, is dependent on the compliance of the battered woman defendant to stereotypical notions of victimization.

Bradfield's analysis exemplifies the tendency of courts to associate battered women's reactions with notions of victimization. Perceiving battered women solely as victims and portraying them as suffering from psychological disorders, the courts provide a narrow account of agency and fail to acknowledge the variety of responses of battered women to violence.

Social science literature on women's lawbreaking links women's crime with low self-esteem[17] (Pollack, 2000). However, associating women's criminal behaviour solely with low self-esteem ignores the social and political context of women's lives. It shifts the focus from the broader societal framework, which is often characterized by racism, discrimination and sexism, to the woman herself, and places the blame for her criminality on her (problematic) mental condition (Pollack, 2000). In analyzing women's criminal behaviour in terms of low self-esteem, and thus emphasizing the women's psychological problems, this approach strengthens the women's victimization and thus, in light of the rigid dichotomy between victimization and agency, denies women's agency. On the other hand, if strength and aggression are manifested in the women's actions and agency is deemed to exist, the oppressive context within which women act and live is rendered invisible (Pollack, 2000, p. 81).

SENTENCING OF BATTERED WOMEN CONVICTED OF MANSLAUGHTER

Sentencing in Canada[18]

Sentencing in Canada, as reflected in *s.718.3(1)*, of the *Criminal Code* is discretionary, except for certain offences that require a minimum sentence. The purpose of sentencing, as presented in *s.718*, is 'to contribute, along with crime prevention initiatives, to respect for the law and the maintenance of a just, peaceful and safe society by imposing just sanctions'. The discretionary nature of sentencing requires that the judge consider mitigating and/or aggravating factors in deciding on a proper sentence; having no prior record (in the case of a first offender), offering a guilty plea and showing remorse are mitigating factors, while any former convictions, or a conviction of an abuse of a spouse are aggravating ones. A relevant section to the discussion of sentencing in general and to the discussion presented in this work in particular is *s.742.1*, which introduces the option of conditional sentencing. For offences with no minimum-penalty requirement, the court can impose imprisonment of less than two years and allow the sentence to be served in the community if satisfied that the accused poses no danger to society. As the following discussion demonstrates, in the majority of the cases introduced in this chapter, conditional sentences were offered to the defendants.

Sentencing Framework for Manslaughter

According to *s.236* of the *Criminal Code*, the punishment for manslaughter is life imprisonment.[19] The courts have consistently acknowledged that sentencing for manslaughter is a complicated task and that the range of sentences available for this offence can vary from case to case, from a lengthy period of imprisonment to a non-custodial sentence. This vast range of sentences is a product of the multiplicity of circumstances in which manslaughter can be committed. The following excerpt from *R. v. Whitteker* (2004) conveys the wide spectrum of sentencing in manslaughter convictions.

> Manslaughter, on the other hand, encompasses very many different factual scenarios. It is necessary that an unlawful act has caused death, but otherwise circumstances range from near accident to near murder… There is a vast range of sentences for the crime of manslaughter depending on the particular circumstances of a case. The various sentencing principles, which the law provides in regard to a sentence for manslaughter, may call for a very substantial period of incarceration in the range of 12 to 15 years at the one extreme and on the other end to a conditional sentence. (2004, para. 22)

Analysis

In order to examine the way themes of victimization, agency and autonomy play out in the legal discourse surrounding sentencing of abused women who kill their abusers or other men, and to further analyze the interrelations between mitigating factors and the above-mentioned notions, I searched the electronic databases (Quick Law, LexisNexis) for cases of manslaughter across Canadian jurisdictions while using certain coding interchangeably, such as battered woman syndrome; battered spouse syndrome; abuse; violence; spouse; and husband; to name some. My goal was to attain as great an inclusive and representative sample of cases as possible. However, some methodological limitations ought to be pointed out. First, an analysis of reported cases is, by its nature, not representative of all the cases that are 'out there' in the system, since many of these cases are never reported. At the same time, a qualitative research is aimed to examine a phenomenon in depth and to provide a rich and detailed account of this phenomenon. My purpose in this work was to provide the readers with a thorough analysis and an in-depth examination of the way notions of victimization and agency are manifested in sentences of battered women who kill.

In order to ensure that my sample covers the relevant reported cases, I also compared my sample to that used by Martha Shaffer in her work on the effect of *Lavallee* on women's self-defence claims.[20] The themes Shaffer drew from her analysis of the cases will be compared later on in the analysis in order to provide a richer account of the sentencing framework.

The search revealed 20 reported cases in which the women defendants were convicted of manslaughter and in which their sentences were mitigated. Three more cases were added to the sample after a comparison with Shaffer's sample of cases. Additionally, 10 more cases in which women were convicted of the manslaughter of their partners were found. However, in these cases the sentences were not mitigated and so they did not form part of the analysis.[21] From the 23 cases in which sentences were mitigated, 15 are presented in this chapter under three thematic categories, as will be discussed below. The eight additional cases do not constitute part of the analysis since the mitigation discourse in these cases did not raise themes of victimization and agency.[22]

The analysis revealed that in all 23 cases, mitigation was a central element. In the majority of the cases the sentences imposed were either conditional sentences or suspended sentences. In a few cases, where imprisonment was imposed, the sentences were also lenient, ranging from seven months to two years.

Three main themes emerge from the analysis of the 15 cases. First, while mitigating the sentences, the courts focus on the mental state of the defendants, stressing their psychological deficiencies and their passivity and helplessness as the primary mitigating factors. In most cases, the courts describe the psychological problems of the women in length, stressing the women's abnormalities as mitigating circumstances. Additionally, it seems that courts are reluctant to acknowledge the rationality in the women's acts of killing, but rather tend to construct their actions as desperate and impulsive acts derived from the mental state of the women and, thus, 'worth' being mitigated.

Secondly, many of the cases are categorized by the judges as unique cases.[23] By constructing each case as particular and distinctive, the courts deny a serious discussion of the broader societal, cultural and economic context of domestic violence. Such a discussion is significant, since it situates the women's acts of killing within a broader context and helps explain the many factors that influence these women's resort to killing. Moreover, the courts overlook the similarities between the cases, which are manifested in the abuse and the violence inflicted on the defendants by their partners. All these cases tell us the stories of abused women and portray the realities of battered women and their difficulties handling the abuse and escaping the abusive relationships. However, by taking the 'case by case' approach, the courts fail to provide an inclusive account of the lives of battered women, and as a result provide a narrow analysis of the problem of domestic violence.

Thirdly, in several cases the courts portray the women as 'victims of circumstances'. The victimization account does not necessarily focus on the mental condition of the women (as in the above-mentioned cases) but includes multiple factors, such as their history of abuse by family members; history of abuse by previous partners; poverty; racism; discrimination; divorce; and more. Notably, many of the defendants in these cases are Aboriginal women, and the courts bring their aboriginality into play by portraying them as victims of a history of colonialism and discrimination. Since Canadian courts are required to consider the history of victimization of Aboriginal offenders in sentencing decisions and to avoid imposing a sentence of incarceration when it is possible under the circumstances (*R. v. Glaude*, 1999; *s.718.2* of the *Criminal Code*), it will be problematic to regard this theme as unique to the discourse of battered women.

Construction of the Cases as Unique

In the following cases the 'uniqueness' of the case serves as a key element in the mitigation of the sentence.

In *R. v. Gatekate* (1998), the accused was charged with first-degree murder and claimed she had acted in self-defence based on the abuse and the terror she had suffered at the hands of her husband. The jury rejected her reliance upon BWS and convicted her of manslaughter. She was sentenced to a conditional sentence of two years less a day, to be served in the community.

When mitigating the sentence, the court stressed that '[t]his is *a unique case* [emphasis added] which must be looked at on its own fact basis' and thus, according to the court, the sentencing imposed could not serve as a precedent to other women who kill their husbands and seek lenient sentences. My contention is that the construction of the case as unique serves as a justification for the lenient sentence imposed. By using particular factors, such as the mental state of the accused, to mitigate the sentence, the court isolates the case from other cases where women kill their violent partners and stresses that it is not reflective of other cases. By doing so, the court can justify and legitimate the lenient sentence imposed. Consequently, the court implicitly rejects any discussion of the broader context of domestic violence, which is necessary in order to acknowledge the societal, cultural and economic factors that influence the resort of many battered women to killing.

A similar approach was taken in *R. v. Chivers* (1987), in which the accused killed her husband, was convicted of manslaughter and was given a two-year suspended sentence and probation. While mitigating the sentence, the judge stressed that this was an exceptional case in which reformation and rehabilitation were the appropriate sentencing 'answer' to the specific situation of the accused.

Notably, the judge referred to the broader context of domestic violence by discussing the lack of shelters and assistance programs for battered women. As mentioned earlier, this contextualization of the abuse is significant, since it illuminates the resort of some women to killing their spouses. By linking the killing to societal factors, this type of analysis shifts the focus from the woman's personality to the broader societal structure as a factor in her resort to killing.

Notwithstanding this analysis, the court depicted the case as having 'extremely unusual features', namely, the mental problems of the defendant. Her problematic psychological situation and her helplessness were used by the court as unique mitigating factors that distinguish this case from other cases of manslaughter.

R. v. Dunlap (1991) was also categorized by the court as an 'exceptional case'. In this case, the accused pleaded guilty to the charge of manslaughter for killing her husband and was sentenced to one year of imprisonment. The violence and the abuse inflicted on the accused constituted the key elements in constructing the case as exceptional. Similar to other 'exceptional' cases, the court structured the violence as a private issue of the accused and thus as a mitigating factor in the sentencing.

Constructing the circumstances of the defendant as distinct and unique is also exemplified in *R. v. D.E.C* (1995). In this case, the accused pleaded guilty to the killing of her husband and was convicted of manslaughter. The killing had been committed 16 years earlier and covered up by the accused. It is important to note that the judge recognized the social and political context of domestic violence and further acknowledged that violence against women and children is not a specific problem of certain people but a reflection of the inequality between women and men in our society. The judge quoted in length from *Lavallee*, and pointed out the prevalent societal attitudes of violence against women at the time of killing. However, albeit an inclusive analysis of domestic violence, the court, while mitigating the sentence, stated that 'in the *particular* and *unique* [emphasis added] circumstances of this case a suspended sentence is appropriate'.

Again, it appears that the court defined the case as unique and distinct in order to justify the lenient sentence imposed. Although the court acknowledged the broader context of the abuse, the judge overlooked the parallels between this case and other cases where battered women kill their abusers and accordingly, categorized the case as exceptional. As distinct and unique, this case was deemed as 'worth' a compassionate approach and, thus, the sentence was mitigated.

R. v. Bennett [No. 1] (1993) demonstrated a similar approach. Notably, in this case the court also offered an in-depth analysis of domestic violence and stressed the implications of domestic violence to abused women's acts of killings. The judge referred to other cases of abused women who kill their abusive partners and analyzed the circumstances of their lives which led these women to kill their partners.

Despite this analysis, the judge still stressed that this was an exceptional case where incarceration was not appropriate. Similar to the above-mentioned cases, by constructing the case as exceptional, the judge could 'allow' herself to mitigate the sentence, arguing that this specific accused did not pose any danger to society.

In *R. v. Cormier* (1974), the Nova Scotia Supreme Court upheld the trial judge's decision to deliver a suspended sentence, stating: 'The learned trial judge was obviously of the opinion that this was one of those *rare* and *exceptional* [emphasis aded] cases justifying a suspension of sentence'.

To wrap up this analysis, it seems that the courts legitimized and validated their decisions to impose lenient sentences in the above-mentioned cases by categorizing these cases as distinct and unique. Classifying the cases as different from other cases in which women kill their abusers, and stressing the distinctive circumstances of the offender and the case, the courts felt comfortable imposing lenient sentences in cases of manslaughter.

Furthermore, even in cases where the courts offered an inclusive analysis of domestic violence that contextualized the killings, and where the courts did not ignore the various themes shared by these cases, they still failed to apply this approach to the specific cases, emphasizing the particular and specific circumstances and characteristics of the defendants.

Focus on the Mental State of the Women

The second theme that emerges in the analysis of the sentencing decisions is the central role played by the mental state of the accused in the mitigating process. The courts base their decisions on the emotional condition of these women, depicting them as pathological, helpless, and suffering from various psychological problems. In many cases, the courts quote psychiatrists' testimonies in length and discuss the mental state of the women in great detail, stressing their abnormalities as mitigating circumstances.

As will be discussed later in this part, placing the mental condition of the women at the core of the mitigation analysis results in lenient sentences – a positive result for all the women discussed. However, doing so also generates a rigid and stereotypical depiction of these women as helpless victims lacking rationality or reasonableness, which can ultimately harm battered women who are charged with killing their abusers.

The courts take into account the abuse that was inflicted on the women as a factor in the sentencing decisions. Considering the abuse is in itself significant, since it acknowledges the realities of battered women and contextualizes the killing by linking it to the violence inflicted on the accused. However, the abuse is conveyed through the psychological deficiencies of the women, and is described using notions of victimization, such as passivity, helplessness, dysfunctionality, unreasonableness and lack of control. Consequently, the women are depicted as victims who lack agency or autonomy and therefore are worthy of the empathy and sympathy of the courts.

Notably, most of the defendants in these cases pleaded guilty to manslaughter for killing their abusers. This fact is important to consider, since a guilty plea serves (in all criminal cases) as a major mitigating factor in sentencing decisions. A guilty plea represents an acknowledgment of the act committed and usually is accompanied by an expression of remorse. It is obvious, therefore, and is further acknowledged by the author, that the mental problems of the defendants do not constitute the sole element in the decision to mitigate the sentences, and that other mitigating factors play out in these cases. Nevertheless, my assertion is that the psychological conditions of the defendants constitute the core part of the mitigation process and, in a way, conceal and minimize other mitigating factors, such as offering a plea of guilty, or being a first offender, conditions which are very much evident in these cases.

A further comment is required here. Convicting the defendants of manslaughter indicates that the acts of killing were not recognized by courts (or juries) as legally reasonable, since otherwise the defendants would have been acquitted on the basis of the claim of self-defence (which requires, according to the Code, that the apprehension of the imminent danger will be *reasonable* [emphasis added] and that the belief of the defendant that she cannot otherwise preserve herself from the danger will be also *reasonable* [emphasis added]).

By criticizing the stereotypical image of unreasonable and irrational women attached to the defendants by the courts in the mitigation process, I do not question whether or not conviction was proper in these cases or whether or not a plea of self-defence was more appropriate than a plea of guilty. My critique, however, focuses on the problematic dichotomy between agency and victimization that is reflected in the courts' decisions. I criticize the use of elements of irrationality and unreasonableness by the courts to portray the women solely as victims who deserve compassion. I challenge the courts' recourse to notions of victimization in order to mitigate the sentences where resistance, strength and power could have served as sufficient mitigating factors.

The discussion below is followed by an alternative analysis, which suggests a different approach to sentencing battered women who kill and may prove to be a solution to some of the problems and difficulties that emerge from the courts' approach.

In *R. v. Gatekate* (1998), which was mentioned earlier, the psychological state of the accused constituted the core of the mitigating analysis and served as a major mitigating factor. The judge described the accused by using the testimonies of three psychiatrists who testified in court. The abuse inflicted on her was conveyed through her psychological deficiencies and her dysfunctionality. Thus, by focusing on her mental state and stressing her 'problems', the court constructed the act of killing as part of the accused's psychological deficiencies and, consequently, portrayed her as a victim who due to her suffering deserved the sympathy of the court.

R. v. Drake (1995) demonstrates a similar approach. The accused was charged with the second-degree murder of her husband. She pleaded guilty to manslaughter, was given a suspended sentence, and was placed on probation for three years. Akin to the previous case, the mitigation of the sentence was based on the mental state of the accused.

The facts of the case are important to mention in light of the court's mitigating analysis. Drake suffered horrific physical, emotional and sexual abuse from her husband for more than 10 years. According to the facts of the case, she was driving the car when she saw her husband walking with another woman after he had not been home for three days when she was pregnant and caring for four children. She made a U-turn and drove up behind him. According to the evidence, the accused appeared frightened, confused and panicky at the time. The evidence also indicates that the deceased was under the effect of cocaine, that he was standing very close to the accused and that he was yelling at her with a tone of anger. There was an argument between them, during which the accused stabbed him.

The court described in detail the testimony of the psychiatrist who testified in court regarding the mental state of the accused. Using the terminology of the BWS, the accused was portrayed as a passive and helpless victim who could do nothing to stop the violence. Her act of killing, accordingly, was analyzed through notions of passivity, helplessness, and submissiveness.

In view of the abuse from which the accused had suffered, and her fear of her husband, along with the nature of the altercation between them – the way her husband stood, talked and acted, and the fact that he was under the effect of drugs – it is not clear why the court resorted to examining the psychological state of the accused in order to explain her act of killing, and thus to mitigate the sentence. Her act could well have been structured as an act of self-preservation and of standing for one's right to safety and security. Moreover, considering the court's acknowledgment that the accused felt that her husband intended to harm her during the altercation, it is not clear why her mental state constituted the key mitigating factor, rather than the reasonableness of her act.

Notably, the accused pleaded guilty to manslaughter and was convicted of this offence. That means that the judge could not declare in his decision that the killing was legally reasonable, since by doing so would have opened the door to the claim of self-defence and closed the door to a plea of guilty. By challenging the resort of the court to the woman's mental state and asserting that the reasonableness of the defendant's act and her resistance should have affected the mitigation, rather then her mental problems, I do not question the conviction or ignore the fact that self-defence was not part of the legal analysis. I do assert, however, that considering the mental condition of the accused as the major mitigating factor obscured her self-resistance, her strength, the rationality in her response to her husband's behaviour, and other elements associated with agency that could well have served as mitigating factors. The court also recognized the anger that the accused felt and the fact that she 'did something she had never done before but 'stood up' to her husband'. However, despite this statement, and the possibility of constructing her response through notions of agency and resistance, her act was depicted through her psychological deficiencies, reflecting her victimization and, accordingly, resulted in mitigation of her sentence.

R. v. Bennett [No. 1] (1993) also illustrates the way notions of victimization and agency are approached in cases of battered women. Although the judge explicitly cautioned against the formation of stereotypes of battered women as passive and helpless, she focused on the mental state of the accused while mitigating the sentence, and further stressed her psychological deficiencies. In doing so, the judge structured the abuse through the mental state of the accused, which, again, was associated with victimization.

Bennett pleaded guilty to manslaughter after killing her husband. She was sentenced to a suspended sentence and three years probation. Considering the sentence, the judge first posed the following question:

> If I accept that Ms. Bennett, in her relationship with Mr. Shaw [her husband], *could be psychologically characterized as suffering from battered woman's syndrome,* [emphasis added] I have no difficulty in imposing a non-custodial sentence. If, *on the other hand,* [emphasis added] Ms. Bennett, as Crown counsel argues, is not quite *the victim she is portrayed to be* [emphasis added] by Dr. Shane, and if her motives in killing Mr. Shaw were drunken revenge and anger, then her actions may be repeated... Ms. Bennett has to serve as an example to others in similar situations that violence cannot be resorted to, and she has to be deterred herself from reacting in a similar way.

In this account the judge clearly distinguishes between two options, which are constructed as opposite: the accused is either a victim or an agent. As a victim, she is 'required' to demonstrate psychological problems. On the other hand, if she reveals anger, she is clearly not a victim and thus, does not deserve the court's sympathy. The message conveyed by the court is that the accused could not suffer from the traumatic effects of the violence and still reacted in a reasonable way against her abuser (e.g., with anger).

Notably, rage and anger have traditionally been denied in characterizations of women in Western societies. Anger and rage represent masculinity, while depression and melancholy are perceived as feminine characteristics[24] (Morrissey, 2003, p. 98). Morrissey acknowledges the problematic implication of associating anger with battered women because 'anger, on the part of such women, is deemed illegitimate, supposedly "proving" that their attacks on their abusers were solely revenge-motivated' (2003, p. 98).

In order to answer her own question, the judge in *R. v. Bennett* invoked the psychological condition of the accused, describing her through the psychiatrist's testimony and using the following terms: 'submissiveness, passivity, vulnerability, learned helplessness, and defensiveness'. The judge also referred to the accused's loss of control, and after acknowledging that she 'suffered' from BWS, went on to describe her difficult childhood and her abusive relationships with men. Taking all of this into account, the judge concluded that the accused suffered from low self-esteem and vulnerability to abusive relationships. In view of this analysis, the sentence was mitigated. Offering Bennett sympathy and empathy due to her being dysfunctional, passive, submissive, helpless, vulnerable, with low self-esteem, the judge denied any element of agency to be associated with her acts.

It is noteworthy to mention that the court referred to the accused's former acts of aggressiveness towards her husband, and cautioned against the construction of a stereotypical image of battered women. Despite the court's general acknowledgment that battered women can act both as agents and victims, the court failed to apply this analysis in this case and chose to focus on one dimension of the accused – that is, her psychological deficiencies – and, thus, stressed her victimization rather than her agency.

Another case where the court uses notions associated with victimization to describe the accused is *R. v. Tran* (1991). Helplessness, acute emotional stress and inability to think clearly are the terms used to portray the accused, to explain the killing and, thus, to mitigate the sentence. At the same time, the judge mentioned the term 'survival' once when describing the killing. However, he did not go further to develop the concepts of agency and resistance. On the contrary, he concluded that the killing was situational, and that it was a product of emotional stress, a state of helplessness, and incapacity to deal with the abuse.

In *R. v. Chivers* (1987), the accused suffered horrific abuse from her husband during their marriage. On the night of the shooting, they had both been drinking and were intoxicated. The deceased beat the accused severely and tried to force her to perform oral sex on him, whereupon she escaped to the washroom. On her return, he was standing with his rifle aiming in her direction; the accused testified that this made her extremely frightened. She somehow succeeded in calming him down, but after he fell asleep, she took the gun and shot him, saying to herself that he would never beat her again.

Although the case was decided prior to *Lavallee*, the court discussed BWS in this case, and stated that the accused fell within the pattern of the syndrome. Referring to the elements of helplessness and passivity, the court structured the act of the killing as 'desperate and spontaneous'. The judge referred to the suicidal tendencies of the defendant and to the 'learned helplessness' that characterized her. In this case, it seems that it is not the abuse suffered by the accused that mitigated her sentence, but rather her psychological situation, mainly her helplessness, which contributed to the leniency of the sentence.

Akin to cases discussed earlier, the focus of the court on the psychological condition of the woman in order to mitigate her sentence is not clear. Considering the horrible abuse from which the accused had suffered for many years, along with the events of the evening, the sentencing could have been mitigated based on the reasonableness of the act. As mentioned earlier, it is recognized that the accused was already convicted, and thus the act could not be structured as legally reasonable. However, the killing could have been constructed by the court as an act of resistance and self-preservation and, thus, as an understandable and explicable act, worthy of mitigation. Focusing on the psychological 'problems' of the accused, rather than on her struggle to secure her life and her children's lives, conveys a message of victimization and not one of agency and, consequently, fails to portray the realities of battered women and their difficulties handling abuse.

The accused in *R. v. Whitten* (1992) was charged with second-degree murder in the killing of her common-law spouse. Her personal history was extremely tragic, and she was physically and emotionally abused by her husband during their relationship. On the night of the killing, she and her husband had consumed alcohol and he had become emotionally abusive towards her. A physical struggle began, during which the husband kicked a table across the room in extreme anger. The accused, fearing for her life based on previous batterings perpetrated by the husband, used a knife she was holding to stab him. She pleaded guilty to manslaughter and was sentenced to a suspended sentence and probation of three years.

The court, in this case, took into consideration several mitigating factors, such as the confession of the accused and her remorse for her actions. The focus, however, was on the psychological condition that resulted from her abuse, along with both her inability to terminate the relationship and the events of the night. The judge got into a detailed discussion of BWS and fit the accused within the syndrome, portraying her as 'immature, dependent and [with] passive personality'. Notably, the court stated that the accused had defended herself at the time of the offence in order to stop her husband's verbal harassment and his threat with a knife. It is questionable why the events of the evening, along with the prior abuse suffered by the accused, were not satisfactory to explain the mitigation of the sentence, and why the court needed to resort to the use of BWS and the psychological problems of the accused in order to mitigate the sentence.

In the following two cases, the defendants were not considered by the courts as victims of domestic violence since no evidence of abuse by their husbands was presented. Notwithstanding the absence of abuse, the courts focused on the mental states of the women and their psychological problems and, thus, opened the door for notions of victimization to constitute the basis of the mitigating decision.

In *R. v. Whitteker* (2004), the accused was portrayed as a passive woman with psychological problems who was lacking self-confidence, and who was 'not yet able to muster the initiative to take care of herself, and to deal with her life fully'. Referring to her alcohol problem and to her dysfunctional behaviour, the court placed an emphasis on her rehabilitation, and so mitigated her sentence. The fact that the accused was under the cumulative effects of sleep deprivation and medication for depression and other conditions, as well as being in an extreme state of intoxication while killing her husband, also contributed to the leniency of the sentence.

In *R. v. Phillips* (1992), the accused killed her partner and was charged with second-degree murder. She pleaded guilty to manslaughter and was sentenced to imprisonment of two years less a day. Although the accused was not abused by her partner, she had suffered abuse in her previous relationships with men, a fact which affected the mitigation of the sentence. Her Aboriginal background also constituted a mitigating factor.

To support the mitigation of the sentence, the court used BWS. The focus of the sentencing analysis is the psychological condition of the accused, 'her sense of utter helplessness and emotional turmoil'. The court stressed the 'tendency' of the accused to engage in abusive relationships by quoting the psychiatrists' testimonies as follows: '[P]ersons such as the accused, who have suffered a lifetime of abuse, have low self-esteem and take a stance of helplessness or submission with their partners to protect themselves from further abuse. These persons are, as is Gloria Phillips, extremely dependency-seeking'.

Mitigating cases of women who killed non-abusive partners is a positive step in advancing women's rights in the legal system. This approach represents the recognition of the effect of abuse on women's responses to violence, and broadens societal recognition of the effect of violence against women on women's lawbreaking. However, it is troubling to witness the extensive use of notions of victimization to describe the defendants in an effort to mitigate the sentence. In the Phillips case, in particular, the court uses a stereotypical description of a battered woman, that is, passive, submissive, dependent, masochistic, and helpless, in order to promote understanding of the defendant's behaviour through a lens of victimization.

In two of the cases studied, the defendants killed men who abused them and were not their partners. In *R. v. Abel* (1986), the accused, while highly intoxicated, killed a man after he sexually assaulted her. This man had also sexually assaulted her 10 days prior to the event of the killing, and in the past had beaten her severely. The court acknowledged that the act of killing was an act of self-preservation and that the accused did not intend to kill the deceased but only to slow him down so that he would not chase her. However, the court stated: 'She must accept at least some measure of responsibility for her state of intoxication, for continually associating with this man – whom she well knew to be violently dangerous to her when drinking – and for remaining alone with him in his home when her other companions had left them together'. Considering the above, the judge sentenced the accused to 10 months' imprisonment.

Notably, in this case the court did not use terminology of victimization but, instead, treated the accused as an active agent by stating that she must accept some measure of responsibility. However, rather than understanding her act as conceptually reasonable, and understandable in view of the prior sexual assault and the beatings, the court uses the notion of agency to require the accused not to be raped or harassed.

In *R. v. Simcoe* (2002), the accused killed her father after he attempted to sexually assault her in front of her friend while she was unconscious from alcohol. The father also shouted obscenities and taunted the accused. The accused had been sexually and emotionally abused by her father for most of her childhood. At the time of the killing, she was suffering from depression and was unable to have children. The trial judge sentenced the accused to four years' imprisonment. The court of appeal reduced the sentence to one year, basing its decision on several factors. The judges of the court of appeal contended that the moral culpability of the accused was diminished due to the provocation of the sexual assault in front of her friend, and also in consideration of the fact that the assault completed a long history of sexual abuse by her father. The court also stated that the accused did not intend to kill her father out of unclear thinking arising from her consumption of alcohol.

Using the doctrine of provocation to mitigate the sentence appears helpful to the defendant in terms of her sentence. However, explaining her behaviour with loss of control and reduced moral culpability overshadows and mutes her agency. The defendant's effort to defend herself from another assault by a father who had abused her sexually and emotionally throughout the years was not structured as reasonable but as an impulsive and uncontrolled reaction deriving from provocation.

It is interesting to reflect on Belinda Morrissey's analysis regarding the use of the defence of diminished responsibility.[25] Morrissey argues that this defence represents a 'feminine' explanation that fits with stereotypical notions of 'good' womanhood, such as, passivity, unknowing, and *diminished* [emphasis in original].

Victims of Circumstances

Similar to the above-mentioned cases, the mental condition of the defendants in the following cases is a dominant feature in the decision to mitigate the sentences. However, the psychological problems of the defendants in these cases are described as part of a broader picture of lives of abuse and torment. The mental condition of the defendants, hence, is not the major mitigating factor, but is perceived by courts as one aspect of their sad life stories that results with mitigation of the sentences. For the courts, being 'pure' victims of circumstances, such as abuse by previous partners, abuse by family members, alcohol, poverty, racism, discrimination, lack of economic opportunities and education, these women deserve to get lenient sentences.

In *R. v. Kahypeasewat* (2006), for example, the court takes into account the accused's tragic upbringing, the murder of one of her children, racism, abuse, addictions, family dislocation, poverty, fragmentation, lack of education and employment, and family dysfunction in the decision to mitigate the sentence. The court also discusses the abuse that was inflicted on the defendant by her partner, and further stresses her helplessness and difficult mental state. Additionally, the court takes into consideration the Aboriginality of the accused, as required by the case law (the *Glaude* factors) and the fact that she was remorseful. Taken altogether, the accused is portrayed as a 'pure' victim who deserves the sympathy of the court.

In *R. v. D.E.C.* (1995), the dichotomy between victimization and agency is clearly exemplified. As stated earlier in the analysis, the accused covered up the killing, which had occurred 16 years earlier. The following is a description of her acts after the killing.

> The following morning she went down to the basement and discovered that V. was dead. She cleansed the body, stripped it of any identification, wrapped it in blankets and plastic, and placed it in a steamer trunk. She then hired a moving contractor to move the

trunk from the basement to her van. She then drove the van to the Hope-Princeton Highway where she dumped it off a cliff.

This paragraph depicts the accused as a determined actor who was trying to regain control of her destiny. This expression of control and agency is overshadowed, however, by the focus of the court on the victimization of the accused and, consequently, her image of an agent is quickly transformed into an image of a victim. The judge resorts to the element of victimization in mitigating the sentence, stating: 'Miss C., who was victimized as a child, victimized in her first marriage, victimized in marriage which led to this tragedy, should not be further victimized by a term of incarceration'.

The court in *R. v. C.L.C.* also depicts the hard life of the accused. The judge refers to the fact that as a child, the accused was a victim of serious physical, sexual and emotional abuse at the hands of her father and her stepmother, and the fact that she was in the care of the Children's Aid Society for five years and lived in foster homes and various institutions. The court also mentions her previous relationship, which was physically, sexually and emotionally abusive. Her act of killing, for the court, was a rash response due to her alcohol consumption and her mental state.

R. v. Phillips (1992), which was mentioned earlier, is also an example of a case in which life of victimization constitute a mitigating factor. In Phillips, however, the mitigation of the sentence is mainly based on the mental condition of the accused while her Aboriginality and her previous abusive relationships are additional mitigating factors.

Although the defendants in the above-mentioned cases were convicted of an offence that may attract a severe punishment, the courts' empathic approach resulted in lenient sentences afforded to them. It is inevitable, thus, to challenge my critique of the courts and to question my course of analysis. After all, the courts showed sympathy and compassion towards the women and acknowledged the role of the abuse inflicted on them in their acts of killing. By offering the women lenient sentences, the goal of the courts was not to further victimize them (as was clearly stated in *R. v. D.E.C.*, for instance). In view of the above, do we really wish to challenge and criticize this judicial approach?

While the approach of the courts to sentencing battered women who kill their abusers and are convicted of manslaughter has proven beneficial to each individual woman in terms of the leniency of the sentences imposed, it raises some serious difficulties to battered women who kill. First, focusing on the mental condition of the women problematizes the claim of battered women who kill to self-defence. By placing the psychological problems of the women at the focal point of the judicial process, the courts create an image of battered women as pathological, irrational and unreasonable. By depicting them solely as victims and obscuring any sense of agency or rationality expressed in their acts, battered women who wish to claim they acted in self-defence may face difficulties convincing the judiciary that they acted reasonably. This victim model, which is based on attributes such as weakness, irrationality, unreasonableness and emotionality, may deny battered women the chance to argue self-defence in similar cases.

Secondly, the construction of the stereotypical image of battered women as dysfunctional and abnormal may also have an effect on the way battered women's credibility is perceived by different actors in the legal system, such as Crown attorneys, defence counsels and the judiciary.

Another implication of this model is the exclusion of women who do not fit this rigid image. In view of the problematic dichotomy between agency and victimization as described in literature on battered women, on the use of BWS, and on women's lawbreaking as discussed earlier, this one-dimensional construction of women in sentencing decisions may result in a situation in which certain women who are not perceived as passive and helpless, but instead are viewed as assertive and strong, would face difficulties and hurdles in efforts to mitigate their sentences. Often these 'certain' women belong to marginalized and discriminated groups, such as Aboriginals or Blacks, who are viewed in a stereotypical and prejudicial way.[26]

Abused women will be required to 'suffer' from mental problems in order to be categorized as worthy victims who deserve the mercy of courts. This approach, thus, creates a dichotomy between women who 'deserve' the sympathy of the courts (victims) and those who don't (agents). The dichotomy between victimization and agency as conveyed in the analysis overlooks the differences between battered women. It ignores the complicated realities of battered women and the various factors that contribute and shape their responses to the abuse, such as limited economic opportunities, limited social services to abused women, and societal views of marriage, motherhood, family, and children, to name a few. To deny battered women who kill emotions of anger, strength, resistance and rationality is to ignore these differences and complexities in their lives.

At the same time, equally problematic would be to ignore the 'sympathy' the courts demonstrate towards the women, along with the sensitivity they express towards their circumstances. It is impossible to ignore the fact that the courts take into account as a mitigating factor the abuse inflicted on the women and thus make an effort to contextualize the killings and to situate these acts within a broader context of abusive relationships. Furthermore, this approach has proven beneficial to each individual defendant given a lenient sentence. Moreover, these women *are* victims and *are* oppressed and abused by their partners. Is this a fact that should be ignored? Should we require the courts to ignore the victimization of the women and their oppression?

My critique of the prevalent use of victimization in the mitigation of the sentences of battered women who kill, on one hand, and the positive outcomes of this approach for particular defendants, on the other hand, raises a significant (and I would say a continual) dilemma of pitting systemic justice against individual justice. This dilemma is very much related to the role, in these cases, of defence counsels.

In view of my own experience in the criminal justice system litigating cases as a Crown prosecutor, and in light of a defence counsel's goal to seek mitigation for her/his clients, I believe that a choice between lenient sentences in cases of battered women convicted of the manslaughter of their partners and a less stereotypical account of battered women will be very simple for defence counsels and their clients, who will invariably choose the former. Considering the favourable legal treatment of battered women who fit the model of a 'pure' victim, who is gentle, weak, submissive, passive and helpless, and considering the dichotomy between victimization and agency,[27] it is inevitable to ask whether defence counsels should give up the use of the concept of victimization in representing battered women who are on trial for killing their abusers. Can defence counsels afford to present nuanced versions of women's experiences while seeking mitigation, when using a model of victimization results in leniency of sentences for women defendants? Would it be too risky, from a defence counsel's perspective and, surely, from that of a defendant, to require the courts not to resort to notions of victimization in the mitigation process when this tool has proven to work for battered women on trial?

For feminist academics and activists who seek to transform the legal discourse of battered women who kill, this is also a dilemma. By criticizing the way courts mitigate sentences of battered women on trial, we may deny battered women the opportunity to actually get lenient sentences. Can we expect women who are on trial for killing their abusers to consider theoretical and broader issues, such as the problematic dichotomy between agency and victimization, when they are fighting for their freedom? Should we seek to eliminate a defence tool which has proven to be a useful mitigating factor in cases of battered women on trial? Should we challenge a framework of sentencing that assists these women in avoiding imprisonment? Are we seeking to achieve justice for all abused women while denying justice for individual abused women?

This dilemma is also associated with the legal route many defence counsels take in defending battered women who are charged with murder. In 16 out of the 23 cases I found (including the ones not discussed in the chapter), the defendants pleaded guilty to manslaughter after being charged with murder. Taking the path of a guilty plea makes it hard on defence counsel to frame a woman's actions as reasonable and rational, since by deserting a self-defence argument, counsel implicitly acknowledges that the woman's act of killing was not reasonable. As a result, it may be hard to portray defendants as resistant and strong actors when seeking mitigation. Thus, the focus of the courts on themes of victimization in the mitigation process is not surprising, and might even be inevitable in view of the guilty pleas. The role of defence counsels and Crown attorneys in framing guilty pleas, and the role of courts in accepting them, are thus significant in analyzing and understanding the sentences of battered women who kill.

The finding that, in the majority of the cases studied, the women pleaded guilty to manslaughter is consistent with Shaffer's and Sheehy's assertion that the introduction of BWS resulted mainly in the mitigation of sentences in cases of battered women on trial for killing their abusers and not so much with their acquittals. Is there a connection between resorting to guilty pleas and stereotypical perceptions of battered women by key actors in the legal system, namely defence counsels, Crown counsels and judges? Do the guilty pleas represent a disinclination by defence counsels to assert reasonableness and rationality on behalf of their women clients? Is the prevalent use of guilty pleas an outcome of stereotypical views of battered women as psychologically defective and as incapable to act reasonably (and thus acquitted on the basis of self-defence)? Or is it that the risks in these cases in arguing self-defence are so high that guilty pleas are a better legal avenue to take? Shaffer suggests in her analysis that a stereotype of the 'deserving' or 'authentic' battered woman may partly explain the choice of guilty pleas in cases that could support arguments of self-defence (Shaffer, 1997, p. 25). In view of the pervasive use of the 'victim model' by the courts, and their focus on the mental problems of the defendants in the cases I found, one can only wonder whether a similar course of analysis should be applied here.

An alternative analysis, which may resolve some of these concerns, would be to shift the focus of the mitigation analysis from the mental problems of the women, and their overall victimization, to other dimensions conveyed in their behaviour, such as their resistance, their strength, their power and determination, and their efforts to preserve their lives. A consideration of these elements is not at odds with the abuse the women suffer, nor does it ignore their harsh lives.

It is vital that the courts consider the abuse and be obliged to take the violence inflicted on battered women into account, either in the sentencing of abused women or in trials. Ignoring these dimensions in the women's lives would take us back to times when abuse of women by their partners was denied and ignored by courts, and would minimize the effects of abuse by male partners on women. However, the abuse can be told in a different voice and can be constructed by courts through notions of agency rather than victimization. Acknowledging dimensions of agency in the women's acts and recognizing the broader framework within which abused women act and react will result in constructing and perceiving the killings as understandable and rational. By transforming the discourse of battered women who kill from a discourse around victimization to one that includes representations of agency, and by stressing signs and notions of agency rather than victimization, battered women will be portrayed differently (not solely as passive victims) and consequently their acts will be described differently.

In such a paradigm, the acts of killing would be perceived, as I term it, as 'conceptually justifiable acts'. Although these acts of killing cannot be considered by courts as legally reasonable since the women have already been convicted of manslaughter, my assertion is that the courts can still construct those acts as understandable and explainable: 'conceptually justifiable and reasonable'. This will be done by using elements and terminology of agency in the mitigating discourse. By exposing and recognizing the aspects of resistance, power, determination and self-preservation demonstrated by these women, the story of their acts of killing can be told using a different narrative than the one used in the above-mentioned cases. These acts can be perceived as reasonable, justifiable, rational, understandable and, thus, as deserving to be mitigated.

Moreover, the abuse should be contextualized through consideration of social and cultural context and via objective factors such as lack of familial support, lack of shelters, poverty and societal inequality between women and men. This will provide an opportunity to view battered women who kill as rational actors. By constructing some of the cases as distinct and ignoring the similarities between these cases, the courts do not allow a discussion of violence against women to emerge, and do not provide an opportunity to situate the acts of killing within a broader societal, cultural and economic framework. By so contextualizing the abuse, the courts will not need to resort to focusing on the mental problems of the women, or to rely solely on them in order to justify the leniency of the sentences.

At the same time, neither the oppression in these women's lives, nor their victimization, ought to be ignored. The abuse and violence these women experience should be part of the mitigating picture, and should inform the courts in their decisions to mitigate the sentences in cases of convicted battered women who kill. However, stressing the resistance of these women, along with their determination and strength, does not mean obscuring their oppression. These notions are two complementing aspects of their lives. They are two sides of the equation. These women can be perceived as agents and still deserve the sympathy of the courts; they can be perceived as victims and still demonstrate strength. Assertiveness and anger, which are associated with agency, do not lessen the extent of the abuse in these women's lives. Strength and resistance do not undermine their oppression.

SUMMARY

'R: They say we have this thing called "learned helplessness..."
Y: Really? I always thought it was when I was getting too *much* [emphasis added] power'.
A conversation between two friends who had violent marriages. (Mahoney, 1991, p. 39)

Expert testimony on BWS was developed to explain the experience of battered women and to provide abused women with a voice to be heard in courts. It attempted to convey to the courts how battered women were affected by the abuse and thus to contextualize their responses to the violence inflicted on them. As discussed in the second part of the chapter, BWS was transformed into a 'separate' defence, which stresses the passivity and irrationality of battered women who kill. Thus, rather than being used to bolster the defence of self-defence for battered women who kill their abusers, by explaining the reasonableness of their acts of killing, and consequently securing an acquittal for these women, BWS has been used to explain the 'failure' of abused women to leave their abusers. It has created a stereotypical, problematic image of a 'good battered woman' who, if she conforms to the portrait created by the syndrome, deserves the protection of the law. Contrary to the expectations of many feminists, as discussed in the introduction to this chapter and as confirmed in the findings of this chapter, BWS has not resulted in a significant number of acquittals in cases of battered woman who kill. Rather, many battered women plead guilty to the lesser offence of manslaughter. BWS, thus, occupies a central role as a mitigating factor in sentencing decisions concerning these women.

In this chapter, I analyzed some of the factors that shape sentencing decisions in cases of battered women who kill, in an attempt to examine the manifestation of agency and victimization in those decisions. The lack of agency and the depiction of the women as suffering from psychological deficiencies form a central observation in this analysis. The centrality of the mitigating arguments in most cases is the psychological problems of the women, along with their helplessness and passivity. To describe the women, the courts often use psychiatrists' testimonies depicting the women as dysfunctional and ignoring any sense of resistance and self-preservation evidenced in their acts.

While this approach has proven beneficial to the women in terms of the leniency of the sentences imposed, it denies them agency and obscures any efforts they may have made to fight the violence. It further perpetuates the categorization of battered women solely as 'victims'. Being victims, battered women are perceived as the 'others', as different from us. By rigidly categorizing battered women who kill, this view fails to develop any serious discussion of domestic violence and abuse of women by their partners in their homes. Furthermore, it problematizes the claim of battered women to equal access to the plea of self-defence. As Morrissey clearly contends 'Women who lack agency also lack the chance to argue in defence of their actions. If they cannot claim that they acted of their own volition in the first place, then they are denied the opportunity to claim that their acts were reasonable and justifiable' (2003, p. 170).

Criticizing the approach taken by the courts in sentencing battered women who kill, I do not intend to argue that these women are not oppressed or victimized by the men they live with. My argument is that solely stressing elements of victimization, denying agency in women who are abused, and perpetuating a stereotypical image of battered women as dysfunctional and abnormal, has harmful implications to battered women, as discussed in length in this chapter. One of these prominent outcomes may be denying battered women who kill their abusers equal access to the argument of self-defence.

The analysis of the sentencing structure offered by the courts also raises several questions to which the answers are not easy. The dilemma between individualized justice and systemic justice for women; the gap between a broader transformation in the discourse of battered women who kill and legal practices; the responsibility of defence counsels in these cases; the role of defence counsels, Crown attorneys and judges in framing guilty pleas in cases of battered women who kill; and the role and limits of criminal law in responding to violence against women are but some of the issues that the analysis generated.

An alternative analysis to that offered by the courts, one that seeks to reframe the mitigation process, was introduced in this chapter. According to this analysis, the narrative used in cases of battered women who kill should be changed, and the discourse of battered women who kill should be transformed to reflect dimensions of agency and resistance. In the suggested discourse, the abuse these women suffer is recognized and acknowledged, but is used to explain and stress the women's urge to self-preservation and thus, the rationality and reasonableness of their acts. The mitigation of the sentences, hence, would be based on the need of the women to preserve their lives and their children's lives, and not on their mental problems and sufferings. The narrative used in these cases would not ignore the victimization in these women's lives, but would portray battered women not only as victims but also as reasonable actors and agents who actively assert themselves. Consequently, battered women would be portrayed in a more inclusive way, one which would use their abuse and victimization to explain and convey the rationality and sense in their responses to the violence.

This narrative should also stress the social context within which battered women act, which is often one of marginalization, racism and sexism. It should take into account the intersection of race, class and culture with gender; it should reject stereotypical perceptions of women and the false distinction between a 'good woman' and a 'bad woman', and it should challenge patriarchal norms of marriage and femininity. These changes may provide battered women with a voice that represents them adequately while acknowledging the differences among them. Moreover, these changes may allow battered women who kill to gain equality in the criminal justice system.

Some questions were left unresolved. Is criminal law the place to explore, question and resolve issues of identity, victimization, agency and autonomy? Can the legal system be expected to lead the public on these issues? Is that its role? How do we solve the dilemma of individualized justice versus systemic justice? Acknowledging these issues and recognizing their importance in this discourse would illuminate the challenges, difficulties and risks in reshaping the mitigating framework in cases of battered women who are on trial for killing their abusers.

NOTES

1. For more statistical information on violence against women, see Measuring Violence against Women, Statistical Trends, 2006; Family Violence in Canada: a Statistical Profile, 2006.

2. Lesbian battering is not included in the discussion of this chapter since lesbian battering has been primarily analyzed in isolation from the legal system (see Mahoney, 1991, pp. 50–54).

3. The cycle theory of violence refers to a three-part cycle: the tension-building phase, in which the abuser expresses hostility towards the woman and abuses her verbally, psychology and physically. In the second phase, called the 'acute battering phase', the abuser physically assaults the woman. In the final phase, called the 'loving contrition' phase, the abuser shows remorse for his actions, promises to reform and generally displays a caring nature. However, the cycle of violence starts all over again and further escalates.

4. According to Walker, as a result of the cycle of violence, a battered woman develops a mental state called 'learned helplessness'. The theory of learned helplessness describes the woman's sense of psychological paralysis. That is, the woman loses her ability to predict that her actions will affect her safety and loses any motivation to alter her situation.

5. The court based its decision on the grounds that the trial judge was mistaken in admitting the expert testimony of BWS. The court also questioned whether Lavallee acted in self-defence.

6. Madame Justice Wilson analyzed the doctrine of self-defence and its inapplicability to women due to its male characteristics. She argued that the gravity of imminence was to be judged according to the battered woman's experience and circumstances, stating that 'the issue is not, however, what an outsider would have reasonably perceived but what the accused reasonably perceived, given her situation and experience' (*Lavallee*, p. 883). She also contended that an outsider could not and should not pass judgment on the fact that a battered woman did not leave the abuser. Madame Justice Wilson also referred to the broader social context as a factor in the decision of many abused women to stay within abusive relationships, and further stressed the notion that battered women do try to escape the relationships or generally show a sense of agency.

7. Elizabeth Schneider contends that as a result of the 'syndromization' of the women's situation, defence lawyers will structure the case around the psychological elements of the woman's situation rather than focus on the woman's particular circumstances and the reasonableness of her act (Schneider, 1996, p. 509).

8. Regina Schuller also argues that by shifting the focus from the woman's reasonable response BWS 'contextualizes her actions within a framework of dysfunction' (Schuller, 2003, p. 232).

9. The following exemplifies this notion: 'Women who are battered may be unable to bring a battering relationship to an end, but they may be constantly planning and asserting themselves – strategizing, in ways that are carefully hidden from the batterer, to contribute to their own safety and to that of their children. They may be negotiating and carefully hiding small but important acts of independence so as to mitigate "separation assault". They may be gathering information, seeking money and support to assist them when they leave, and succeeding in breaking away only after multiple attempts' (Schneider, 2000, pp. 84–85).

10. On this point, Marry Anne Dutton contends that psychological realities of battered women are broad and, thus, it is impossible to limit their reactions to a singular model (Dutton, 1993, p. 1196).

11. In the case of Black women, it has been noted that various stereotypes associated with Black women in North American society, such as: 'the angry Black woman', 'the strong Black woman' and the 'promiscuous and immoral woman' deny Black battered women the protection of the law of self-defence. These negative prejudicial images categorize Black women as 'the others' and, hence, as the 'bad' women (Allard, 1991; Fenton, 1998; Martinson, 2001). Allard puts it as follows: 'The passive, gentle white woman is automatically more like the "good" fairy tale princess stereotype than a Black woman, who as the 'other' may be seen as the "bad" witch' (Allard, 1991, p. 194). Thus, while white battered women have to face the hurdle of proving that they deserve the protection of the law, Black battered women face extra hurdles doing so due to the various negative images associated with being Black. Notably, this analysis is also relevant to other marginalized groups of women who are viewed as 'different' than the (white) norm.

12. On this point, Schneider contends that in order to equalize battered women's rights to trial, the elements and the circumstances of each case ought to be examined in light of the existence of gender bias in the criminal justice system. However, rather than examining the impact of gender bias on each particular case of a battered woman who kills, defence lawyers refer to BWS as a separate defence regardless of the broader context of gender bias (Schneider, 1996, pp. 487, 497).

13. For a discussion of two of the leading liberal theorists, writing on autonomy: Dworkin and Feinberg, see Kathryn Abrams (1999, pp. 808–813). Feinberg defines autonomy as the liberal self, portrayed as autonomous, who holds the following qualities: 'authenticity, integrity, and distinct self-identity'. For Dworkin autonomy is a combination of two elements: authenticity and procedural independence.

14. The conception of autonomy is varied among different branches of feminism. Although the common understanding among feminist scholars writing about autonomy is the movement beyond traditional liberal assumptions of autonomy towards a broader conception of this notion, they varied in their approach to defining and conceptualizing autonomy (see Abrams, 1999).

15. Dutton describes three categories of strategies: personal, informal and formal. Some of these strategies are talking to the batterer about stopping the violence, temporarily escaping from the batterer's presence, looking for help from family and neighbours, calling the police, seeking help from a divorce lawyer and so on.

16. According to liberal philosophy, self-direction is an aspect of autonomy, which refers to the direction of one's own path. The complement aspect is self-definition.

17. Pollack uses the following paragraph, written by the Canadian Task Force on Federally Sentenced Women from 1990, as an example: 'Low self-esteem reduces a woman's ability to cope. It increases self-destructive behavior… It can contribute to violence against others. Low self-esteem reduces a person's ability to plan for the future, to take responsibility for her actions, and to believe she can make meaningful choices that will help her live with respect and dignity'. Notably, Pollack states that this type of analysis is not exclusive to women who break the law but became an integral part of a social policy discourse.

18. For a detailed discussion of the nature of sentencing in Canada and the legal principles that shape the process of sentencing in Canada see Allan Monson (2001). *The Law of Sentencing*. Toronto: Irwin Law.

19. Where a firearm is used in the commission of the offence, the law states a minimum punishment of imprisonment for a term of four years.

20. Shaffer found 35 cases (19 of these cases were reported and 16 cases were collected from newspaper reports) in which counsel raised BWS as a defence to a criminal charge or as a factor in sentencing. Notably, Shaffer did not focus solely on cases where the women killed their partners but analyzed cases of fraud, assault and more.

21. It will be interesting, in a future work, to proceed to examine the manifestation of agency and victimization in these cases and explore the reasons for non-mitigation in view of the discourse of agency and victimization. The cases are *R. v. Chicksi* [1988] N.W.T.J. No. 24; *R. v. Aquiatusuk* [1991] N.W.T.J. No. 16; *R. v. Glaude* 119 C.C.C.; *R. v. Whynot* [1996] N.S.J. No. 12; *R. v. G.A.M.* [1996] N.S.J. No. 52; *R. v. W.L.Q.* [2005] S.J. No. 13; *R. v. Fisher* [2004] 60 W.C.B. (2d) 404; *R. v. Machiskinic* [2004] W.C.B.J. LEXIS 1619; *R. v. Mcdow* [1996] 30 W.C.B.(2d) 77. The sentences in these cases ranged from three years to eleven years of imprisonment.

22. Notably, in most of these cases the abuse inflicted on the women *was* a significant factor in the mitigation and BWS *was* used to mitigate the sentences. However, the courts did not extend the discussion beyond mentioning the abuse. Moreover, the abuse was but one of various other factors, such as children, alcohol consumption, lack of criminal record, and volunteer work at the community. The cases are *R. v. Cabrera* [2003] O.J. No. 4510; *R. v. Emard* [1999] W.C.B.J. 2906; *R. v. Oretel* [1992] 18 W.C.B. (2d) 36; *R. v. Trimble* [1992] O.J. No. 3287; *R. v. Brown* [1992] 18 W.C.B. (2d) 37; *R .v.Gilpin* [2002] B.C.J. No. 3230; *R. v. Ferguson* [1997] O.J. No. 2488; *R. v. Neyelle* [1992] N.W.T.J. No. 18; and *R. v. Cowley* [1995] O.J. No. 592 – in view of the discussion of victimization and agency, some of the terms of the probation imposed on the accused in this case are worthy of mention: developing self-sufficiency skills, improving self-esteem, and dealing with co-dependency issues (para 8).

23. Based on Bradfield's discussion of 'exceptional cases' in the Australian context, I was interested to find out whether this notion is also manifested in the Canadian context.

24. Morrissey further argues that battered women who were interviewed by Lenore Walker stated that their own anger in a threatening and violent situation caused them to forget their fear and to act. Morrissey adds that Walker, however, contended that anger in battered women, followed the killing and did not precede it.

25. There is no statutory defence of diminished responsibility in Canada.

26. See text accompanying note 11.

27. See discussion at part three, pp. 12–18.

ACKNOWLEDGMENTS

I would like to thank Liz Sheehy for suggesting this topic and Janet Mosher for reading and commenting on this chapter. Thank you, both.

REFERENCES

Abrams, K. (1999). From autonomy to agency: Feminist perspectives on self-direction. *William and Mary Law Review, 40*, 805.

Allard, S. A. (1991). Rethinking battered woman syndrome: A black feminist perspective. *UCLA Women's Law Journal, 1*, 191.

Bell, M., & Mosher, J. (1998). (Re)fashioning medicine's response to wife abuse. In: S. Sherwin (Ed.), *The politics of women's health: Exploring agency and autonomy* (pp. 205–233). Philadelphia: Temple University Press.

Bradfield, R. (2002) *The treatment of women who kill their violent male partners within the Australian criminal justice system.* Unpublished PhD Thesis, University of Tasmania, Faculty of Law.

Chewter, C. L. (2003). Violence against women and children: Some legal issues. *Canadian Journal of Family Law, 20*, 99.

Crocker, P. L. (1985). The meaning of equality for battered women who kill men in self defence. *Harvard Women's Law Journal, 8*, 121.

Dutton, M. A. (1993). Understanding women's responses to domestic violence: A redefinition of battered woman syndrome. *Hofstra Law Review, 21*, 1191.

Fenton, Z. F. (1998). Domestic violence in black and white: Racialized gender stereotypes in gender violence. *Columbia Journal of Gender and the Law, 8*, 1.

Mahoney, M. (1991). Legal images of battered women: Redefining the question of separation. *Michigan Law Review, 90*, 1.

Mahoney, M. R. (1994). Victimization or oppression? Women's lives, violence, and agency. In: A. F. Martha & M. Roxanne (Eds), *The public nature of private violence: The discovery of domestic abuse.* New York, London: Routledge.

Martinson, L. (2001). An analysis of racism and resources for African-American female victims of domestic violence in Wisconsin. *Wisconsin Women's Law Journal, 16*, 259.

Monson, A. (2001). *The Law of Sentencing.* Toronto: Irwin Law.

Morrissey, B. (2003). *When women kill: Questions of agency and subjectivity.* London: Routledge.

Pollack, S. (2000). Reconceptualizing women's agency and empowerment: Challenges to self-esteem discourse and women's lawbreaking. *Women and Criminal Justice, 12*, 75.

Schneider, E. (1996). Self defence and relations of domination. Moral and legal perspectives on battered women who KILL: Resistance to equality. *University of Pittsburgh Law Review, 57*, 477.

Schneider, E. (2000). *Battered Women and Feminist Lawmaking.* New Haven and London: Yale University Press.

Schuller, R. A. (2003). Expert evidence and its impact on jurors' decisions in homicide trials involving battered women. *Duke Journal of Gender Law and Policy, 10*, 225.

Shaffer, M. (1997). The battered woman syndrome revisited: Some complicating thoughts five years after *R. v. Lavallee. University of Toronto Law Journal, 47*, 1.

Sheehy, E. (1994). Battered women syndrome: Developments in Canadian law after *R. v. Lavallee.* In: J. Stubbs (Ed.), *Women, Male Violence & the Law.* Sydney: Institute of Criminology.

Sheehy, E. (2001). Battered women and mandatory minimum sentence. *Osgoode Hall Law Journal, 39*, 529.

Sheehy, E., Stubbs, J., & Tolmie, J. (1992). Defending battered women on trial: The battered woman syndrome and its Limitations. *Criminal Law Journal, 16*, 369.

Sherwin, S. (1998). A relational approach to autonomy in health care. In: S. Sherwin (Ed.), *The politics of women's health: Exploring agency and autonomy.* Philadelphia: Temple University Press.

Stubbs, J., & Tolmie, J. (1994). Battered woman syndrome in Australia: A challenge to gender bias in the law? In: J. Stubbs (Ed.), *Women, Male Violence & the Law.* Sydney: Institute of Criminology.

United Nation Population Fund. (2005). http://www.unfpa.org/swp/2005/english/ch7/index.htm

Walker, L. (2000). *The battered woman syndrome* (2d ed.). New York: Springer.

Cases

R. v. Abel [1986] N.W.T.J. No. 55.

R. v. Aquiatusuk [1991] N.W.T.J. No. 16.

R. v. Bennett [1993] O.J. No. 1011 (Ont. Provincial ct.).

R. v. Brown [1992] 18 W.C.B. (2d) 37.

R. v. Cabrera [2003] O.J. No. 4510.

R. v. Chicksi [1988] N.W.T.J. No. 24.

R. v. Chivers [1987] N.W.T.J. No. 118.

R. v. Cormier [1974] 9 N.S.R. (2d) 687.

R. v. Cowley [1995] O.J. No. 592.

R. v. D.E.C. [1995] B.C.J. No. 1074.

R. v. Drake [1995] O.J. No. 4375 (Ont. ct. GD.).

R. v. Dunlap [1991] N.S.J. No. 77.

R. v. Emard [1999] W.C.B.J. 2906.

R. v. Ferguson [1997] O.J. No. 2488 (Ont. ct. GD.).

R. v. Fisher [2004] 60 W.C.B. (2d) 404.

R. v. G.A.M. [1996] N.S.J. No.52.

R. v. Gatekate [1998] O.J. No. 6329 (Ont. Ct. GD).

R. v. Gilpin [2002] B.C.J. No. 3230.

R. v. Glaude [1999] 119 C.C.C. (3d) 481.

R. v. Kahypeasewat [2006] S. J. No. 587.

R. v. Machiskinic [2004] W.C.B.J. LEXIS 1619.

R. v. Mcdow [1996] 30 W.C.B. (2d) 77.

R. v. Neyelle [1992] N.W.T.J. No. 18.

R. v. Oretel [1992] 18 W.C.B. (2d) 36.

R. v. Phillips [1992] O.J. No. 2716 (Ont. Ct. GD.).

R. v. Simcoe [2002] O.J. No. 884.

R. v. Tran [1991] O.J. No. 2052 (Ont. ct. GD.).

R. v. Trimble [1992] O.J. No. 3287.

R. v. Whitteker [2004] O.J. No. 1415 (Ont. S.C.J.).

R. v. Whitten [1992] N.S.J. No. 105.

R. v. W.L.Q. [2005] S.J. No. 13.

R. v. Whynot [1996] N.S.J. No. 12.

CONTEXTUAL CONSTRAINTS ON DEFENDANTS' APOLOGIES AT SENTENCING

M. Catherine Gruber

ABSTRACT

This chapter explores some of the risks and constraints associated with defendants' apologies during allocution at sentencing. It argues that defendants' stigmatized institutional role identities in conjunction with the constraints imposed by the discursive context of allocution function to limit both the effectiveness with which defendants can speak on their own behalf and the kinds of things that they can say. Allocution has long been understood as a protection for defendants. This chapter proposes that the ideologies associated with this turn at talk have functioned to obscure the ways in which allocution preserves existing power configurations instead of challenging them.

The practice of giving defendants the opportunity to address the court at sentencing is known as the right of allocution. The right of allocution is recognized in more than half of the American jurisdictions (*McGautha v. California*, 402 U.S. 183 (1971)); in U.S. District Courts, the Federal Rules of Criminal Procedure make it required. Allocution is viewed primarily as a benefit for defendants because, according to the Supreme Court's holding in

Studies in Law, Politics, and Society, Volume 45, 47–74
Copyright © 2008 by Emerald Group Publishing Limited
All rights of reproduction in any form reserved
ISSN: 1059-4337/doi:10.1016/S1059-4337(08)45002-0

Green v. United States, 365 U.S. 301 (1961), it provides the defendant the opportunity "to make a statement in his own behalf" and "to present any information in mitigation of punishment" (Wright, King, & Klein, 2004, p. 152). Allocution also comes with risks, however. Well-known risks concern the possibility that the defendant could speak in such a way that would suggest that she had not fully accepted responsibility for the crime (Natapoff, 2005; O'Hear, 1997). Because defendants often offer some kind of apology during allocution, another risk concerns the production of an apology by a defendant who might want to appeal her conviction. This is problematic due to the way in which an apology is understood as conveying the speaker's acceptance of responsibility for the offense.

This chapter calls attention to a set of risks facing defendants that are less well known. They concern the ways in which the context of the sentencing hearing constrains both the kinds of things that a defendant can say on his own behalf and the degree to which he can speak in an effective manner. We first examine the impact that defendants' stigmatized role identities have on their ability to speak effectively on their own behalf. Defendants' role identities function in another way in that they limit the topics that are available for an allocution: thus, although allocution is understood as providing defendants the opportunity to present information that could mitigate the sentence, it appears to be inadvisable for defendants to highlight aspects of the crime – even uncontested ones – that position them in a less blameworthy light. Further, we show how, although an apology appears to be expected, the numerous ways in which the context of the sentencing hearing differs from more typical contexts in which apologies are produced function to undermine the effectiveness of the apologies produced during allocution. We close with a discussion of an atypical allocution which suggests that the limited nature of the interaction between defendant and judge constrains defendants' options for speaking about "lessons learned." We propose that the language ideologies associated with allocution – specifically, that allocution serves as a protection for defendants – obscures the ways in which allocution functions to reify the distinctions which the criminal justice system imposes upon those whom it processes. It appears that defendants who most closely approximate the criminal defendant stereotype are least able to make use of the opportunity to speak on their own behalf due to the stigmatizing effects of inhabiting this institutional role identity.

This chapter integrates data from two different kinds of sources: (1) ethnographic research conducted in U.S. District Courts and (2) the findings of sociolinguists and other socio-oriented research on identity management and the ways in which apologies are understood to function. Before turning to the heart of the chapter, we briefly review the 1961 case of *Green v. United States*, which provided the grounds for understanding allocution in a new way and we introduce the term, "language ideologies." We describe federal sentencing hearings and the rules that have been developed with regard to the administration of the right of allocution. After that we turn to the subject of apologies and we identify some of the benefits and risks associated with apologizing during allocution. We then describe the way in which the data used in this chapter were acquired and we give a brief overview of the patterns which shaped the defendant allocutions that were examined. The remainder of the chapter is devoted to a discussion of the ways in which defendants' stigmatized institutional role identities and the discursive features of allocution constrain both what defendants say and the degree to which they can speak effectively on their own behalf.

Although the right of allocution in American courts has deep roots in the common law, the purpose allocution was intended to serve has changed over time. As the *Harvard Law Review* (1968) article "Procedural Due Process at Judicial Sentencing for Felony" notes, under the common law of England, the point of asking a defendant whether he had "any thing to offer why judgment should not be awarded against him" was not to offer the defendant the opportunity to present mitigating evidence or to plead for leniency, but

> to give the defendant a formal opportunity to present one of the strictly defined legal reasons which required the avoidance or delay of sentencing: he was not the person convicted, he had benefit of clergy or a pardon, he was insane, or if a woman, she was pregnant. (pp. 832–833)

In *Green*, the Court observed that although the circumstances for American defendants in the mid-twentieth century had improved, the right to speak on one's own behalf was still valuable.

> We are not unmindful of the relevant major changes that have evolved in criminal procedure since the seventeenth century – the sharp decrease in the number of crimes which were punishable by death, the right of the defendant to testify on his own behalf, and the right to counsel. But we see no reason why a procedural rule should be limited to the circumstances under which it arose if reasons for the right it protects remain. None of these modern innovations lessens the need for the defendant, personally, to have the opportunity to present to the court his plea in mitigation. (*Green v. United States*, 1961)

The language of *Green* reflects an understanding of allocution primarily as a benefit for defendants. In fact, *Green* makes this point even more explicitly when it states: "[t]he most persuasive counsel may not be able to speak for a defendant as the defendant might, with halting eloquence, speak for himself" (*Green v. United States*, 1961). Because the right of allocution is understood as providing a benefit for defendants, it has come to serve as an index of the fairness of the criminal justice system.

The description provided by *American Jurisprudence 2d* (1998) reflects allocution's dual nature: "Allocution is a plea for mercy; it is not intended to advance or dispute facts. The purpose of allocution is two-fold: first, it reflects the belief that civilization should afford every defendant the opportunity to ask for mercy, and, second, it permits the defendant to impress the jury with his or her feelings of remorse" (21A: §811).

These comments reflect the ways in which allocution has become incorporated into the set of ideologies associated with language in legal contexts. Linguistic anthropologists have contributed much to our understanding of language ideologies. Silverstein (1979) observes that language ideologies are "sets of beliefs about language articulated by users as a rationalization or justification of perceived language structure and use" (p. 193). Woolard (1998) elaborates this notion, claiming that "ideology is seen as ideas, discourse, or signifying practices in the service of the struggle to acquire or maintain power" (p. 7). Silverstein (1981) and Hill (1998) discuss some of the ways in which a set of beliefs about language can obscure a native speaker's awareness of those parts of her linguistic system that fall outside of the components accounted for by the ideology. This obscurity can apply to both the structural system (i.e., structural features of grammar) and to ways in which language functions in the real world. In "Today there is no respect," Hill (1998) identifies distortions associated with an ideological system that is different from the one that is dominant in English and other European languages. (Each set of language ideologies comes with its own set of distortions.) Her work with Mexicano speakers in the Malinche Volcano region of Central Mexico reveals consistent patterns of mismatch between what particular sets of speakers say about certain ways of speaking and what they actually do. She found that the speakers who most bemoaned the lack of respect in current, Spanish-influenced speaking styles and specifically the mixing of Mexicano and Spanish themselves made the most use of Spanish loan words. This chapter argues, along the same lines, that the ideological filter of viewing allocution as a benefit for defendants obscures the ways in which the context constrains what defendants can say and how effectively they can say it.

At federal sentencing hearings, unless a statutory sentence is ruled to apply, the judge generally imposes a sentence based on the Federal Sentencing Guidelines, which link ranges of months of imprisonment with

43 offense levels and 6 criminal history categories. Defendants get assigned to a particular range of months based on the intersection of their total offense level and their criminal history category. A defendant's total offense level is determined by the base offense level associated with the particular crime (e.g., the base offense level for robbery is 20); the base offense level is then increased and/or decreased based on the presence of additional aggravating or mitigating factors. For example, committing the robbery at a financial institution and/or using a firearm during the offense constitute aggravating factors; in addition, defendants who are judged to be ringleaders of the offense, or who are labeled "career criminals" face additional increases to their total offense levels. In drug cases, the weight of the drugs constitutes another aggravating factor: a heavier cache of confiscated drugs will increase a defendant's offense level depending on where that weight falls in the Guidelines' table which links weights and offense levels.

One of the few downward adjustments that can lower a defendant's total offense level involves a two- or three-point deduction (three points become available if the total offense level is 16 or higher) if the defendant has demonstrated "acceptance of responsibility" for the crime. As Winstead (1996–1997) observes, this deduction was included in the Federal Sentencing Guidelines because, traditionally, "offenders who displayed true remorse for their acts received less severe sentences." (p. 1030) According to Hutchinson, Yellen, Hoffman, and Young's *Federal Sentencing Law and Practice* (2004), actions that offenders could take that are held as indicating that they have accepted responsibility for their actions include

(a) truthfully admitting the conduct comprising the offense(s) of conviction and truthfully admitting or not falsely denying any additional relevant conduct for which the defendant is accountable...;

(b) voluntary termination or withdrawal from criminal conduct or association;

(c) voluntary payment of restitution prior to adjudication of guilt;

(d) voluntary surrender to authorities promptly after commission of the offense;

(e) voluntary assistance to authorities in the recovery of the fruits and instrumentalities of the offense;

(f) post-offense rehabilitative efforts; and

(g) the timeliness of the defendant's conduct in manifesting the acceptance of responsibility (p. 1358).

O'Hear (1997) argues that district and appellate courts tend to have conflicting interpretations of what "acceptance of responsibility" means. O'Hear claims that appellate courts tend to link the acceptance of responsibility benefit to a defendant's remorse, while district courts tend to apply the deduction in response for a defendant's cooperation, that is, a guilty plea. One reason that remorse in defendants is valued is because it is viewed as an index of rehabilitative potential. In her 2005 article, "Speechless: The Silencing of Criminal Defendants," Natapoff writes

> Acceptance of responsibility and rehabilitation are intertwined, central goals of the criminal justice process. A defendant's acceptance of responsibility or remorse for his crime is usually seen as a necessary precursor to rehabilitation because it reflects an internalization of the wrongfulness of his actions. According to the Supreme Court, "[a]cceptance of responsibility ... demonstrates that an offender 'is ready and willing to admit his crime and to enter the correctional system in a frame of mind that affords hope for success in rehabilitation over a shorter period of time than might otherwise be necessary.'" (2005, pp. 1494–1495)

For sentencing ranges that exceed 24 months, the maximum of a sentencing range does not exceed the minimum by more than 25%. In January 2005, in the case of *United States v. Booker* (2005), the Supreme Court held that the Federal Sentencing Guidelines were no longer mandatory; as a result, a judge now has greater leeway to impose a sentence that is below the guidelines when she feels such a sentence is warranted.[1] Based upon the *Sourcebook of Federal Sentencing Statistics* (2005), however, the Guidelines appear to be used in much the same way that they were before *Booker*.[2] (In support of this claim, on February 20, Linda Greenhouse (2007) noted in the *New York Times* that a study by the United States Sentencing Commission last year reports that "judges have continued to impose sentences within the guidelines ... in 86% of all sentences.") In most cases then, it is that 25% of the lower end of the range that the judge exercises her discretion over, and on which a defendant's allocution can have an effect.

Over the years, case law has provided guidelines for the way in which the right of allocution is to be administered. According to *U.S. v. Mata-Grullon* (887 F.2d 23 (1989)), judges have to appear to be open to what the defendant is saying; specifically, a judge should not give the appearance that she has already made up her mind regarding the sentence. Additionally, a judge should not intimidate a defendant or prevent him from speaking freely (*U.S. v. Sparrow*, 673 F.2d 862 (1982); *U.S. v. Sarno*, 73 F.3d 1470 (1995)) and on the topic of his choice (*U.S. v. De Alba Pagan*, 33 F.3d 125 (1994); *U.S. v. Murphy*, 530 F.2d 1,2 (1976)). There are also some limits, however: according to *U.S. v. Mitchell*, the Court of Appeals for the Second Circuit noted that allocution does not entitle a defendant to "enter into a diatribe of the sentencing Judge" or of any other judicial body. Similarly, allocution should not be used for political, philosophical, or religious platform speeches (*U.S. v. Mitchell*, 392 F.2d 214 (1968)). If defendants choose to address the court by means of an allocution, they may do so, generally for as long as they like (*U.S. v. Li*, 115 F.3d 125 (1997)).

Typically a sentencing judge does not explicitly respond to a defendant's allocution. Instead, the judge's sentence is understood as responding to all of the preceding elements of the sentencing hearing – in fact, possibly all of the elements of the defendant's conviction – not just the defendant's allocution. This discursive feature of speaking without receiving a response makes allocution a largely monologic speech event. O'Hear (1997) suggests that one reason why many judges avoid asking defendants follow-up questions after allocution is to minimize defendants' risk of self-incrimination.

Defendants often use their allocution to make some sort of apology to the judge, their families, the victim(s), and/or the government. Apologies have been defined in many ways. For example, apologies have been treated as speech acts, acts "in which to *say* something is to *do* something" (Austin, 1962, p.12). As Austin (1962), Searle (1975), and others have observed, apologies involve the expression of emotions and feelings in a way that most other speech acts do not; as a result, the perceived sincerity of a speaker in producing an apology is critically important to an apology's success. Apologies have also been defined on the basis of their function: according to Goffman (1971), apologies constitute one of several types of "remedies" which function to restore harmony to an interpersonal breach. O'Hara and Yarn (2002) and Gill (2000) distinguish apologies from other kinds of remedies. This study follows Gill in holding that an apology differs from excuses and justifications in that it "involves both acceptance of responsibility for the act and an acknowledgment of its wrongfulness" (2000, p. 12).

Offering some kind of apology during allocution is a natural choice for a number of reasons. According to statistics provided by the Administrative Office of U.S. Courts for the year between October 1, 2004 and September 30, 2005, the national average of guilty pleas was 96%. Thus, the vast majority of federal criminal defendants have admitted their guilt prior to sentencing. In this way, the criterion of responsibility for the offense that is necessary for an apology has been met. According to the definition provided by Gill and others (cf. O'Hara & Yarn, 2002), apologies also communicate an acknowledgement of the wrongfulness of the action. Thus, apologies provide a means for displaying remorse, and, as noted above, remorse is linked to "acceptance of responsibility" – and the two- to three-level deduction in total offense level. At the highest offense levels, a reduction of three levels can mean a difference of eight years in prison. This makes apologizing a rhetorically savvy strategy for defendants. It can also be argued that the judge's invitation to allocute, which typically takes a form such as, "Mr./Ms. X, is there anything you would like to say on your own behalf before I sentence you today?," functions in a priming capacity for an apology: the judge's, "is there anything you'd like to say?," plausibly harkens back to parents' methods of eliciting apologies from their children. From this perspective, an apology could be understood as expected during allocution.

Apologizing during allocution also carries risks, however. A number of legal studies on apologies have developed the connections between an apology and responsibility for the offense. On the one hand, as Cohen (1999) and O'Hara and Yarn (2002) point out, in many situations an apology can function to bring about a resolution to a conflict and sometimes prevent legal action on the part of the injured party. On the other hand, an apology given by the offending party could be admitted as evidence at trial to establish the liability of the transgressor (O'Hara & Yarn, 2002, p. 1181). This fact might make an offending party unwilling to apologize even when she feels responsible for the offense and regrets her actions. As Cohen notes, some auto insurance companies counsel those whom they insure that coverage is contingent upon the insured party's not voluntarily assuming any liability – which in turn is understood as telling the insured party to not apologize in an accident situation (1999, pp. 1025–1026). This has ramifications for apologizing during allocution because, if a defendant who was convicted by a jury (after claiming to be innocent) apologizes for her offense at sentencing, her chances of successfully appealing the conviction could be harmed. Under the heading 'Practice guide,' *American Jurisprudence* develops this point explicitly.

> Counsel should advise the defendant of the right of allocution, if any, and to the possible dangers of making a judicial confession during allocution which might tend to prejudice an appeal or give the sentencing judge an opportunity to decide that the defendant lied at the trial and use it at sentencing. (75B, §1946)

Not apologizing during allocution also carries risks: if, for example, a defendant uses his allocution to maintain his innocence after having been found guilty, a judge might increase the severity of the sentence that is imposed. This is what happened in *U.S. v. Clemmons*, 48 F.3d 1020 (1995), a case decided in 1995 by the U.S. Court of Appeals for the Seventh Circuit. In response to Clemmons' allocutory claim that he never intended to commit fraud, the judge replied:

> I was set to be sympathetic for a plea for the low end of the guidelines, but I don't think you deserve that now. And I intend to sentence you to the maximum because I don't think you learned a thing. (*U.S. v. Clemmons*)

For defendants who have pleaded guilty, apologizing during allocution still carries risks. For these defendants, the risk of allocution lies in defendant statements that are inconsistent with the inhabitance of "the role of wrongdoer" (Emerson, 1969, p. 192). Emerson's observation with regard to juvenile delinquents has relevance for adult criminal defendants as well.

> In general, mere verbal expressions of remorse and contrition do not adequately communicate the commitment to the role of wrongdoer expected by court officials. A totally consistent performance is required, and this demands that the repentant delinquent convey a properly deferential and remorseful attitude by his demeanor. (1969, p. 192)

Goffman (1971) and Bach and Harnish (1979) observe that apologies are also ritual speech acts. According to Robinson (2006), ritual speech acts have to be in conformance with fairly strict rules; in this way they contrast with common speech acts, which are governed by much looser conventions (e.g., inviting someone to do something). As a result of these constraints, "[a]ll members of a community are expected to perform these speech acts in the appropriate circumstances, and are sanctioned if they fail to do so (or fail to perform them properly)" (p. 88). As a result of these general rules governing the production of apologies, defendants who produce a weak apology, or one that is perceived as insincere risk swaying the judge in the opposite direction and receiving the maximum sentence. Natapoff (2005) sums up the situation: "The stakes are as high as they can be: A defendant who gets it 'wrong' gets a longer sentence. For some defendants, this threat is enough to dissuade them from speaking at all" (p. 1466).

Even waiving the right of allocution, however, is not a completely safe choice: judges appear to vary in terms of how they understand a defendant's decision to decline the opportunity to address the court. One of the judges in this study went so far as to reassure defendants that he would not hold it against them if they chose not to speak. It appears that allocution is not viewed so neutrally by all judges, however. In the case of *Minnick v. Mississippi* 111 S. Ct. 486, 498 (1990), the Supreme Court asserted: "[w]hile every person is entitled to stand silent, it is more virtuous for the wrongdoer to admit his offense and accept the punishment he deserves."

Before addressing the additional ways in which the context of the sentencing hearing constrains what defendants can say during allocution, we briefly describe the data used for this study. The analysis offered here is based on the integration of two types of data: (1) studies by (socio)linguists and sociologists on identity management and the ways in which apologies have been observed to function and (2) ethnographic data from 52 sentencing hearings held between November 2004 and March 2006 in U.S. District Courts.[3] As part of my dissertation project, I collected 52 apologetic allocutions in three different courtrooms which are referred to here as the courtrooms of Judge X, Judge Y, and Judge Z.[4] I collected 17 allocutions in Judge X's courtroom, 17 allocutions in Judge Y's courtroom, and 18 allocutions in Judge Z's courtroom. I attended and took notes on each of the sentencing hearings and afterwards used recordings of the hearings to make my own transcripts for analysis. According to Walker (1990), and my own observations, the transcripts produced by court reporters are "cleaned up" in myriad ways – at a minimum, paralinguistic information such as hesitations, false starts, and crying is not represented, but on a deeper level, grammar deemed less than perfect (especially the grammar of attorneys and judges, but sometimes that of defendants, too) is often standardized for the printed version.

The 52 defendants consisted of 41 men and 11 women. Their ages ranged from 20 to 56, with a median age of 30. In terms of race, 26 of the defendants (50%) were Caucasian; 16 (31%) were African-American; 8 (15%) were Native American; 1 (2%) was Hispanic; and 1 (2%) was Asian.[5] Of the 49 defendants for whom I was able to obtain information regarding their educational history, the education level of 36 of the defendants (73%) consisted of a high school degree or less. Of the 52 defendants, 48 (92%) had pleaded guilty and 4 had gone to trial and been adjudged guilty by a jury.[6] Fifteen of the 52 defendants (29%) retained their own attorney; the remaining 37 (71%) had counsel that was appointed by the court.

In order to be sentenced under the Federal Sentencing Guidelines, the probation officer who prepares the Pre-Sentence Investigation report assigns defendants a criminal history category of I–VI: in this dataset, 18 defendants (34%) were assigned the lowest category, category I; 4 defendants (8%) were assigned to category II; 14 defendants (27%) were assigned to category III; 3 defendants (6%) were assigned to criminal history category IV; 4 defendants (8%) to category V; and 9 defendants (17%) to the highest category, VI. The crimes for which defendants were sentenced varied, but more defendants were charged with drug-related crimes than with any other category of crime (24 defendants). Firearm charges accounted for the largest group after drug crimes (14 defendants); after that came non-violent money-related crimes, such as theft, embezzlement, or fraud (6 defendants).

Nine of the 52 allocutions (17%) were prepared in advance and were read aloud by defendants at the sentencing hearing; the majority of the allocutions (43/52 – 83%) were delivered extemporaneously. The apology narratives ranged from 4 seconds to 186 seconds in length of time that they occupied. The median allocution time was 29.5 seconds. The kinds of things that defendants said during their allocutions varied, but I was able to capture the commonalities among them with 8 different codes and 26 subcodes. Briefly, defendants (1) accepted the opportunity to address the court, sometimes with markers of politeness ("Thank you") and deference ("Your Honor"); (2) they criticized their actions or offered a personal reaction to the offense, often by means of some sort of apology; (3) they talked about how they had changed or how they had learned a lesson from the experience; (4) they offered information in mitigation of a harsh sentence, such as by making mention of positive things they had done – either earlier in life, or during the commission of the crime; (5) they thanked family and friends for their support; (6) they made reference to the sentence that was about to be imposed – sometimes requesting leniency, other times conveying their acceptance of whatever sentence would be imposed; (7) they broke the frame of allocution by making reference to the context of the sentencing hearing; and (8) they ended their turn at talk, sometimes with politeness markers and honorific terms for the judge. If we define a token as an utterance consisting of an optional subject, a verb (or verbs if they are conjoined) and its object(s), which is usually demarcated by pauses, the majority of defendants' allocutions employed varying numbers of tokens of between three and five of the above-mentioned eight elements. Fifty-one of 52 allocutions (98%) made reference to the offense itself in way that cast blame on themselves or they offered a personal response to the offense, such as by means of a conventionalized apology (e.g., "Uh, I would just like to say to my family, I'm sorry for what I've put you guys through for the last few years" (X4: 1–2)).

The remainder of this chapter is devoted to a discussion of some additional risks and constraints associated with allocution that are less well-known. We address the assumption of *Green* (and other legal sources) that allocution provides an opportunity for effective speech on one's own behalf and we propose to qualify the understanding that allocution provides an opportunity to speak in mitigation of the sentence, and on any topic of the defendant's choice. It is important to expose these constraints because they challenge the assumptions prevalent in much of the official literature on allocution. In fact, this chapter proposes that the ideological construction of allocution as a benefit for defendants functions to obscure the constraints that the context of sentencing imposes on the exercise of the right of allocution. We will identify and discuss four ways in which the opportunities to address the court are considerably more limited than the linguistic ideologies surrounding allocution would suggest. The first two ways concern the degree to which defendants' stigmatized institutional identities limit the degree to which they can speak effectively on their own behalf as well as the kinds of things that can be offered in mitigation of punishment. The second two are linked to the discursive context of the sentencing hearing: we propose that the numerous ways in which the context of allocution differs from more prototypical contexts in which apologies are offered, as well as the judge's (typical) lack of response to an allocution, function to undercut the potential effectiveness of an allocution and limit the kinds of topics that can be addressed. We begin by examining the interplay between defendants' individual and role identities in the context of the courtroom.

We know from Goffman's study of social situations and his attention to shifting interactional roles that a speaker and addressee are always in some kind of role relationship with one another (Goffman, 1959, 1971, 1981). In the institutional context of the courtroom, defendants inhabit multiple identities simultaneously: they are gendered individuals; they are addressing someone with whom they have (typically) had very little previous interaction (possibly only the plea hearing); and they are also defined by their stigmatized institutional identity, that of criminal defendant (Goffman, 1963). Because the interaction takes place in an institutional context in which the furniture, the clothing of courtroom actors, and their physical positioning vis-à-vis one another serve to magnify their relative institutional statuses (cf. Hazard, 1962), the defendant's stigmatized institutional identity is brought to the foreground and his individual identity is pushed to the background.

The purpose of the institutional event taking place supplies another context-defining component: sentencing hearings are held for the purpose of imposing sentence on defendants. Given the growth of prison populations in recent years (see, e.g., Uggen, Manza, & Thompson, 2006) and the problems of prison violence (O'Connor, 2000, among many others) it will be presumed that defendants seek to minimize their sentences of imprisonment. As a result, when defendants make apologetic allocutions – as most of those who make an allocution appear to do – the metapragmatic framing supplied by the context of the courtroom functions so as to skew what defendants say towards the pole of self-interestedness. This is a problem because self-interestedness conflicts on a fundamental level with the perception of sincerity. Defendants who are understood as speaking out of self-interest will not be viewed as being sincerely remorseful, and, as was noted earlier, it is remorse that case law suggests is a reason for which a judge might sentence a defendant more leniently.

A defendant speaking in a way that is heard as fundamentally self-interested with regard to the sentence faces a substantial handicap in achieving persuasive eloquence. In this way, the realities of the courtroom conflict with the premise underlying the paean to allocution in *Green*. In order for a defendant to be able to tap into the rhetorical efficacy achieved by speaking on his own behalf, the defendant has to have the opportunity to speak in some kind of individual capacity. *Green* does not take into account the constraints that are imposed by inhabiting a stigmatized institutional identity. Thus, the degree to which a defendant is able to foreground his individual identity over his institutional identity in the context of the courtroom and tap into the benefits of allocution touted by *Green* is questionable.

Further, defendants whose criminal history category positions them as other than first-time offenders would appear to face an even bigger hurdle in this regard. Part of this has to do with the way in which apologies work: as Owen (1983) observes, "apologies seem to take on a 'commissive' aspect and to relate to future acts, not just past ones" (p. 119). Defendants with lengthy criminal records have most likely appeared in court before and could be presumed to have offered an apology, with at least an implicit promise of better behavior in the future: appearing in court for a second (or third, etc.) time casts doubt on the defendant's sincerity in making the previous apology, which in turn undermines the sincerity of the current apology. In this way, the weight of past offenses could function to foreground a defendant's institutional role identity to an even greater degree. This would result in a substantial restriction of the benefits of allocution and would suggest that allocution offers the most potential for defendants whose records frame them as least like a stereotypical criminal as possible. In this way, ideas about allocution function in the ways described of language ideologies: under a banner which labels it as a protection for defendants (presumably all defendants), allocution instead appears to reify the distinctions which the criminal justice system imposes upon those whom it processes. Defendants who most closely approximate the criminal defendant stereotype appear to be least able to make use of the opportunity to speak on their own behalf due to the stigmatizing effects of inhabiting this institutional role identity; in other words, the more that defendants are associated with this role identity, the greater the stigmatizing effect.

In the context of the sentencing hearing, defendants' role identities function in another way: they limit the topics that are available for an allocution. As noted above, Rule 32(i)(4)(A)(ii) affords the defendant two rights: "to make a statement in his own behalf" and "to present any information in mitigation of punishment." Examples of the kinds of things that might serve to mitigate punishment include the defendant's good record, a difficult childhood, or the defendant's feelings of remorse. In this dataset, four defendants appeared to try to mitigate their offense by asserting that certain socially disapproved of actions that are understood as typically occurring in the commission of the defendants' particular crimes did not, according to them, take place. These attempts at mitigation did not appear to have the desired effect of framing the defendants' actions in a better light. Two examples are presented below. The mitigating elements being referred to are underlined; the entire allocutions are provided for context.

In the transcribed utterances, the following symbols are used:

~	Pseudonym
#	Unintelligible; 1 per syllable
#word	Transcribed word is uncertain
#word_#word	Uncertain which of two words is heard
.	A pause (when it occurs mid-sentence)
Word	Bold-face indicates emphasis via loudness or contrastive pitch

Mr. XH was a 35-year-old Caucasian man who was being sentenced for producing and selling methamphetamine, to which he had pleaded guilty. He was classified as having the highest possible criminal history category: VI. In Judge X's courtroom, the defendant was typically given the right of allocution before the attorneys made their recommendation for sentence; in this particular case, however, Mr. XH's attorney arranged that Mr. XH would make his statement after he finished making his recommendation.[7]

X8. Def. Atty; ~ Mr. H wants to say something to you.
     ~ Judge X; Yes, and I want to ask him to say – ~ Mr. H:
1   ~ Mr. H; . Uh, yeah, um .
2   I mean if I could go back and do this over, I'd do a whole lot of things different,

3   Uh, . I can't say it would change the outcome of it
a whole lot so, . Um .

4   People I've hurt, . um, more than any of 'em my family, . my friends, .

5   um, . uh, . the community,

6   As far as the environmental thing um, .

7   I guess the way it's written, I'm . basically guilty of it .

8   but uh, . one thing I did I-I was . – regardless of **what**
I did out there, I was

9   always careful not to dump any #methamphetamine #out #there #I
#mean

10   [Judge X interrupts for clarification here]

11   I was always careful **not** to damage the environment – that's one thing
I did **try**

12   not to do – I mean, I . – I love to fish and hunt and . outside, you
know.

13   If-if you look further in the reports, my chemicals were all put back in
the

14   containers . and were dropped off at recycling centers.

15   I haven't dumped any on the ground, or . polluted anything in that
way.

16   Um, . Whatever you give me, I'm gonna do it, I'm gonna make the
best of it,

17   I'm gonna try and . do whatever school programs
I can while I'm there . and all,

18   make sure this doesn't happen again.

19   I'm hoping that . I can end up somewhere . close to home so I can at
least see

20   my mother?

21   Um, . yeah, I just apologize to the court for takin up your
time, .

22   and the community, for what I've done, . um, .

23   anybody that was harmed in any way by what I did.

24   I mean I . I didn't mean to hurt **any**body. .

25   And that's . t's about it. .

26   I just apologize.

27   Judge X; Thank you.

After the prosecuting attorney made his recommendation for sentence, Judge X delivered her closing remarks. She noted that Mr. XH had engaged in producing and selling methamphetamine in the past. In addition, as if in response to Mr. XH's allocutory claims of environmentalism, Judge X noted that "a clandestine lab cleanup crew was needed to remove the anhydrous ammonia that was improperly stored in the unlocked propane tank and to clean up other chemicals related to the manufacturing process." On one level, Mr. XH's claim about dropping off chemicals at recycling centers is not mutually incompatible with the meth lab containing improperly stored anhydrous ammonia. It was the metamessage that Mr. XH was environmentally conscious and a "good citizen," that Judge X challenged with her comment. Thus, while Mr. XH appeared to be trying to frame his crime (and himself) in a less blameworthy light, Judge X's assertion rendered his attempt ultimately unsuccessful. Due to the procedure of who speaks when at the sentencing hearing, Judge X got to have the last word on Mr. XH's environmentalism.

Mr. YE was a 30-year-old African-American man. He was being sentenced for robbing a bank and had previously entered a guilty plea. Mr. YE's criminal history category was I (the lowest category).

Y5.	~ Judge Y; ~ Mr. E, do you wish to be heard . prior to sentencing?
1	~ Mr. E; Yes, Sir.
2	~ Judge Y; You may proceed.
3	~ Mr. E; . It's . hard to explain the words, the conviction I feel . about what I've done,
4	but . I do realize that . it was the wrong way to go about getting money .
5	and scaring people and puttin their lives in danger . **is serious**.
6	Although I didn't pull a gun out, .
7	it should be taken serious, because I could've –
8	I **did** put people's lives in danger.
9	Um, . I know firsthand how the people felt – . well, they felt pretty shooken up, .
10	'cause I was a victim of robbery in a-uh-um . carjackin that took place a coupla
11	years back. .
12	And I know how much it shook me up.
13	So I **did** ask myself, . I'm sayin why would I put somebody else through
14	#this_#the same situation,
15	and the main thing that came to mind was, that I was just thinkin about myself at

16   the time
17   – I wasn't thinkin about the people in the bank,
18   I wasn't thinkin about my family,
19   I wasn't even thinkin about God that sees all,
20   I was just thinkin about what I can gain at the
      time .
21   because I was about to lose my business,
22   and I know I had borrowed money from other people, and owed
      them.
23   Um, . I know the [Presentence Report] recommended . I think four to
      five years,
24   but, . I'll be thirty-one next month .
25   and uh-um, . I've been sittin in jail for seven months on this
      case .
26   and I've had a lotta time to think about what I've done .
27   and I've gotten a lotta good out of it and have
      a different outlook on life.
28   And I – so I hope you . think what I'm sayin **is** sincere because it is.
29   And, . basically, . I hope that you'll let deserve
      a reduced sentence or even
30   released on supervision if you will.
31   I do regret what I've done.
32   I know I – . done people wrong and .
33   I sorry about that.
34   Thanks.
35   Judge Y; ∼ Mr. Smith, anything on behalf of the government?

Mr. YE's attempt at mitigation was problematic in the same way that Mr. XH's had been in that he tried to offer a version of the events of the crime that positioned himself in a less blameworthy light. What made Mr. YE's attempt at mitigation different from Mr. XH's was that he went to considerable lengths to allocate blame to himself for frightening the tellers at the bank. It appeared that his attempt to "undo" the damage caused by his attempt at mitigation was unsuccessful, however. After Mr. YE's attorney, Mr. YE, and the prosecuting attorney had made their statements, Judge Y said, as part of his closing remarks.

And you will recall the – uh, the – uh, uh, plea at which time he did stipulate to that threatening conduct where he entered the bank with a gun, jumped on a teller's counter, threatened to kill and/or shoot the bank employees.

In this way, Judge Y communicates that whether or not Mr. YE actually pulled the gun out is irrelevant. In both of these examples, the defendants have offered crime-related information that has no bearing on the legal categorization – and hence, the accompanying consequences – of the crime. Although the content that defendants offer in these examples is technically irrelevant, the fact that defendants are understood as attempting to frame their criminal actions in a better light is not.

Although defendants are accepted authorities with regard to recounting positive actions they have performed in the past (just as individuals are culturally accepted authorities with regard to how they feel about things (Labov & Fanshel, 1977; Oatley, 1992), they are not accepted as authorities on the topic of the crime. As a result of having been processed by the criminal justice system (in conjunction with their guilty plea), other people, that is, the prosecutor, the undercover detective, etc. now have the authority to tell the story of "what happened" (cf. Merry, 1990), and the defendant is accorded the status of a distinctly unreliable narrator. For a defendant to attempt to recast at sentencing the story of what happened or didn't happen as part of the crime is really not his to tell any more; attempting to do so in the face of these unspoken rules can subject the defendant to character-damaging implications that could have a negative influence on the judge – and, as a result, the sentence.

In all four of the cases in which defendants appeared to attempt to mitigate their offenses by highlighting the absence of a blameworthy element of the crime, the defendants received some sort of rebuke or challenge by the judge during closing remarks. In the examples presented here, the judges recast the defendants' versions of the crime in more blameworthy ways during their closing remarks. What was at issue was not the falsity of the mitigating statements themselves: Mr. XH may indeed have practiced recycling and Mr. YE might not have pulled the gun out. At issue was the defendants' attempts to portray their crimes – and hence, themselves – in a more flattering light. With regard to the sentences they received, Mr. YE (Y5) was assigned a sentence at the upper end of the guideline range (63 months from a range of 51–63 months) and Mr. XH (X8) received the statutory maximum for his crime (120 months). Of course, many factors go in to the assignment of a sentence. Nonetheless, in these cases it seems safe to posit that the defendants' allocutions did not help their positions and may, in fact, have hurt them.[8]

What we find then, is a mismatch between the ideologies associated with allocution and the constraints that are supplied by the context of the sentencing hearing. According to Rule 32, the defendant is invited to speak on his own behalf and present information in mitigation of the sentence. Given that the defendant is being sentenced on the basis of particular crimes he has been convicted of committing, the topic of those crimes would, on face value, seem to be a relevant topic for allocution. In fact, however, for the defendant to recount his version of events when his version portrays him in a less blameworthy way (or worse, conflicts with the officially sanctioned version) is, in practice, off-limits – especially if the defendant has already pleaded guilty.

I have identified two ways in which defendants' institutional role identities function to limit the ways in which they can make use of the right of allocution to speak effectively on their own behalf. Next we turn to constraints that are associated with the discursive context of allocution. As has been noted, defendants often use their allocution to make some sort of apology to the judge, their families, the victim(s), and/or the government. Allocution constitutes a non-prototypical context for the production of an apology in a number of different ways (cf. Komter, 1998). First, the person to whom the defendant is addressing her apology was not directly affected by the defendant's actions. In addition, in typical apologies the apology follows the offense within a relatively short period of time and is in turn followed by a response from the addressee. In the context of the sentencing hearing, many months can intervene between the offense and the apology produced at sentencing; furthermore, as noted above the judge usually does not respond to the apology narrative produced by the defendant in the way that addressees of apologies are typically expected to respond, for example, "that's OK"; "I accept your apology"; or by means of some further exchange: "do you really mean it?"

The context constrains defendants' allocutions in another way, as well. As Owen (1983) observes, "…apologi[z]ing is one of a class of acts that are expected to be performed without prompting." (p. 136) Thus, the "best" apologies should be those which are unprompted. Because of the rules of courtroom interaction (i.e., the judge controls the conversational floor to a high degree), this option is not available for defendants. Thus, at the same time that the judge invites the defendant to allocute, she deprives him of the opportunity for making a truly unprompted apology. Judges are most certainly aware that an unprompted apology is not an option for defendants in this context, but this awareness does not preclude a defendant's apology from being tainted by this circumstance in some way. It is possible that the prompting frames in which defendants' apology narratives are always encased in this context subtly undermine the sincerity of the apologies that are produced. Additionally, although the defendant will be formally addressing a single person (the judge), the presence of other persons in the courtroom – especially, perhaps, the court reporter who is converting evanescent speech into text before the defendant's eyes – could function to inhibit the display of emotion. According to Tavuchis (1991), the presence of multiple parties fosters the creation of a punitive atmosphere (p. 52).

In many ways, then, the apologies produced in the context of sentencing hearings are unlike those that are produced in more interpersonal contexts. We propose that the mismatch between the addressee and the person(s) who was/were harmed, the time lapse between offense and apology, the prompting frame in which the apology is produced, the formal context, and defendants' self-interest in the impending sentence function to weaken defendants' apologies. As producers of weak-sounding apologies, defendants are additionally subject to the taint of insincerity. In spite of these drawbacks, 51 of 52 defendants produced statements which involved acceptance of responsibility for the offense and an acknowledgment that it was wrong. Thus, defendants face a double-bind at sentencing: an apology appears to be expected, but the discursive and situational constraints in which the apology is produced function in such a way as to undermine the effectiveness of that apology.

The discursive context in which allocutions are produced limits what defendants can say during allocution in another way. As Coulmas (1981) observed, apologies typically occur in a three-part sequence: the misdeed, the apology, and some kind of response by the addressee.[9] Earlier, we observed that allocution provides an atypical context for the production of an apology because judges usually do not respond to the content of defendants' allocutions. After defendants finished delivering their allocutions, Judge X and Judge Z usually said only, "Thank you"; Judge Y usually called the name of the prosecuting attorney, thereby inviting him or her to give a recommendation for sentencing. This means that defendants who apologize during allocution are producing a fundamentally dialogic speech act in a monologic context. This atypical discursive context is bound to impact the way in which an apology is understood.

The monologic context of allocution appears to have another effect, as well: it limits what defendants say on the topic of "lessons learned." This effect, in all likelihood, would have remained hidden, if it hadn't been for one unusual hearing in which the monologic structure of allocution was broken. (Basing a claim on the strength of a single interaction is, of course, risky; however, if the pattern of monologic allocutions is the norm, we cannot expect to find many examples of the divergent and revealing pattern.) In the case of X12, Ms. XL, a 41-year-old Caucasian woman, had been convicted of taking an envelope containing a check for $2,000 while working for the U.S. Postal Service. Ms. XL's allocution was quite short. In response to Judge X's question, "Ms. L, is there anything you'd like to say on your own behalf before I sentence you?" Ms. XL said, "Well, I know I made a mistake . and . I'm sorry for that. Um, I can't go back and change what I did but I . have learned from it. And um, . this #thing will never happen again." At this point Judge X broke the frame of monologicality and asked Ms. XL to elaborate, saying: "And what do you think you've learned?" In response, Ms. XL said, "That . things aren't . as bad as you think they are. There's always people out there that can help #me."

This example is interesting for many reasons. First, it was the only case in which a judge asked a question that had real bearing on the content of the defendant's allocution and was not simply a point-of-information question or one oriented towards building rapport with the defendant.[10] Judge X's question was real and Ms. XL's answer had potentially real significance – in other words, she could have answered badly. Given that this interchange was exceptional, it is worth examining that factors that made this case different from others. Although O'Hear (1997) suggests that many judges avoid asking defendants follow-up questions so as to minimize their opportunities to incriminate themselves, Ms. XL appeared to be a model defendant, and as a result, unlikely to aggravate her situation. This was a first offense for Ms. XL, who had a strong employment record. In addition, her offense level was the lowest offense level in my dataset. (A total of three defendants (including Ms. XL) had the same offense level.) The fact that she had committed a white-collar crime as opposed to the drug crimes that populated the dockets is worth mentioning, as is her gender, due to the relative infrequency of women who inhabit the role of criminal defendant. This case was also one of the 25% of the 52 cases in the dataset in which defendant and judge belonged to the same categories of gender and race. After Ms. XL delivered her allocution, her attorney personally attested to Ms. XL's sincerity, saying: "…I think of all the defendants that I have represented that she really feels the worst about committing this crime."[11] All of these factors suggest that Ms. XL was a highly unusual defendant and a good candidate for a more personal exchange at sentencing.

The break in monologicality is interesting for another reason: Judge X appeared to find Ms. XL's answer to her follow-up question very insightful. In 15 of 16 cases, Judge X responded to defendants' allocutions with "Thank you;" in response to Ms. XL's allocution however, Judge X said appreciatively, "That's very valuable."[12] She also paused for nearly three and a half seconds before responding. This was the longest pause among the 17 allocutions in the dataset that took place in Judge X's courtroom.

One way to identify what distinguished Ms. XL's answer with regard to what she said she learned from the kinds of things that other defendants said is to look at the other cases in which defendants used "lesson-learned" type language and the allocutory material that followed it. In all of these examples, defendants proceeded on to the topic of forbearance.

X1:	28	I have learned my lesson
	29	I promise I will not stand in front of you again.
X12:	4	but I . have learned from it.
	5	And um, . this #thing will never happen again.
X16:	7	I've definitely learned from it, you know.
	8	I guarantee myself that I would – . next time anyone hears about me or anything
	9	like that, it's . gonna be in a positive manner, you know, in a positive direction, so
Y9:	3	I learned, from bein incarcerated, . that
	4	that . never do this again.
	5	It's not **worth** it – it's not worth losin my daughter.
Y14:	9	I have learned a lesson
	10	and will **not** repeat this mistake ever again.

Although the numbers are small, there is a striking pattern: after defendants make claims to have learned from the preceding, crime-related events, what comes next is a statement about the future that depicts a change in the defendant's actions. We might say that in the genre of courtroom apologies, claims about "lessons learned" during allocution appear to be linked to statements regarding how that lesson will translate into changed (and "better") behavior in the future.

When defendants use different language for their "lessons learned" statements and talk about "realizations" that they have had, these realizations tend to be focused on their criminal actions and similarly framed in moral/evaluative terms such as "right" and "wrong": for example, "First of all, . I now realize . my actions that led me here . were wrong." (X17: 3) What we don't see in naturally occurring allocutions is defendants offering the kinds of lessons that Ms. XL offered in response to

Judge X's question in an unelicited context. In fact, during her allocution, Ms. XL exemplified the pattern that appears to be typical.

X12:   3   Um, I can't go back and change what I did
        4   but I . have learned from it.
        5   And um, . this #thing will never happen again.

After claiming to have learned from what happened (line 4), Ms. XL offered a future, forbearance-related statement: "And um, . this #thing will never happen again" (line 5). It was Judge X's question, "And what do you think you've learned?" that appeared to provide the frame which allowed Ms. XL to share what appeared to be a real insight (or "lesson") that she had gained from her experience. This pattern, although preliminary, of course, suggests that a monologic context is not conducive to the sharing of certain kinds of more personal information.

The guideline range under which Ms. XL was sentenced was 0–6 months; she was assigned a non-prison sentence and was required to spend two months in a Community Corrections Center.[13] (All of the defendants were assigned terms of varying length of supervision after they finished serving their sentences.) This rare exchange dramatically reveals the ways in which different frames for speaking – monologic versus dialogic – can constrain or make available resources for constructing the self.

Allocution is understood as providing defendants with the opportunity to speak on their own behalf at sentencing and to offer information in mitigation of the sentence. For these reasons, this long-standing sentencing tradition is understood as a benefit for defendants. Understood in this way, allocution reflects linguistic ideologies – sets of beliefs about language articulated as a rationalization of perceived language use. As linguistic ideologies provide speakers with channels for accessing some aspects of the ways that language functions, they also obscure other aspects of language function. It was proposed that the belief that allocution serves defendants' interests obscures the ways in which the context of sentencing hearings constrains both what defendants can say and the degree to which they can speak effectively on their own behalf.

We have discussed four ways in which the context of sentencing hearings constrains the possibilities for making a successful allocution. In the context of the courtroom, defendants' stigmatized institutional role identities tend to privilege a reading of defendants' apologies as motivated by self-interest as opposed to sincere remorse, which undermines the sincerity that has been judged as essential for a successful apology. Relatedly, we proposed that the more a defendant's record and background approaches the stereotype of "career criminal," the less potential allocution offers for making an effective statement on one's own behalf. Second, although the definition of allocution invites defendants to offer information in mitigation of punishment, as criminal defendants they are no longer authorized to narrate the events of the crime in a way that reduces the culpability of the offense, even if the mitigating facts that are offered are uncontested. Based on the data I have collected, defendants who emphasized potentially mitigating aspect of their crimes risked being corrected by the sentencing judge during the judge's final remarks; they also risked receiving sentences that were above the minimum prescribed by the Federal Sentencing Guidelines. The discursive context in which allocutions are produced also impacts what defendants say and how their statements are received. Specifically, we proposed that the context of sentencing hearings undercuts the degree to which defendants can apologize "well" in many different ways. Lastly, the monologic nature of allocution also appears to impose limits on the kinds of things that defendants can say. We examined one anomalous case in which there was a break-through to dialogicality between defendant and judge, and argued that the dialogical frame allowed the defendant to share a true lesson of her experience in a way that does not appear to be available for defendants speaking in a monologic context.

The ways in which defendants might harm their position by saying the "wrong" thing at sentencing have been discussed in the literature; the ways in which the context handicaps defendants' allocutions have received much less attention. If lawmakers and judges believe that defendants can speak freely and on any topic of their choice and are unaware of the constraints that the context of allocution imposes on the statements made therein, what defendants actually say could be assessed relative to an impossible standard.

NOTES

1. Before *Booker*, a judge could depart from the Guidelines only when the court found that there was "an aggravating or mitigating circumstance of a kind, or to a degree, not adequately taken into consideration by the Sentencing Commission in promulgating the Guidelines" (*American Jurisprudence 2d*, 21A, §840).

2. The 2005 Sourcebook reports that from October 1, 2004 until January 11, 2005, 70.9% of all federal sentences imposed fell within the guideline range that applied. In the eight and a half months remaining in the court's calendar year after *Booker*, 61.6% of all federal sentences fell within the guideline range. Because the rate of above-the-guideline sentences was under 1%, we know that the increase in non-guideline sentences post-*Booker* consisted largely of below-the-guideline sentences. The difference in below-the-guideline sentences after *Booker* was approximately 10%.

3. I am very grateful for a dissertation improvement grant from the National Science Foundation's Law and Social Science Program which covered the costs of travel and the purchase of official transcripts. I am also grateful to the University of Chicago's Language Laboratories and Archives and especially Barbara Need for permission to borrow recording equipment.

4. In order to protect the identities of all of the persons involved in this study, the names of all courtroom actors have been changed.

5. Information regarding defendants' race (and the racial categories themselves) came from public documents available for the cases in Judge X's and Judge Y's courtrooms; for the defendants in Judge Z's courtroom (for whom these public records were not available), I assigned defendants a race based on their appearance.

6. This rate of 92% of defendants in the data set who pleaded guilty is lower than the national average: according to government statistics from 10/1/04–9/30/05, 96% of all convictions of federal defendants resulted from guilty pleas. See http://www.uscourts.gov/judbus2005/appendices/d7.pdf

7. The relative sequential position in which the defendant's allocution occurred in the sentencing hearing differed across the three courtrooms. If we identify the major sentencing hearing events as: P – prosecuting attorney makes recommendation for sentence; D – defense attorney makes recommendation for sentence; and A – defendant's allocution, in Judge X's courtroom, the order was A, D, P; in Judge Y's courtroom, the order was D, A, P; and in Judge Z's courtroom, the order of events was P, D, A.

8. Another defendant (not included in the discussion here) recast the events of his crime in a way that conflicted with the government's version. This turned out to be a more harmful strategy than mentioning mitigating aspects of the crime that were not necessarily false. After the sentencing hearing, this defendant was immediately taken into custody. Typically, defendants who had been free on bond to appear for sentencing remained free until the start date of their sentence.

9. It is an open question whether apologies that precede a misdeed are true apologies or some kind of hybrid speech act. This chapter does not take a position on this point.

10. In the data set there were only three cases (X12, Z1, and Z3) in which the judge engaged the defendant in some way so as to follow up on something that the defendant said during allocution. In the cases of Z1 and Z3, Judge Z asked point-of-information questions. Additionally there were brief exchanges between judge and defendant that were not related to the allocution in Y6, Z5, and Z16. In Judge Z's courtroom the exchanges appeared to be rapport-oriented.

11. This quote was taken from the official transcript of the hearing.

12. In the 16th case, Judge X's responded by saying the name of the defense attorney, thereby inviting him to make a recommendation with regard to the sentence that should be imposed.

13. Sentences to Community Correction Centers typically required defendants to be present in the facility unless they were working or attending rehabilitative programs.

ACKNOWLEDGEMENTS

I am grateful to Valentina Tikoff and Ben Williams and two anonymous reviewers for valuable feedback on earlier drafts of this chapter. Thanks are also extended to Austin Sarat for encouraging me to submit this chapter.

REFERENCES

American Jurisprudence 2d. (1998). Rochester, NY: Lawyers Cooperative Publishing Company.

Austin, J. L. (1962). *How to do things with words*. Cambridge, MA: Harvard University Press.

Bach, K., & Harnish, R. P. (1979). *Linguistic communication and speech acts*. Cambridge, MA: MIT Press.

Cohen, J. (1999). Advising clients to apologize. *Southern California Law Review, 72*, 1009–1069.

Coulmas, F. (1981). Poison to your soul. Thanks and apologies contrastively viewed. In: F. Coulmas (Ed.), *Conversational Routine* (pp. 69–92). The Hague: Mouton.

Emerson, R. (1969). *Judging delinquents*. New York: Aldine.

Gill, K. (2000). The moral functions of an apology. *The Philosophical Forum, XXXI*, 11–27.

Goffman, E. (1959). *The presentation of self in everyday life*. New York: Doubleday.

Goffman, E. (1963). *Stigma*. New York: Simon and Schuster, Inc.

Goffman, E. (1971). *Relations in public. Microstudies of the public order*. New York: Basic Books, Inc.

Goffman, E. (1981). *Forms of talk*. Philadelphia: University of Pennsylvania Press.

Greenhouse, L. (February 20, 2007). Justices to revisit thorny issue of sentencing guidelines in first cases after recess. *New York Times*.

Harvard Law Review. (1968). Note: Procedural due process at judicial sentencing for felony. *Harvard Law Review, 81*, 821–846.

Hazard, J. N. (1962). Furniture arrangement as a symbol of judicial roles. *Etc.: A Review of General Semantics, XIX*, 181–188.

Hill, J. (1998). "Today there is no respect": Nostalgia, "respect", and oppositional discourse in Mexicano (Nahuatl) language ideology. In: B. Schieffelin, K. Wollard & P. Kroskrity (Eds), *Language ideologies: Practice and theory* (pp. 68–86). New York: Oxford University Press.

Hutchinson, T., Yellen, D., Hoffman, P., & Young, D. (Eds). (2004). *Federal sentencing law and practice.* St. Paul: West Group.

Komter, M. L. (1998). *Dilemmas in the courtroom. A study of trials of violent crime in the Netherlands.* Mahwah, NJ: Lawrence Erlbaum Associates, Inc.

Labov, W., & Fanshel, D. (1977). *Therapeutic discourse.* New York: Academic Press.

Merry, S. E. (1990). *Getting justice and getting even. Legal consciousness among working-class Americans.* Chicago: University of Chicago Press.

Natapoff, A. (2005). Speechless: The silencing of criminal defendants. *New York University Law Review, 80,* 1449–1504.

O'Connor, P. (2000). *Speaking of crime. Narratives of prisoners.* Lincoln: University of Nebraska Press.

O'Hara, E., & Yarn, D. (2002). On apology and consilience. *Washington Law Review, 77,* 1121–1192.

O'Hear, M. (1997). Remorse, cooperation, and "acceptance of responsibility": The structure, implementation, and reform of Section 3E1.1 of the federal sentencing guidelines. *Northwestern University Law Review, 91,* 1507–1573.

Oatley, K. (1992). *Best laid schemes. The psychology of emotions.* Paris: Cambridge University Press.

Owen, M. (1983). *Apologies and remedial interchanges. A study of language use in social interaction.* Berlin: Mouton.

Robinson, D. (2006). *Introducing performative pragmatics.* New York: Routledge.

Searle, J. R. (1975). A taxonomy of illocutionary acts. In: K. Gunderson (Ed.), *Minnesota studies in the philosophy of science* (Vol. VII, Language, Mind and Knowledge, pp. 344–369). Minneapolis: University of Minnesota Press.

Silverstein, M. (1979). Language structure and linguistic ideology. In: P. R. Clyne, W. F. Hanks & C. L. Hofbauer (Eds), *The elements: A Parasession on linguistic units and levels* (pp. 193–247). Chicago: Chicago Linguistic Society.

Silverstein, M. (1981). The limits of awareness. In: *Working papers in sociolinguistics* (Numbers 81–87, Number 84, pp. 1–30). Austin, TX: Southwest Educational Development Laboratory.

Sourcebook of Federal Sentencing Statistics. (2005). U.S. Sentencing Commission.

Tavuchis, N. (1991). *Mea Culpa. A sociology of apology and reconciliation.* Stanford: Stanford University Press.

Uggen, C., Manza, J., & Thompson, M. (2006). Citizenship, democracy, and the civic reintegration of criminal offenders. *Annals of the American Academy of Political and Social Science, 605,* 281–310.

Walker, A. G. (1990). Language at work in the law. The customs, conventions, and appellate consequences of court reporting. In: J. N. Levi & A. G. Walker (Eds), *Language and the Judicial Process* (pp. 203–244). New York: Plenum Press.

Winstead, J. (1996–1997). *Nuñez-Rodriguez* and a defendant's acceptance of responsibility: A jailbreak from the confinement of the federal sentencing guidelines? *Kentucky Law Journal, 85,* 1021–1041.

Woolard, K. (1998). Introduction: Language ideology as a field of inquiry. In: B. Schieffelin, K. Woolard & P. Kroskrity (Eds), *Language ideologies. Practice and theory* (pp. 3–47). Oxford: Oxford University Press.

Wright, C. A., King, N. J., & Klein, S. R. (Eds). (2004). *Federal practice and procedure: Criminal 3d.* Thomson/West.

Cases Cited

Green v. United States, 365 U.S. 301 (1961)
McGautha v. California, 402 U.S. 183 (1971)
Minnick v. Mississippi, 111 S. Ct. 486, 498 (1990)
U.S. v. Booker, 125 U.S. 738 (2005)
U.S. v. Clemmons, 48 F.3d 1020 (1995)
U.S. v. De Alba Pagan, 33 F.3d 125 (1994)
U.S. v. Li, 115 F.3d 125 (1997)
U.S. v. Mata-Grullon, 887 F.2d 23 (1989)
U.S. v. Mitchell, 392 F.2d 214 (1968)
U.S. v. Murphy, 530 F.2d 1,2 (1976)
U.S. v. Sarno, 73 F.3d 1470 (1995)
U.S. v. Sparrow, 673 F.2d 862 (1982)

BLOOD RELATIONS: COLLECTIVE MEMORY, CULTURAL TRAUMA, AND THE PROSECUTION AND EXECUTION OF TIMOTHY McVEIGH

Jody Lyneé Madeira

ABSTRACT

Based on interviews with 27 victims' family members and survivors, this chapter explores how memory of the Oklahoma City bombing was constructed through participation in groups formed after the bombing and participation in the trials of Timothy McVeigh and Terry Nichols. It first addresses the efficacy of a collective memory perspective. It then describes the mental context in which interviewees joined groups after the bombing, the recovery functions groups played, and their impact on punishment expectations. Next, it discusses a media-initiated involuntary relationship between McVeigh and interviewees. Finally, this chapter examines execution witnesses' perceptions of communication with McVeigh in his trial and execution.

Studies in Law, Politics, and Society, Volume 45, 75–138
ISSN: 1059-4337/doi:10.1016/S1059-4337(08)45003-2

1. INTRODUCTION

On April 19, 1995, thousands of pounds of fuel oil and fertilizer brought down the nine-story Alfred P. Murrah Federal Building. A total of 842 persons were injured or killed as a direct result of this tragedy; 168 of the 842 were killed, 19 of whom were children (Sitterle & Gurwitch, 1999, p. 163). The blast left 462 homeless and damaged 312 buildings and businesses (Sitterle & Gurwitch, pp. 163–164). In the weeks and months following the bombing, several groups emerged and became extraordinarily active, serving as magnets for community membership and resources; formative among them were the Oklahoma City National Memorial Task Force, charged with overseeing the building of the Oklahoma City National Memorial, and a group comprised of family members and survivors seeking to shorten the lengthy habeas appeals process so as to bring peace to victims' families. In subsequent trials, Timothy McVeigh and Terry Nichols were indicted and charged with eight counts of first-degree murder for the deaths of federal officials as well as several other federal charges, including conspiracy. While McVeigh was convicted in June 1997 on all counts and sentenced to death, the jury in Nichols' trial found him guilty of involuntary manslaughter and conspiracy after deliberating for 41 hours, failing to reach a unanimous verdict on whether Nichols planned the bombing "with the intent to kill." After being sentenced to life in prison without possibility of parole, Nichols was tried and convicted in 2004 of 162 counts for first-degree murder in Oklahoma state court, but again escaped the death penalty.

The legal aftermath of the Oklahoma City Bombing culminated in the execution of Timothy McVeigh. On June 12, 2001, 232 witnesses – 10 in the death house at the state penitentiary in Terre Haute, Indiana and 222 at a remote viewing location in Oklahoma City – prepared for an event that all hoped would bring some ending to an unspeakable period in their lives. Whereas "live" witnesses viewed a side profile of McVeigh, "remote" witnesses observed the closed circuit feed from a camera positioned on the ceiling directly over McVeigh's face. Although the remarks of Attorney General John Ashcroft emphasized "closure," most witnesses found some element of the execution disappointing. Sue Ashford, a survivor who witnessed the execution via closed-circuit transmission, stated "the man just went to sleep" (Romano, 2001). Paul Howell, another witness, lamented, "We didn't get anything from his face. His facial expressions were just about as calm as they could be" (Romano). Larry Whicher said that "it doesn't provide as much as I thought it would" (Romano).

Dramatic and tragic deaths are cultural traumas that require explanation. In their wake, understandings are formed collectively through such processes as interpersonal discussion and media coverage. "Interest" groups form in the aftermath of traumatic events to facilitate collective information-gathering and mourning. In the context of the Oklahoma City bombing, memory of the bombing as a culturally traumatic event was constructed through social processes, and ties formed out of bloodshed that both helped and hindered family members' and survivors reconstructions of meaning. Rapport that developed between members of prominent task-oriented community groups which formed in the days and weeks after the bombing was a key source of mnemetic energy, and these bonds were often felt to be as strong as those of blood kinship. In addition, an involuntary association between victims' families and survivors and perpetrators Timothy McVeigh and Terry Nichols crystallized at 9:02 a.m. on April 19, 1995. If voluntary relationships between members of community groups were strengthening and constructive ties, then this involuntary victim-offender relationship was a destructive and confining tie that trussed victims to the bombing as an event.

To study these relationships, their construction and representative effects, is to step into a realm where research has yet to shed light. This article considers how family members and survivors made sense of the bombing through both group membership and participation in legal proceedings. Engaging in collective memory work, their responses to the bombing were shaped by two primary relationships: the positive, healing, unmediated relationships formed between group members and the negative, destructive, mediated relationships between family members/survivors and Timothy McVeigh. Specifically, it poses three research questions. First, in the wake of collective cultural trauma, what impact, if any, does advocacy group membership have upon memory? Second, when pursuing accountability for criminal perpetrators of collective trauma, how do victims' family members and survivors negotiate institutional constraints to form perceptions of these perpetrators and conclusions about the "meaning" of the traumatic event? Finally, how do victims' family members and survivors react to the execution of a criminal perpetrator, and what factors are "meaningful" in the reactions they have?

In endeavoring to answer these important questions, I conducted in-depth, face-to-face open-ended interviews with 27 individuals who were either victims' family members or survivors of the Oklahoma City bombing. Throughout this chapter, I refer to these interviewees as research "participants." This interviewing technique allowed me to conversationally guide participants through accounts of how the bombing, trials, and McVeigh's execution impacted their lives while granting participants complete freedom of response and allowing me the flexibility to ask follow-up questions. Interviews were conducted at any site in Oklahoma City that was comfortable for the participant, and most were conducted in participants' residences. Three interviews with participants who did not reside in Oklahoma were conducted electronically via land-line telephone. All interviews were recorded with participants' permission and transcribed for analysis. A total of 30 participants were interviewed; however, two were not included because they were rescue workers, and not victims' family members or survivors present at the moment of the bombing. More specific information on individual participants' characteristics is included in the Appendix. Research participants were recruited through two methods. First, letters were mailed anonymously[1] to individuals on the mailing list of the Murrah Federal Building Survivors Association; these letters described the research project and requested that interested individual contact me directly to participate. Second, other prospective research participants were contacted by individuals who had already been interviewed; these participants in turn contacted me directly to schedule interviews. The final participant sample was composed of 17 females and 10 males. Of the 27 participants, 26 were Caucasian and 1 was African-American. This demographic composition parallels both the overwhelmingly white member-ship of the post bombing groups, including the Murrah Building Survivor's Association, and that of the larger victim population. All participants were over 18 years of age (participants' ages ranged from mid-30s to low-70s) and thus were able to legally consent to participation. Because this project was exploratory and no a priori theory existed to guide my inquiry, I adopted a grounded theory methodology from its inception.

   This chapter will first explore the efficacy of a collective memory and cultural trauma perspective for analyzing collective processes of sense-making through group membership and legal proceedings. It will then briefly describe the mental context in which family members and survivors joined groups in the wake of the bombing, and the functions those groups played in trauma recovery, after which it will summarize the impact of group membership on punishment expectations. Thereafter, this chapter will detail an involuntary relationship which formed between McVeigh and family members and survivors and which was predicated on the basis of constructed social and media representations. Finally, this chapter will examine family members' and survivors' perceptions of communicative interchange with McVeigh in the venues of the trial and execution.

Throughout, victims' family members and survivors are referred to by number instead of name to preserve their anonymity.

2. COLLECTIVE MEMORY, CULTURAL TRAUMA, AND THE LAW

With memory set smarting like a reopened wound, a man's past is not simply a dead history, an outworn preparation of the present: it is not a repented error shaken loose from the life: it is a still quivering part of himself, bringing shudders and bitter flavours and the tinglings of a merited shame. (Eliot, 2003, p. 653)

As George Eliot astutely observed, memory is a *living* concept, one that is not merely alive and evolving but *social*, capable of triggering emotions such as shame that only have meaning within a collective. Thus, in the aftermath of culturally traumatic events, there is a need to study the creation of meaning from a collective memory perspective that focuses upon the collision between victims' demands and law's institutional needs for rule adherence and legitimacy. Communication scholars recognize that "memory is not simply a mental operation that a person uses or that she or he can refine and improve" but is instead a "phenomenon of community" (Blair, 2006, p. 52). Memory has been "a major preoccupation for social thinkers since the Greeks" (Olick & Robbins, 1998, p. 106). Yet, a *social* perspective on memory only took root in the late nineteenth and early twentieth century, with the work of Henri Bergson, Sigmund Freud, Walter Benjamin, and Frederic Bartlett (Olick & Robbins). Contemporary usage of the term is traced to Maurice Halbwachs, and the 1950 publication of his essay on collective memory, *Les mémoires collectives* (Olick & Robbins). Halbwachs (1992[1941], p. 43) posited that collectives enable memory, such that "no memory as possible outside frameworks used by people living in society to determine and retrieve their recollections." Since 1980, there has been a "pursuit, rescue, and celebration of collective memory," perhaps due to political developments such as multiculturalism, the decline and fall of Communism, and movements of victimization and victim's rights;[2] this focus upon collective memory has been "less in texts than in the spoken word, images, gestures, rituals and festivals" (Le Goff, 1992, p. 95).

Memory work, then, is the process of working through and narrating experiences. As such, it is always interpretive and constructive, and concerned with reaching closure about past events. Through memory work, individuals gain distance from a life event that is necessary to understand and contextualize them and place them in causal relationships to other life occurrences – in other words, to position themselves in relation to that event. Memory work is collective in the sense that individuals share many life events, and collaborative interpretations of these events may take shape as individuals gather and share memories and interpretations, with the result that individual perceptions are in turn reshaped by these communal exchanges. Groups may therefore perform memory work by constructing areas of common knowledge which create social bonds between members.

A collective memory perspective is the most appropriate lens through which to scrutinize the roles that behaviors such as group joining and attendance and participation in legal proceedings played in helping victims' families and survivors to recover from the Oklahoma City bombing. In essence, memory offers a form and content for addressing the Oklahoma City bombing in that it both structures and explains the evolving understandings of the bombing and its perpetrators formed by individuals and groups. This conclusion is also compelled by the nature of trauma, which acquires its horrific proportions from its ability to destroy not only an individual's sense of normality but the normality of the collectives that constitute that individual's social support network. Trauma has profound consequences for communities as well as individuals, and memory work has been shown to be central to the recovery or "working through" of the collective, which may require processes of sense-making, accountability and restitution, often procured through collective institutional means such as trials and truth commissions. Most importantly, traumas affect collectives long after their survivors have passed on; the bombing of Hiroshima and Nagasaki and Holocaust death camps are just two examples of traumas which happened over 60 years ago but which remain problems with which American collective memory must grapple. Surely, then, trauma as a phenomenon is not reducible merely to individual proportions since its effects resonate most pervasively and permanently in the culture of a collective. "Collective" here denotes victims' family members and survivors of the Oklahoma City bombing.

The theoretical mirror I hold up to this data, however, is not simply framed by collective memory. The type of event structured by collective memory is also significant; traumatic events such as the Oklahoma City bombing call into play a theoretical subcategory of collective memory known as cultural trauma. In analyzing the creation and reconstruction of meaning in the aftermath of the Oklahoma City bombing, I document the evolution of a specific culture of interpretation and rehabilitation formed *against a larger national cultural backdrop* that prompts American citizens to feel "compelled to honor those ... who have been murdered for an unjust cause" (Alexander, 2003, p. 3). As Alexander states, "those collective forces that are not *compulsory*, the social forces to which we enthusiastically and voluntarily respond.... We do not mourn mass murder unless we have already identified with the victims, and this only happens once in a while, when the symbols are aligned in the right way" (Alexander, p. 3). According to Alexander, a recent leader in developing a theory of cultural trauma under the rubric of "cultural sociology," cultural trauma "occurs when members of the collectivity feel they have been subjected to a horrendous event that leaves indelible marks on their group consciousness, marking their memories forever in changing their future identity in fundamental and irrevocable ways" (Alexander, p. 85). Cultural trauma provides a means by which collectives can begin to address an event perceived as traumatic, to "not only cognitively identify the existence and source of human suffering but 'take on board' some significant [moral] responsibility for it" (Alexander, p. 85). In this way, collectives formulate and demonstrate "solidary relationships in ways that, in principle, allow them to share the sufferings of others ... societies expand the circle of the we" (Alexander, p. 85). Notably, cultural trauma is, like collective memory, a *collective* process of construction; as Smelser (2004, p. 43) notes, "a collective trauma, affecting a group with definable membership, will, of necessity, also be associated with that group's collective identity." And cultural trauma is also explicitly trauma of *culture* – what Sztompka (2004, p. 161) terms the "axio-normative and symbolic belief systems of a society."[3] Finally, because trauma is socially mediated, collectivities sense trauma in much the same way as a spider senses a fly in the web, by disturbing vibrations that disrupt the "patterned meanings of the collectivity" (Alexander, p. 92). But these "patterned meanings" that are disturbed must be meanings that penetrate to and are bound into the core of collective identity, so that that core is imperiled when those meanings are stretched too taut or broken altogether.

Of course, trauma claims-making – like other forms of "linguistic action" – is "powerfully mediated by the nature of the institutional arenas within which it occurs" (Alexander, 2003, p. 97). This includes the institutions of the law and of mass media, each of which shape trauma claims in particular ways, and impose particular institutional consequences. The legal institution is particularly significant for victims' family members, who must rely on its proceedings to hold an offender accountable – a key step in working through the trauma of the crime. According to Alexander (p. 97), when the "cultural classification" of an event as traumatic "enters the *legal* realm, it will be disciplined by the demand to issue a definitive judgment of legally binding responsibilities and to distribute punishments and material reparations."

The institutional effect of law, then, is to narrow trauma claims to specific stages of the mnemetic process, such as the attribution of responsibility (Alexander, 2003, p. 98). Similarly, the ways in which the mass media as an institution affects claims of trauma enable the mnemetic process to gain new narrative "opportunities" but at the cost of becoming subject to "distinctive kinds of restrictions" (Alexander, p. 100). As a form of mediation, mass communication may provide heretofore inaccessible outlets for the dramatization of trauma, and may provide a vehicle for one interpretation to gain an edge over other competing interpretations (Alexander, p. 100). Yet, processes of constructing trauma "become subject to the restrictions of news reporting, with their demand for concision, ethical neutrality, and perspectival balance," and may be "exaggerated and distorted" due to the competition between news outlets (Alexander, p. 100).

Law as an institution, then, mediates cultural trauma and is a forum for the formation of collective memory. There is a contemporary perception that, in the words of Elias Canetti, the dead "are nourished by judgment," and that criminal law is a "means of recompensing the slain through a deliberative act" (Douglas, 2001, p. 1). As do other institutions, law has a collective memory of its own, particularly as a site for the communication and construction of cultural authority (Halbwachs, 1992[1941], p. 140). The rule of law itself is a product of collective memory; the boundaries between the legal and the extra-legal are maintained through the judicial tradition – "a tradition that pervades all its members to a high degree" – which cumulatively "represent the collective work of a line of jurists and eminent magistrates" (Halbwachs, p. 140). Oliver Wendell Holmes infamously noted that "the life of the law has not been logic: it has been experience," and stated that "the law embodies the story of a nation's development through many centuries," so that "the degree to which it is able to work out desired results depend very much on its past" (Holmes, 1881, pp. 1–2). Significantly, law is product of social and well as legal actors; jurists always remain members of the social collective even after they put on the robes of advocacy or office.[4]

Trials, including criminal prosecutions, belong within the category of rituals designated by Turner as "social dramas"; criminal law is especially comparable to the formation of collective memory since its deterrence concerns are oriented in the future, where collective memory locates greater social solidarity, but its retributive concerns are situated in the past, where collective memory finds its narrative content (Osiel, 1999, p. 18). Garland

(1990, pp. 67, 57) notes that the rituals of criminal justice – the courtroom trial, the passing of sentence, the execution of punishments – are, in effect, the formalized embodiment of the *conscience collective*, which is "protected by a strict code of penal law, which – unlike most law in modern society – *does* evoke deep-seated emotions and a sense of the sacred." Thus, the act of imposing punishment becomes a process of working through an event which imperils a collective (Garland, p. 67). "Justice" becomes the operative concept for social solidarity, involving a consensus both that certain acts committed are wrong and must be punished.

Collective memory is furthered by the delivery of legal stories. In the criminal trial, the prosecutor serves as a public spokesman who "tell[s] the stories through which such sentiments are elicited and such membership consolidated" (Osiel, 1999, p. 28). In these stories, the culpability of the perpetrator assumes primary importance, since it the illegal exercise of the offender's free will that dictates the outcome of the story and bring about the victim's death (Osiel, p. 72). After conviction, punishment "signals the greater or lesser presence of collective memory in a society"; disciplining those who commit the most socially unacceptable acts reinforces our awareness of what acts are proscribed (Osiel, p. 31). The ability to enunciate and fix stories in legal frames, then, becomes an important source of social power.

But the efficacy of legal proceedings as a trigger for collective memory formation is constrained by two concepts: law's modesty, or its superficial unwillingness to play such a formative mnemonic role; and its practices, rules and traditions that narrow the breadth and depth of inquiry to binary categories such as guilty or not guilty. Because of law's storying potential, citizens may expect legal proceedings to take a formative role in adjudicating history, leading to judicial protest. In socially potent trials such as that of Adolf Eichmann, courts have explicitly invoked judicial modesty in rejecting such a definitive role, pleading shortsightedness and the lack of cultural authority. But while courts pay lip service to judicial modesty, they cater to processes of collective memory formation despite themselves.[5]

But legal doctrine certainly limits its efficacy for collective resolution of cultural trauma. Criminal prosecutions are formulated to hear and adjudicate evidence on whether a given suspect committed a criminal act – an inquiry with a very limited scope which is unlikely to reach the social implications of that criminal behavior. Legal conclusions are inherently professionalized, derived through the application of legal principles to decide disputes on the basis of evidence introduced and evaluated in accordance with legal doctrine, all orchestrated by procedural rules. Stretching a conviction into a social statement may actually distort collective memory; a conviction, though comprehensive enough for professional purposes, is but the product of a necessarily narrow professional inquiry into a unique set of facts and may not be elastic enough to stretch to fit into a collective memory frame. And that assumes that specialized legal practices translate into or are meaningful within a social collective. Law may also be focused on minute evidentiary details that may seem meaningless to a public hungry for dramatic developments. The danger is not in boredom per se but in how it affects a trial's impact upon collective memory, as it decreases the likelihood that significant attention will be paid to legal developments and thereby diminishes the impact of such proceedings on collective memory.

Finally, the very legal practices through which an event is interrogated may constrain the impact of a trial upon collective memory. Evidentiary and procedural rules mandate that evidence be introduced in very specific ways, and limit elicited testimony to forms of questioning acceptable on direct or cross-examination. A criminal prosecution is the story of a crime, and not a story of that crime's effects, which means that the victims' story is left out, or at least put aside until sentencing. Attendants at legal proceedings hear about the defendant and sometimes hear from the defendant as well, but information about the victim is largely confined to "objective" evidence such as the nature and characteristics of injuries and markings, and rarely if ever hear about the victim or the victim's family before sentencing, when victim impact testimony may be given. Thus, the legal narrative is a necessarily incomplete narrative. Other institutional actors, such as historians or sociologists, must step in to supplement the historical record of events whose memory consists largely of a legal record focused on objective proof of the crime and not the subjective experience of the event. When subjective testimony is permitted into legal inquiry, confrontational means of eliciting and challenging testimony may directly contrast with the sacrosanct status that testimony – and witnesses – are accorded in collective memory, where proof is not prioritized (Osiel, 1999, p. 104). Finally, law does not explicitly acknowledge its socially constructed nature, unlike "fickle" collective memory (Osiel, p. 217). Legal reluctance to acknowledge the primacy of social construction stems from its needs for finality and fixation; legal doctrines such as "res judicata, collateral estoppel, stare decisis, double jeopardy, mandatory joinder, statutes of limitations, and restrictive standards of appellate review" are designed to discourage or thwart altogether the subsequent reinterpretation of precedent (Osiel, p. 216).

The only situation in which legal practitioners overtly acknowledge constructive processes is the act of legal interpretation (Osiel, p. 242).

As a result of the mismatch between the means to law's ends and the formation of collective memory, law is caught between a need to maintain the legitimacy of its institutional narratives and satisfying diverse justice "needs." Law as an institution, then, cannot bear the weight of collective memory alone. Instead, law contributes to organic processes of collective sense-making. As law sees itself as an institution with the potential to shape collective memory, it becomes changed by that potential, aware of and thus more vulnerable to the same movements that influence collective memory formation. Postmodernism has brought new challenges to the collective sense-making processes, including problematizing the primacy of legal proceedings as a storying forum. Similarly, law has subjected itself to obligations owed to new, previously excluded populations such as victims' families. Legal conclusions must now "affirm as well-warranted the victims' feelings of resentment and indignation, for this affirmation is the only way for society at large to show that it acknowledges and take seriously their condition *as* victims" (Osiel, 1999, p. 273).

3. VOLUNTARY BLOOD RELATIONS

The focus of our attention must now shift from the social construction of memory to mnemetic processes themselves, what Halbwachs termed the social frameworks of memory, because the act of social construction – the social articulation and maintenance of memory – occurs in groups.[6] The memory practices of groups constitute attempts to interpret and assign meaning to culturally contested issues. Here, "collective" denotes the membership of communal groups organized almost immediately after the Oklahoma City bombing. The bombing as an event abruptly birthed a memorial collective whose members were immediately instantaneously bound to one another by the ties of loss and the shared experience of suffering.[7] It was within this memorial community that "interest" groups formed to pursue defined goals such as reforming habeas law or building a memorial. In mediating cultural trauma, group membership became a form of "active grief" behavior through which "family members and survivors formed new communities to offer support to each other" (Linenthal, 2001, p. 98). This article will focus on two of the most effective mnemetic groups formed in the wake of the Oklahoma City bombing: the Oklahoma City National Memorial Task Force, which organized the construction of the

Oklahoma City National Memorial from 1995 to 2000, and a "habeas" group of family members and survivors who sought speedier executions and whose lobbying efforts culminated in the passage of the Antiterrorism and Effective Death Penalty Act of 1996 (Senate Resolution 735, 104th Congress, 1996).[8] Several members of the habeas group later banded together to lobby for the passage of the Victim Allocution Clarification Act of 1997 (House Resolution 924, 105th Congress, 1997) clarifying the rights of victims set forth in the 1990 Victims Rights and Restitution Act (better known as the "Victims Bill of Rights") so as to allow victim impact witnesses to both observe a trial and offer impact testimony.[9]

3.1. Members' Mental State upon Joining

Group joining behaviors took place at a time when family members and survivors were in an extremely vulnerable mental state. Complicated or traumatic grief[10] was rampant, and trauma also resulted from the loss of a perceived "just world" prior to the bombing.[11] Simply put, murder is disorder.[12] Common emotional experiences of participants[13] prior to group membership include feelings of alienation and loss of control, simplification of moral categories, a need for information about the bombing, and anger towards the perpetrators. Crucially, participants were joined groups either to overcome these emotional obstacles or to find positive outlets for potentially destructive energies.

Survivors of traumatic events, including murder victims' family members, often feel increasingly alienated in their wake, and perceive that they are unable to connect with the everyday world around them.[14] This pervasive helplessness and loneliness may take forms that are physical, such as the inability to control physical behavior (e.g., spontaneous weeping in "inappropriate" locales), or social, such as loss of established routines and avoidance by former social acquaintances immediately after the event or at a point where victims fail to "bounce back" as expected (Rock, 1998, pp. 31–42). Homicide also creates a sense of "unfinished emotional and practical business which will cloud subsequent recollections, prevent the possibility of a fitting farewell, and lead to a continuing sense of the presence of the dead" (Rock, p. 39). In an effort to restore control and prevent future losses, survivors may adopt a practice of "keeping vigil" for the dead, behaviors that maintain the traumatic pitch of post-disaster life as well as create needs to protest injustice, to keep others safe from harm, and to resist loss of meaning, and to remember and represent the dead or wounded (Wattenberg, Unger, Foy, & Glynn, 2006, p. 568).

In addition; complex moral schemas break down in the collapse of meaning following homicide, devolving into radically stripped and simplified evaluative mechanisms that paint the world in absolutist tones of good and evil.[15] Survivors, then, are defined in opposition not to the deceased victim but to the perpetrator, and each evolves its meaning from its relationship to the other. Significantly, survivors perceive this relationship as inequitable. Survivors also experience a desperate need for information, which is perceived as a key ingredient in undertaking life reconstruction. Because one cannot move forward without thoroughly understanding insofar as possible the circumstances of the murder, information about the crime and perpetrator is precious. Information is power, and the best way of gathering it is often by attending legal proceedings.[16] Finally, anger is of course the prototypical survivor response; one thinks of survivors as angry voices demanding vengeance against the murderer. Anger, then, is not only an emotion but an activity of "self assertion and of accusation" (Rock, p. 101). Anger is purposive and "intentional; establishing not only the angry subject but also the object against which the anger is directed" (Rock, p. 102). Anger is an important activity for survivors simply because it motivates and orients survivors toward a goal; encouraging them to once again assert control. Thus, in acting from anger, survivors perform anger, and live in the anger experience (Rock, p. 49).

3.2. Group Functions

Groups formed in the wake of the Oklahoma City bombing served three primary mnemetic functions for their members: providing companionship; serving as sites for narrative and norm construction, and providing opportunities for action and goal accomplishment. Regarding companionship, group bonding can be a powerful antidote to feelings of isolation or alienation, offering companionate stability and solidarity. Theories of group therapy for those afflicted by traumatic grief are based on the understanding that members may feel the kind of understanding and safety that is often missing from their natural social network (Shear, Zuckoff, Melhem, & Gorscak, 2006, p. 327). Attending group meetings was the first time in which participants took stock of their social network in the sense of realizing who else had survived the bombing; or how everyone else was faring physically and emotionally; in the words of participants, group meetings were "reunions." For family members, meeting survivors who had known their loved ones was especially important. In addition, after the bombing, participants' paramount need was to speak with other survivors or family members. For five participants, the bonds of companionship were so strong that fellow group members became "family," and often replaced family support networks that were weakened or altogether absent. When asked about the benefits of group membership, nine participants reported that family members either did not want to talk about the bombing, did not understand the true impact of the bombing upon their lives, or placed ill-fitting limits upon "proper" coping strategies. Groups also provided listening ears to satisfy the imperative to share experiences of loss. Coming together as a group, however, was not always an easy or productive process; the first years after the bombing were marked by tensions between family members and survivors and between supporters and opponents of the death penalty.

In addition to being sources of companionship and camaraderie, groups that formed in the wake of the Oklahoma City bombing were also "storying" sites where narratives of the bombing and of its perpetrators were continually constructed. Key to mnemetic processes were members' ability to meet others with similar experiences, to join a normative community, and to gather information. In addition to playing an important companionship role, talking through the event with others who "were there" was important in sense-making processes. The need to find others with similar experiences is so integral to recovery that it is one of the chief purposes of group therapy for traumatic grief (Shear et al., 2006, p. 326). Exchanging stories also created a set of normative expectations or assumptions as to "who" a group was and what it stood for. Simplified moral schemas developed by homicide survivors very soon after losing a loved one to murder actually become incorporated into homicide survivor groups; and perpetuated within group culture (Rock, 1998, p. 103). Finally; group meetings also were forums where members could learn of and discuss the latest developments in memorial construction and in the prosecutions of McVeigh and Nichols. Information gathering and commensurate sense-making was an important part of initiating mnemetic processes, what participants spoke of as "putting the pieces of a puzzle back together." As a result of interaction, participants were able to collectively impose a narrative meaning upon grief, and describe learning how to speak of the bombing and exchanging stories with others as "healing" and "cathartic."

Finally, processes of life reconstruction became enmeshed with group goals. Accomplishing a goal such as the passage of habeas legislation or the building of the memorial provided an outlet for anger-motivated activity. Family members of victims killed in other instances of terrorism have used anger as a unifying force; Rock remarks that "it was with anger that people came together.... Lockerbie relatives group was formed in March within a few months and the first few meetings" (Rock, 1998, p. 47). When united; survivors and family members were a potent advocacy force, as families of homicide victims have often been (Rock, p. xiii). Members were able to see how particular group goals both aligned with members' unique interests after the bombing and fulfilled members' personal needs for certain kinds of activity. Accomplishing group goals aided members to once more regain a sense of control and overcome perceived helplessness; for instance, participants describe being empowered by the habeas group's successful lobbying for the passage of habeas reform. Significantly, different groups fulfilled different functions. Whereas the memorial task force allowed participants to remember murdered victims, the habeas group was about achieving justice. Of course, group goals were also seen by members as worthy accomplishments in their own right independent of their healing potential; participants described the memorial as a truth-telling mechanism, a site that was symbolic of the culture of Oklahoma City, and as a monument to a creative use of destructive forces and to the healing process itself. Group members themselves remain intensely proud of goal accomplishment, describing the passage of the AEDPA in 1996 was "a miracle in most of our eyes;" and participation in the memorial process as "quite an honor." Goal achievement as a point in time also designated an appropriate moment for members to transition into lives reconstructed in the process of trying to accomplish a certain end; as beneficial as group membership was, there came a time when some members felt that involvement was no longer necessary. Moving forward often created the incentive to cease intense involvement on bombing-related activities.

3.3. Effects of Group Membership on Perceived "Justice Needs"

Groups – and group goals – affected the degree to which members felt that attending various stages of legal proceedings; including McVeigh's execution, was personally meaningful, particularly in comparison with other possible activities such as work, involvement in non-legal activities, and family time. In essence, then, members' "justice needs" – consisting of the hoped-for outcomes of the legal proceedings, attainment of account-ability, and the desired impact of proceedings upon finality, remembrance and recovery – were partially constructed through the formation of group identity and the selection of group goals.

The memorial task force indisputably had a very different focus than the habeas group; it endeavored to remember and represent murdered victims as well as living survivors and rescue workers, and focused on making these memorial constructions as full and robust as possible. Thus, the memorial task force pursued a goal centered around creating and ensuring a *presence*, not an absence. In so doing, it strove to give voice to the dead and the living, a voice that emphasized tragedy and turmoil but also rebirth and rebuilding through remembrance. Significantly, these voices belonged only to those victimized by the bombing; the Oklahoma City Memorial marginalized the presence of McVeigh and Nichols. The only museum display describing prosecutory proceedings is a two-panel installation entitled "Justice" that includes chronological timelines of the prosecutions along with sketches from the trials and blowups of three newspaper articles. There is no mention of McVeigh's execution with the exception of a nondescript 4-by-8-inch bronze plaque that was installed within an hour of McVeigh's death. The habeas group; in contrast, may have pursued death penalty reform in the names of murdered loved ones, but its primary focus was on what surviving family members of murder victims had to endure through waiting as long as seventeen years for an offender's execution to be carried out. Thus, the habeas group prioritized the *justice* of eradicating opportunities for offenders such as McVeigh to pursue additional appeals which prolonged execution – a focus on the offender and on the need to expeditiously carry out death sentences, albeit one pursued in the names of murder victims and their families.

In keeping with these goals, core members of the memorial group were likely to find the building of the memorial *or* the guilty verdict in the McVeigh trial more meaningful than the execution. By the time of the execution in June of 2001; more memorial task force members stated that they were too involved in family or work or other activities that they perceived as positive and "healthy" to attend the execution. Habeas group members, on the other hand, were more likely to see both the trial and execution as meaningful, and characterized the execution as the culmination of legal proceedings. Habeas group members not only spoke of a need to *see* as much of the legal proceedings as possible, but also verbalized a need to be *involved* in proceedings for reasons of completion and because members had struggled to ensure broader access to proceedings (i.e., ensuring that victim impact witnesses could attend evidence presentation in the case in chief, ensuring that the trial was broadcast back to Oklahoma City after the change of venue, ensuring that the execution would be broadcast back to Oklahoma City from Terra Haute). Thus, since group goals were healing, choosing a goal for many members defined not only a major mnemetic focus, but also defined a moment in time – the accomplishment of the goal – after which members felt comfortable leaving behind both intense involvement with the group and preoccupation with the bombing and its legacy. As Participant 27 stated, "after about the fifth anniversary, when they opened the Memorial, and the Memorial got off and running, I sort of didn't feel like it was as therapeutic anymore." Reconstruction was complete only after the building of the memorial or McVeigh's trial and/or execution. Group goals also influenced which institution would "enable" healing, namely the memorial or the criminal justice system. Goal selection also reflected informed judgments about what was the most appropriate way to memorialize the bombing, those murdered, and the bombing's impact on survivors, rescue workers, and family members.

The difference between the memorial group and the habeas group can most conservatively be characterized as a rhetorical difference – in how members spoke of the meaningfulness of legal proceedings versus other possible time investments. It is not surprising that memorial task force members who opposed the death penalty stated that they did not need an execution for "justice" to be attained. It is surprising, however, that whereas all habeas group members speak of a need to attend and be involved in legal proceedings for various reasons, some memorial task force members who either supported the death penalty either all the time, held "no opinion," or supported it on a case-by-case basis do not mention that the trial and execution were particularly meaningful proceedings. In contrast, *all* participants who were members of the habeas group felt that attending the trial and/or execution were important steps in being "involved" in the process or "made a difference." Habeas members' widespread support for legal proceedings is not shocking; the habeas group, which at an approximate maximum membership of 30 was much smaller than the memorial group with its hundreds of members; was explicitly formed to be an advocacy group and was comprised of individuals who literally dedicated themselves to that end. The memorial goals of the memorial task force did not overlap with legal proceedings against McVeigh and Nichols; the task force only had to conceive of a way to represent these proceedings in a display that illustrated their significance to the Oklahoma City community and indeed to the national and international community. In contrast, members of the habeas group explicitly sought to change legal proceedings in several different ways and so from its inception the group focus was *on* legal proceedings. Thus, statements made by habeas group members attesting to the importance of attending McVeigh's trial and execution directly contrast with the statements of memorial task force members who elected not to attend the trial and/or the execution, choosing instead to prioritize of other concerns such as work and family.

4. INVOLUNTARY BLOOD RELATIONS

4.1. The Source of the Involuntary Victim–Offender Relationship

Collective memory usually derives from more traditional group formations; such as the memorial task force and habeas group. But another type of relationship also proved to be significant in the context of the Oklahoma City bombing. The reconstruction of memory in the wake of the bombing was also heavily influenced by an involuntary relationship that existed between family members and survivors on the one hand and McVeigh and Nichols on the other, a relationship that existed even though neither party knew the other prior to the murderous act, a relationship that like any other is communicative, structured through speech and silence. This relationship is rarely tacitly acknowledged let alone explicitly defined in criminological scholarship, and is a concept that is completely logical when one looks at factors that affect the presence and strength of this relationship – publicity about the offender and the murder, the victims' families' need to know "why" and "how" the crime occurred and the necessity of understanding the offender to answer those questions at least in part. How could victims' families help but feel they know an offender through the plethora of intimate details that emerges through contemporary media coverage? Sharp notes that coverage of Jeffrey Dahmer's murders extended to the most banal details of his personal life: "the type of beer he drank, his cigarette preference, the types of potato chips he ate, and the brand of baking soda he used in his refrigerator" (Sharp, 2005, p. 1). This relationship may extend to offenders' families as well; offenders and their families (and even offenders' communities) may be roped together into a category of otherness, set apart by disgust and hatred, with offenders' family members experiencing intensely negative publicity (Sharp, p. 36). In the context of the Oklahoma City bombing, this was a relationship in which victims' impressions of McVeigh as a man and, in some cases, as a monster contextualized his mannerisms and his statements. It was a relationship characterized by perceptions of communicative iniquity, inequity and inequality, in which victims/survivors perceived they had little communicative control over McVeigh, where

McVeigh was seen to have great communicative agency and an ability to communicate with victims/survivors despite their antipathy towards such efforts, while victims had to settle for channeling their own communications through media or through victim impact testimony. It was a relationship pregnant with communicative necessity and perceived obligation, in which victims very much wanted to hear "why" and how McVeigh carried out the bombing and yearned in many cases[17] to speak with him in person. Finally, it was a relationship whose only possibility of termination lay in the death of McVeigh or of victims themselves.

In addition, this involuntary relationship between McVeigh and family members and survivors profoundly influenced the formation of collective memory and the resolution of cultural trauma because it was perceived as a challenge to the reconstruction of identity through group and individual processes such as those discussed in the previous chapter. As will be discussed shortly, because of the constructed understandings of McVeigh that participants evolved, 10 participants directly referred to McVeigh's continued existence and media communications as barriers on the road to "recovery" and resolution and connected his execution with the need to silence him.[18] A living Timothy McVeigh was simultaneously a reminder of his potential to "jab" at victims, a reminder of the bombing, and a reminder of injustice. In occupying one camp in the involuntary relationship between victim's family/survivor and offender, and therefore bound to victims' family members and survivors, McVeigh became a part *of* the collective, instead of being cast outside it. The inclusion of McVeigh in the collective was traumatizing to family members and survivors because it directly affected the narrative resolution of the trauma and delayed family members' and survivors' control over the resolution process because at any time a message could issue from McVeigh that could potentially aggravate wounds just starting to scab over. Communication could not cease and the relationship could not be terminated until McVeigh was dead. Thus, the collective memory of homicide – including the collective memory of the Oklahoma City bombing – is shaped not only by the events of the murder but also for the duration of the involuntary relationship between offender and family members/survivors.

It is possible to describe the tie between family members and survivors and McVeigh in other ways besides terming it a "relationship." Framing it in relational terms, however, is most fitting because of it captures the profound way in which these ties colored family members' and survivors' processes of sense-making, particularly in formulating their preferred legal resolution to the bombing – what punishment was deserved. Focusing research on the victim–offender relationship also appropriately recognizes that victims and survivors define as well as become defined by the experiences of survivorship, that they act upon and are acted upon in turn. It implies an exchange, a give and take of activity and passivity, and recognizes that processes of sense-making are mutually constructive and cyclical, and not self-constructive and linear. Victims change and alter conceptions of grieving in the course of healing; they are active participants in the trial with the potential to change its practices and potentials; and they challenge representations of victims in addition to conforming to existing representations. Finally, refocusing research on the victim–offender relationship also effectively organizes how participants made sense of the chaos of post-bombing social relations. It explains why the vast majority of participants regardless of political views on the death penalty felt relief in the wake of the execution which terminated the involuntary relationship that had begun six years before.

In the wake of the bombing, family members and survivors became involuntarily and intimately linked to McVeigh and Nichols through the offense, so that they must "live with" them to a greater or lesser extent until death – either the offender's, or their own. As Janice Smith, a nonparticipant and nonwitness family member whose brother was murdered in the bombing, stated in a media interview after McVeigh's execution on June 11, 2001, "It's over. We don't have to continue with him any more" (Bryant, 2001). There may even be a sense that family members and survivors are an offender's "audience" and an interactive positioning based on this perception. Constance Richardson, a nonparticipant family member whose 20-year old daughter was murdered in the bombing, chose to visit the memorial on the morning of June 11, 2001 instead of witnessing the execution by closed-circuit, stating "I didn't want to be part of his audience" (Bryant).

Intensive interviews with family members and survivors reveal a perception that statements made by McVeigh were targeted to these individuals to further wound them. Participant 21 states, "like every time he turned around, he was doing some thing to jab at us and it was just very painful because he could sit there behind those bars and get us three squares a day and everything and not have all these worries and, and he kept jabbing at us in his own little way." After McVeigh was executed, however, the "jabbing" ceased; as Participant 15 explains, "I never think about McVeigh now that he's been executed cause he's not in the media now. You know he played the media and the media played him and he was there… . I've quit completely, stopped thinking about him the day they executed him. He's you know he's hurt me enough and he doesn't care. Not at all." Participant 25's comments are most illustrative of this point.

> McVeigh, even though he knew that he was getting the death sentence, he was defiant all the way up to the point where it actually happened, okay? He would speak out to the media…. And everything that he did was doing nothing but hurting the family members here in Oklahoma…. Nichols, Nichols is a little different because since he's been tried and convicted, you don't hear about him…. I can live with him being in prison for the rest of his life, for the simple reason that he is not defiant and he's not going out and getting on the news and so forth and trying to hurt the family members.[19]

Participants also perceived that this relationship was intimate in the sense that McVeigh as a communicative agent made statements *to* family members and survivors in an attempt to further wound them. Participants speak of McVeigh jabbing "at us," of McVeigh hurting "me" and "telling the families," and of McVeigh and Nichols having "access to the family members, survivors through the media, through books." In addition, participants seem at times to assert that they "knew" what McVeigh would do in a given situation; 13 participants, for instance, remarked that McVeigh would not have sincerely meant any apology that he may have given at his execution.

It is considerably easier to understand the interpersonal process of collective memory construction in a social setting such as the memorial task force or the habeas group, where most communicative interaction is face-to-face, and not mediated. It is more difficult to comprehend a "relationship" that forms in a completely mediated context, in the utter absence of direct communication. Such a relationship is not "interpersonal" in the traditional sense of the term, involving "at least two communicators; intentionally orienting toward each other; as both subject and object; whose actions embody each other's perspectives both toward self and toward other" (Bochner, 1989, p. 336). Yet, there is a tangible perception on the part of family members of survivors of intimacy, of "knowing" McVeigh and Nichols that would be present in an interpersonal relationship.

4.2. McVeigh as Para-Social Enemy

This relationship bears a strong resemblance to *para-social interaction*, a concept devised in 1956 by Horton and Wohl (1956) to explain the phenomenon of television viewers' perceived relationship to television personalities, defined as "the illusion of face-to-face relationship with the performer" in which "the conditions of response to the performer are analogous to those in a primary group" (p. 188). This relationship is built upon a cumulative "exchange" of affective messages between the personality, termed the "persona," and the audience, whereby the audience is "subtly insinuated into the program's action and internal social relationships and, by dint of this kind of staging, is ambiguously transformed into a group which observes and participate in the show by turns" (Horton & Wohl, p. 189). Para-social relationships are characterized by a "lack of effective reciprocity" since "the interaction, characteristically, is one-sided, nondialectical, controlled by the performer, and not susceptible of mutual development"; thus, "the audience is free to choose among the relationships offered, but it cannot create new ones" (Horton & Wohl, p. 189). Other ways in which audience members may communicate to the persona or to show producers, such as letters or telephone calls, "lie outside the para-social interaction itself" (Horton & Wohl, p. 189). Despite the lack of communicative give and take, the persona who is the focus of the para-social relationship becomes integrated into the audience member's social circle as a familiar presence (Horton & Wohl, p. 190). Significantly, this presence is above all a reliable presence (Horton & Wohl, p. 190). But however artless this relationship may appear, it is also a strategic and constant one (Horton & Wohl, p. 191). Producers formulate the persona's character specifically to enhance audience members' loyalty to the persona, with respect to the personality's image, "its major theme is that the performer should be loved and admired" (Horton & Wohl, p. 195). Audience members are expected to adapt to the engineered relational format with the persona as it is offered; they may not alter it, and so must continue the relation on those inflexible terms (Horton & Wohl, p. 194). Thus, audience members must be susceptible to a "coaching of attitudes" (Horton & Wohl, pp. 195, 196). But audience members' willingness to be susceptible to this coaching is entailed in audience membership itself, since that role entails some level of identification. Subsequent research into para-social relationships further suggests that this illusory intimacy, the subjective creation of audience members, is actually taken as "real" (Levy, 1979, p. 185).[20] Para-social relationships continue to pervade media usage today.[21]

It is abundantly clear that researchers have construed the persona that is the target of the para-social relation as being in the position of a para-social "friend," someone who is likeable and trustworthy. Thus, this type of investiture can be termed a "positive" para-social relationship, or a investiture of positive affect in a persona. But logically, if one can have relationships with para-social "friends," then one may also have relationships with para-social "enemies," opening the door to the formation of "negative" para-social relationships. Negative para-social relations have the same characteristics as their positive counterparts, though these characteristics form an identification that is the inverse of that encouraged by the positive relation. As in Herbert and Wohl's conception of the positive para-social relation that prompts audience members to be loyal to a media persona, a para-social relation with an "enemy" likewise frames spectators' perceptions of the performer, enabling persistent dislike and animosity. Whereas the positive para-social persona is an "ingroup" member, a desirable associate, the para-social enemy is an outsider, a deviant Other. Victims are as encouraged to be loyal to their hatred of criminal personas as audience members are encouraged to admire their media personas. The criminal persona is as enduring a figure as a positive persona, engendered to predictably inspire loathing. And audience members who form negative attachments to para-social enemies also must accept the relational format imposed by the media "producers" who construct that persona. Realizing how negative para-social relations are cultivated also necessitates broadening the concepts of "media" and "media producer," extending them from application in the narrower context of mass media to application in the broader context of social institutions who may take on strategic mediating roles – including the criminal justice system. This means that the producers of para-social enemies in the context of homicide are not only the producers of hit television crime dramas but also criminal justice officials who orchestrate the arrest and trial of criminal offenders from the "perp walk" to incarceration or execution, the public rituals for exposing and judging "enemies of the system."

But gauging from participants' attributions of malicious communicative intent to McVeigh and the degree to which their responses attributed a dialogic character to their interactions with McVeigh, it is clear that there is ample evidence of a negative para-social relation between family members and survivors and McVeigh. McVeigh is their para-social enemy, the one who, however mediated his communications may be, both has the potential to communicate and actually communicates with the intent of inflicting further harm on an especially vulnerable and wounded population.

The intimacy of this negative para-social relation is particularly ironic in light of the impersonal nature of the Oklahoma City bombing itself. McVeigh saw himself as standing in opposition to the United States government, at the narrowest opposing the government agencies involved in Waco and Ruby Ridge, and explained that he chose to bomb the Murrah Federal Building because he thought that it would make a spectacular media target, not out of personal animosity toward anyone who worked in the building or anything housed in the building. Yet, the bombing immediately became intensely personal, as images brought to life stories such as the iconic image of the dead Baylee Almon, the one-year-old baby girl cradled in the arms of Oklahoma City firefighter Chris Fields. The impersonality of the bombing was an incomprehensible affront to family members and survivors, who could not see it as impersonal, and in asking the unanswerable question "why," sought to learn, "why us."

Because para-social identification is enhanced or discouraged by the construction of mediated images of a persona, the visual technology of mediated images plays a key role in the formation of such relationships. Joshua Meyrowitz contends that an affective relationship can be encouraged by the composition of a television shot, arguing that the para-social identification of viewers with viewed personae is enhanced by technological reproduction of key interpersonal proxemic distances. According to Meyrowitz (1979, p. 225), there is a "visual 'relationship' between the viewer and the image" which exists for the duration of the television viewing. This relationship is altered by the "framing variable," or the distance at which a shot places the viewer from the viewed (Meyrowitz, p. 225). Each variety of shot has a para-social consequence: "actions in long shots, for example, tend to be viewed in terms of abstract 'events,' while close-ups focus attention on personal characteristics and response" (Meyrowitz, p. 229). Meyrowitz (p. 227) further divides television views of subjects into two categories, "portrayed objective distance" which "'maintains the role of a detached observer' of the action" and "portrayed subjective distance" which "assumes the point of view of one of the characters'" and "shows the viewer what one person within the action sees."

Applying these theories to media coverage of McVeigh facilitates insight into how McVeigh came to be constructed as a para-social enemy. Media coverage of McVeigh can be limited to two "moments": shots of McVeigh being escorted to and from the courthouse in Oklahoma City by law enforcement, and an Emmy-award winning interview that aired March 13, 2000 that Ed Bradley conducted with McVeigh for "Sixty Minutes" while McVeigh was incarcerated on death row in federal prison. The "perp walk" shots most certainly portrayed McVeigh in the "front region" role of criminal and social enemy. Thus, it is not surprising that McVeigh's profile from these "perp walk" shots later became the centerpiece of news graphics headlining execution stories. Ed Bradley's "60 Minutes" interview, on the other hand, allowed McVeigh to explain himself in his own words, yet the interview alternated between camera shots of McVeigh captured over

Bradley's shoulder, positioning the viewer in the interrogator's chair, and close-ups of McVeigh's facial expression. In addition, the image from McVeigh's Oklahoma "perp walk" was the dominant photograph of him used in media coverage of the Oklahoma City bombing, and was often incorporated into news graphics. McVeigh's gaze was also highlighted by textual descriptions of these very same images. Early media stories described McVeigh's expression as that of "hard eyes unlit by the faintest flicker of emotion," the look of a man whose "name didn't mean much then but the image did," the stare of "a poker-faced killer in a crewcut" (Handlin, 2001). This first impression resurfaced continually, including on the morning of his execution: "[i]n his last moments, his face was as blank as it was that April day six years ago when America first saw him escorted out of an Oklahoma jail" (Associated Press, 2001). Thus, early media constructions of McVeigh were cyclically incorporated into subsequent constructions, snowballing upon one another to produce a coherent image of McVeigh as para-social enemy.

The degree to which McVeigh's stare is incorporated into media images and the way in which McVeigh himself was framed during the "60 Minutes" interview illustrates how crucial this gaze became in the construction of McVeigh as a para-social enemy. The heavy media focus on the "perp walk" images could very easily have influenced the early impression formation of family members and survivors, socially constructing expectancies regarding the import of his communicative behaviors. Impression formation upon initial acquaintance is rapid, or even instant, as the subconscious makes its "highly stereotypic" impressions (Burgoon & Hoobler, 2002, p. 262). Because what can be gleaned from introductory verbal exchanges is restricted by convention, nonverbal cues such as "stable physical appearance and kinesic and vocalic cues" are especially significant in "shaping interpersonal expectations and in generating a frame for the parties' interpretation of subsequent behavior. Fortunately, "thin slice" methodology[22] has shown that interactants require only very brief glimpses of behavior to form "fairly accurate and strong" judgments of actors (Burgoon & Hoobler, p. 262). The rapidity of impression formation is necessary because humans are "driven by an underlying need for uncertainty reduction" and by a need for sense-making (Burgoon & Hoobler, p. 262).

Thus, the moment when family members and survivors were "introduced" to McVeigh via media broadcast of the "perp walk" was very likely the moment that they formed initial impressions. Significantly, this footage or still shots from it were rebroadcast extremely frequently in ensuing years, thus reinforcing the visual cues from which the initial impression was formed. Three of the eight execution witnesses remarked on the similarities between McVeigh's gaze during the execution and his gaze on previous occasions captured and aired on television; as Participant 22 recalled, "[h]e didn't just look. He had that same look in his eyes when they arrested him. Do you remember him coming out of the courthouse and that stern look on his face? That's the look he had… . Like defiant."[23] Such comments reveal not only that witnesses were aware of how McVeigh was constructed in and by the news media as a person and an offender, but that they found these constructions meaningful.

5. ENDURING PARA-SOCIAL LEGACIES: IMPRESSIONS OF McVEIGH'S CONDUCT AT TRIAL

Family members' and survivors' initial impressions of McVeigh formed as a result of pre-trial images such as the "perp walk" were "confirmed" by their impressions of his behavior at trial. The most frequent characterizations of McVeigh at his trial all reflect an "inappropriate" emotion or reaction to the trial event; McVeigh is described variously as inappropriately jocular, sarcastic, arrogant, unemotional, and unremorseful. Presumably, the ideal defendant should be solemn, respectful, remorseful, and intimidated by the machinations of justice moving against him. These very same qualities appear in the most frequent characterizations of Nichols, wherein Nichols is emotional, shamed, quiet, and nervous.

5.1. Perceptions of McVeigh's Conduct at Trial

One of the most pervasive trial witness characterizations of McVeigh was as an unemotional defendant whose reactions were nonexistent or impossible to interpret, and connected this blankness of expression to moral failing such as dishonesty, arrogance, callousness, and even evil.[24] This coldness also evoked an impression of arrogance; Participant 8 stated, "He is a cold son-of-a-bitch and he sat there arrogant and looking like he was enjoying the show," and 24 noted, "He was almost proud, I felt like, proud of what he had accomplished, what he had done."

Seven participants recall being struck by McVeigh's perceived jocularity.[25] These moments of perceived jocularity and informality contrasted with other moments in which participants apprehended that McVeigh was paying a great deal of attention to the proceedings.[26]

5.2. Perceptions of Nichols' Conduct at Trial

Trial witnesses characterized Nichols' conduct as the opposite of McVeigh's behavior. Participant 25 noticed a "very definite" difference between McVeigh's and Nichols' courtroom presences, and perceived that that difference individualized the defendants: "it made us look at both of them as individuals. ... So you could tell that they was two different individuals altogether." Participants reported that Nichols was more emotional than McVeigh. Participants 2 and 24 stated that of Nichols that "he seemed to be more emotional," and Participant 8 stated that "you could see emotions on his face." According to Participant 24, this emotion was elicited by the trial: "I felt like things that were said or done not necessarily by me during my testimony but by maybe others, victim impact, that kind of thing, that there were times when he was very emotional."

Participants also credited Nichols with displaying situationally appropriate emotions. Participant 8 stated that Nichols appeared to be "uncomfortable, scared, guilty ... He looked very frightened." Participant 25 also characterized Nichols as afraid: "But most of the time he was, how would you say, he was ... looked like he was a little afraid about what was going to happen than anything." And Participant 28 described Nichols as "a little more nervous." Participant 24 stated that Nichols may have felt shame: "I also felt like that McVeigh was proud of what he did and I felt like that Nichols was maybe more ashamed of what he couldn't have stopped from doing." For Participant 29, this display of emotion was a sign of humanity: "And I hate to give him credit for this but you kind of see a person in Nichols." Nichols was also quieter, according to Participant 25: "more the quiet, refined individual, who sat there and didn't say a heck of a lot or didn't do a lot. He would write notes to his lawyer every once in a while." Participant 28 stated that he was more serious: "He didn't ... he wasn't the jokester whatever. I mean he was just ... he didn't ... he did lean over and talk to his attorneys and but he didn't do the waving at people and the laughing and you know, he did not do that. He was much more serious." Participant 29 described Nichols as "resigned."

5.3. Dissatisfaction with Limited Access to McVeigh through Trial Proceedings

Participants often wanted to meet with McVeigh outside of the trial forum. This suggests that the constraints placed upon the victim–offender relationship and the accountability process by the criminal justice institution also unfortunately constrained memory work, and that participants wanted to escape these institutional constraints to gain access to McVeigh and/or to ask different types of queries. This indicates an unwillingness to entirely defer to the criminal justice system as arbiter of guilt and innocence. There was a sense that seeing McVeigh in person would confirm guilt; for instance, Participant 8 attended trial proceedings in person because "I had to see for myself I mean all the media was telling you was that he was guilty but I had to look at him and know and I knew if I looked at him I'd know if he was guilty or not no matter what the jury came back with..." Other participants expressed disappointment with the questioning limitations of the trial's narrow guilt/innocence inquiry; Participant 25 wanted to ask other questions that had not yet been answered: "I wanted to find out why, with the questions that I had, not some lawyer or the judge or whatever asking him. I wanted to ask my own questions." Finally, the fact that trial attendees' access to McVeigh was mediated by the trial forum and direct access was foreclosed could be frustrating to participants; three participants spontaneously remarked on the constraints imposed by legal procedures and in legal venues. Participant 25 stated, "it would have been nice to have been able to ask, personally ask and not have to, you know, go through a lawyer ... just to say you know, why did you do that? What were you thinking? What did you think you were going to accomplish?" These reactions to encountering McVeigh through the trial forum illustrate the limited efficacy of criminal trials as vehicles of individual, and therefore collective, memory.

6. THE COMMUNICATIVE RAMIFICATIONS OF McVEIGH'S EXECUTION

Like McVeigh's conduct during media interviews and trial, his behaviors at the execution continued to heavily influence family members' and survivors' collective memory of his identity as a perpetrator of the bombing (Was he repentant? Was he defiant?) and thus to color the ways in which they made sense of the final legal stages of the bombing.[27]

6.1. Understanding the Execution as Communicative Interaction

It may seem odd at first to speak of an execution as a communicative act, which will herein be defined as a specific episode in which someone is engaged in meaning-making by drawing on enculturated systems of communicative practices, the underlying sociocultural systems or toolboxes from which we strategically choose spoke, written, or gestural behaviors. Human communication is not a transmission of transparent meaning but a negotiated exchange of meaning. Communication does not take place in a vacuum but in a social context seething with entities that may either facilitate or hinder human interaction. Differing cultural backgrounds or ideological assumptions may result in deviating perceptions as easily as does a noisy environment or technological malfunction. A communicative framework of action and reaction is the ideal means by which to address punishment in general, capital punishment in particular, and the execution as a specific imposition of capital punishment. Criminal law's efficacy itself presumes the existence of communication, expressions that some actions are illegal and that those commit crimes will be punished. That we all understand what actions are illegal is proof that those concepts have been successfully communicated to us. As a state-instituted ritual, punishment is a social act, and capital punishment is its most extreme form.

Thus, an execution is both communicative action and an event with social consequences. An execution is the enactment of the pronounced death sentence. The state is the primary actor in the execution ritual that outlines, regulates, and supervises the execution though the execution is carried out in the name of the people. The state actor communicates both with and through the condemned to reach the immediate witnesses and more remote audiences exposed to the execution through media. The state's expression to the condemned is a unique punitive message. Usually punishment is meant to express censure, and a "don't do it again" warning. Here, the object of the punishment won't live to learn his lesson, so one can infer that the state's ultimate communicative target is not the condemned but the witnesses to the execution.

The condemned plays a remarkably passive role in the execution process. The execution is designed to subordinate the will of the individual to the will of the state, reenacting the contract between the governed and the governing. Punitive acts, then, are the means by which the state seeks to "prevent the despotic spirit ... from plunging the laws of society into its original chaos" (Beccaria, 1963[1764], p. 12). Executions are the ultimate confirmation of this reposited popular power over the body of the infractor. The state has codified its gatekeeping role in carrying out the execution, most notably for our purposes in 28 C.F.R. § 26.4(f), which prohibits photographic, audio, and visual recording devices at federal executions.

Significantly, "execution finally puts the body beyond the possibility of social control" (Giddens, 1991, p. 162). Social control over the social *person* must cease upon death, but social control over the *body* can continue in perpetuity. But until the moment of execution, the body is the site and target of the most rigid forms of social control. The state imprisons the condemned until the date of his death, and impresses additional restrictions upon his final moments. Since the days of public hangings, prisoners have often been hooded or masked "to spare spectators the sight of the condemned person's distorted or disfigured features," and after the electric chair replaced the noose, leather face masks concealed the condemned's features (Bessler, 1997, p. 151). When lethal injection is used, the prisoner's body is often sanitized by a sheet cover, and the prisoner lays supine upon a gurney so that witnesses see only one side of his features. In McVeigh's execution, the closed-circuit camera was suspended directly over his head, so that witnesses had an unobstructed view of his features.

The state also restrains the condemned's final expressions and actions. Formerly, "at large spectacles and at small private executions as well, the prisoner was made a part of the ritual by being offered an opportunity to deliver his final words" (Lifton & Mitchell, 2000, p. 182). Now, however, this privilege has been "gradually withdrawn" because "there is a fear that he will say something nasty that will disrupt the proceedings," and in some cases, the prisoner is only permitted to write his last words (Lifton & Mitchell, p. 182).

Finally, the physical space in which the execution is carried out further emphasizes that the state is the primary actor and others but incidentally connected to the act. According to Foucalt, the execution, once a "pure event" and "collective spectacle," moved out of view with the invention of the prison organization. Death was dissected into silent and rehearsed routine processes, "a sequence of technical modifications" to make it "instantaneous" and "unobtrusive" (Giddens, 1991, p. 162). The very existence of the witness room distances witnesses from the invocation and metaphysical and physical consequences of the execution; witnesses become bystanders because of the distance imposed by concrete and glass. The layout of the witness rooms further regulates witnesses' impressions and responses and structures the execution as a distant communicative event, allowing the state to "minimize the fascination of looking by effecting death as mechanically and as precisely as possible" (Sarat, 2001, p. 189).

6.2. Deconstructing the Gaze

6.2.1. The Marked Gaze
Witnesses literally attend and attend to an execution on the basis of general communicative expectancies. Such dynamics are activated when the

condemned invites or opens an interaction by either looking into the witness rooms or by addressing witnesses through "last words." Often, the condemned does make some communicative endeavors, but rarely makes the gestures that witnesses most desire. In exploring the interactive dimensions of the McVeigh execution, we come first to the importance of his visual awareness of witnesses established through gaze. Witnesses in the death chamber reported that, when the curtain was opened, McVeigh physically lifted his head and slowly stared into three of the four witness rooms wherein sat his own witnesses, bombing victims, and media witnesses. There is some question whether McVeigh stared into the room reserved for government witnesses. Persons in all of these rooms but the offender witness room were concealed by a one-way glass. McVeigh then lay back down and stared up at the ceiling, into the closed circuit camera. This active visual engagement with witnesses was noted by all three participants who witnessed the execution live in Terra Haute, and all five remote witnesses believed that McVeigh was staring directly at them.

Execution witnesses are often intensely interested in watching the offender's face throughout the procedure, to the point that corrective measures may have to be taken when logistics such as the location of the gurney vis-à-vis the victim witnessing room and the girth of the defendant combine to make this impossible.[28] Interviews with witnesses who viewed McVeigh's execution by closed circuit reveal that witnesses felt that the placement of the camera directly over the gurney in Terre Haute was ideal because it allowed them to clearly see McVeigh's facial expressions. The desire to see McVeigh face-to-face fueled some witnesses' desire to view the execution. When asked about the desire to see the execution in person, Participant 25 remarked in a media interview five days before the execution:

> I'm hoping that if I can see his face maybe I can get some kind of idea exactly who he is and what he thinks.... . Stare him in the eye and I hope he stares me back. I'm hoping that if I can see his face maybe I can get some kind of idea exactly who he is and what he thinks. (CNN Breaking News, 2001)

Closed circuit witnesses report being "shocked" or "jarred" by the sudden sight of McVeigh' face on the screen. But this shock did not prevent most witnesses from unhesitatingly endorsing this placement. Participant 5's spouse states, "I'm glad I saw him that close up and everything, cause that way I knew from his eyes and his expression what he was feeling." Participant 15 stated, "I wanted to see his face." Participant 21 credits a spiritual experience of forgiveness that she underwent during the execution to being able to see McVeigh's face: "I think the face thing is what, really brought it to reality with me … it was a face-to-face thing and I think that's probably what drew me in to what I needed to go through." The two closed circuit witnesses who wanted to see a more inclusive picture stated that they wanted to see more of what was going on in the execution chamber.

Interviews with witnesses manifest that McVeigh's gazing behaviors gave rise to an intense perception among closed circuit witnesses that McVeigh was aware that his death was being witnessed, that he wanted to create a certain image, and that his gazing behavior produced an interactional expectancy. Closed circuit witnesses believed that McVeigh was staring at them through the camera and that he was conscious of their presence. Larry Whicher, a closed circuit witness, stated in a media interview immediately after the execution that McVeigh "actually lifted his head and looked directly into the camera and it was as if he was looking directly at us." Whicher described his stare as "totally expressionless, blank stare – and his eyes were unblinking,…he didn't need to make a statement. I truly believe that his eyes were telling me he had a look of defiance and that if he could he'd do it all again" (CNN Live Event, 2001). Participant 5's spouse also sensed that McVeigh was aware that he was being watched: "He knew that people were looking at him, watching him…" When McVeigh's face appeared on the screen, it seemed to Participant 7 that he was looking at the witnesses in the viewing rooms.[29] Not only did witnesses feel that McVeigh was aware of live and closed circuit witnesses, but there was a definite perception that McVeigh was actually and purposefully *looking at* all witnesses, whether they viewed live or by closed circuit. Participant 21 stated that "he raised his head up and I mean he kind of did like this and it was almost like he was just staring at each person … and it was something he did on purpose." 21 described the sight of McVeigh's face as intimate, stating "It's almost like it was a face-to-face contact with him." Participant 22 stated that when McVeigh's face, 22's reaction was, "there's his face *looking at you*" (emphasis added). Participant 28 perceived that McVeigh was not only aware of witnesses' presence and that his gaze seemed to penetrate through the mediated images to reach witnesses:

> And as he stared at the camera, knowing that we were watching, I mean he knew, he knew… . And but I … you know, he … he would just stare at that camera. And it was just … like it was just he was just staring right through you. I mean absolutely everyone said the same thing. It looked like he was looking right at you, like he was looking right at me.

Witnesses in the death chamber in Terre Haute had a different experience of McVeigh than witnesses who viewed via closed-circuit television.

Participant 25 stated that McVeigh "glared into the room, you know, trying
to figure out who was who, who was in there and where we were standing
at." Participant 29 recalled that McVeigh raised his head in an effort to look
at victim witnesses, although it was unexpected: "I never expected him to
look at us. And then ... it was like drum roll. His head turns to his right. He
rolls over and he looks at all of us. Or at our window. Four, maybe five
second and then turns his head back." Live witnesses, then, only had
seconds of perceived eye contact with McVeigh.

In the closed-circuit image, McVeigh was lying on his back and so his gaze
defaulted to the ceiling, making it unclear whether he was looking at the
camera, the ceiling, the remote witnesses, both, or neither. The remote
witnesses, however, did impose meaning upon that gaze, and perhaps even
felt its full impact even though they were the most removed. As closed
circuit witness Larry Whicher stated in a media interview immediately
following the execution: "I think that stare in the camera is something that
will stay with me... . It won't haunt me, but I think it will be a memory that
will stay with me and make me think there are others like that in the world"
(Horne, 2001).

6.2.2. The Social Consequences of the Gaze

For sighted people, gaze is an important social behavior (Argyle & Cook,
1976, p. ix). Of course, "looking at others and being looked by them, is of
central importance in social behavior, for those who can see" (Argyle &
Cook, p. ix). Above all else, a gaze conveys visual attention (Argyle & Cook,
p. ix). In a classic 1967 study of eye gaze, Kendon proposed that eye contact
had three functions, the first two of which are directly relevant here: to
express emotion, monitor others' actions, and regulate conversational flow
(Kendon, 1967). Similarly, Argyle found that eye contact signaled the level
of intimacy which existed between two interactants; the greater the eye
contact, the closer the relationship between them (Argyle, 1988). Mutual
gaze is also physiologically arousing; Mazur et al. found that mutual gaze
between experimental participants caused more arousal (measured by
"strong, significant, and consistent drops" in thumb blood volume, or TBV,
which measures the quantity of blood moving from the "periphery of the
body to the heart, lungs, and large muscles") than control conditions of
nonmutual gaze (Mazur et al., 1980, pp. 62, 71).

Because of McVeigh's gazing behavior, witnesses perceived that he was
both conscious of and paid careful attention to their presence. McVeigh's
staring behavior was likely marked for closed circuit witnesses because
it was interpreted as unexpected behavior or a breach of social norms

(Argyle & Cook, 1976, p. 83). According to Kendon, 11 out of 20 subjects in an experimental interview situation spontaneously commented on variations in an interviewer's gaze pattern when it deviated from normal, whereas none mentioned the gaze when the interviewer's gaze patterns remained normal (Argyle & Cook, p. 83). If these findings with respect to gaze in an interpersonal context may be extended to other non-face-to-face interactions, then attendees' frequent commentary on McVeigh's gaze may be an indication that his gaze was an unexpected behavior, or that it was interpreted as deviant or in breach of social norms.

Having established that McVeigh's gaze was socially significant, we may begin to explore what exactly it signified and how it positioned McVeigh vis-à-vis the witnesses; in other words, we may explicate the social consequences of the gaze. The most obvious element that a gaze conveys is visual attention (Argyle & Cook, 1976, p. 84). It is McVeigh's gesture of straining to gaze into each witness room that informed witnesses of his conscious and careful attention to and awareness of their presence. Logically, witnesses who were in the death chamber in Terre Haute may have had a more immediate or intimate encounter with McVeigh than witnesses who viewed the execution via closed-circuit television because of the close physical proximity. McVeigh was reclining on his back so that his gaze was directed upwards to the ceiling as a matter of course, and so it is unclear whether his upturned gaze into the camera (and through its lens to the witnesses in Oklahoma City) was targeted at the ceiling, the remote witnesses, both, or neither. However, it was the remote witnesses who viewed McVeigh's face throughout the entire procedure who imposed the meaning upon that gaze, just as the death chamber witnesses assigned meaning to McVeigh's physical gaze into the witness rooms. Ironically, it was the remote witnesses who felt the full impact of McVeigh's gaze.

Thus, visual attention can act as a summons, and an attentive gaze may be the indication that a communicative interaction is starting or is likely to start. Because of its attentive properties, a gaze unites persons who were previously inattentive both towards each other and to the interactive potential that arrived with an awareness of the gaze. This interpersonal unity is there even if the motivation that engendered the gaze divides its participants, as in the case of an openly hostile stare. When a gaze thus serves as a trigger for attention, communicative expectancies are a logical corollary (Argyle & Cook, 1976, p. 85). In effect, then, the gaze constitutes a summons to pay attention *because* the gazer is paying attention, implying that attention is a reciprocal behavior.

The attentive gaze also objectifies its target. According to Merleau-Ponty, people can be "stripped of existence" or "transformed into an object" by "being looked at by someone who dares not strike up any relationship" (Argyle & Cook, 1976, p. 85). Thus, a gaze that is an invitation to attention (and therefore to awareness of attention) but is not an invitation to further communicative interaction is a truly objectifying gaze, a behavior which has significant social consequences and positioning effects for its target.

A gaze may also signify an attempt to establish dominance. Evidence suggests that status is determined very soon within an interaction, from the first 15 seconds to 1 minute, instead of emerging over a longer term.[30] Staring behavior is commonly interpreted as assertive in a wide range of cultures, and empirical research has illustrated shown that staring behavior can be perceived as threatening or dominating.[31] Stares are likely to be perceived as showing anger, aggression or assertiveness when accompanied by lowered eyebrows (Mazur et al., 1980, p. 63). The experimental findings of Mazur et al. (p. 64) suggest that mutual gazes accompanied by lowered brows were more physiologically arousing than mutual gazes accompanied by raised brows; declines in subjects' TBV were "significantly deeper" in the lowered brow situations. Mazur et al. (p. 70) found that participants' level of comfort with staring behavior was a "strong predictor" of dominance in subsequent interactions, with participants who reported being more comfortable with the scale taking a dominant role in subsequent conversation and decision-making tasks. In a communicative purpose related to assertions of dominance, gazes can also communicate threat or challenge (Smith, Sanford, & Goldman, 1977).

The positioning effect of a gaze can also result from an active "staring down" which puts the subject "in her place," or it may result from deviant behavior that violates norms of interaction and thus provides discomfort in the subject. For instance, "staring on the part of strangers constitutes a bizarre piece of rule-breaking, whose meaning is unclear, from which the person stared at might well want to escape" (Argyle, 1988, p. 93). The interpretation of a gaze, like the meaning of other nonverbal signals, is heavily dependent on its social context, how actors define the situation (Mazur et al., 1980). An execution setting is not the same type of interaction as a friendly chat between friends; the condemned's past behavior has in some way opposed him to those who witness his execution either because they were somehow harmed by him (survivors or family members of victims) or because they are there to commemorate the consequences of his transgression (media and government witnesses). This explains why McVeigh's gaze was interpreted as confrontational or defiant, particularly when interpreted in light of his silence at the warden's request for "last words." Such a confrontational gaze connotes animosity and dominance and implies emotion and power roles: "looks can express aggression and hostility, and can also evoke it" (Argyle, p. 74).

Witness responses suggest that McVeigh's gaze could have been perceived as one of two particularly aggressive gazing behaviors, a "stare down" or a "hate stare." A stare down is a "dominance encounter" in which one party decides to hold another's gaze so that it becomes a staring contest in which each interactant attempt to outstress the other that ends only when one party looks away (Mazur et al., 1980, p. 52). Participant 8 wanted to stare down McVeigh when 8 attended his trial in Denver: "I just stared at him I said I'm gonna stare at you until you look me in the eye and he did. And I said I'm not going to, you're going to look away before I do." An especially antagonistic gaze that Goffman termed the "hate stare" is a deliberate breach of the nonstaring accord between strangers that Goffman terms "civil inattention" (Argyle, 1988, p. 74). The hate stare is "insulting partly because it implies the person stared at doesn't really count as a person at all" (Argyle, p. 75). This perspective prioritizes the "deliberate breaking of the social norm" (Argyle, p. 75). Both of the consequences of the hate stare parallel likely consequences of McVeigh's gaze: objectifying the targets of the gaze, and its deviance from social norms. Such a gaze implies that the gazer is dominant and has the right to stare at and impose upon the target of his gaze. In studies of dominance, increased looking by a person makes him or her appear more dominant to others.

6.2.3. Witnesses' Perception of a Communicative Gaze

The execution did indeed have communicative dimensions for most witnesses, so much so that one journalist was prompted to refer to McVeigh's gaze as "a look they will long remember, the long hard stare into the camera," that was comprised of a "blankness" and an "unblinking gaze" (Horne, 2001). Closed circuit witnesses most certainly perceived that McVeigh was attempting to send a message. Witnesses described McVeigh's expression as either confrontational ("staring" into the camera), or "stern" or "defiant" ("I've seen it a lot in my grandchildren. You know that kind of defiance of ah, you can whip me if you want to but it's not hurting.") or as overtly malicious, terming it a "go to hell" or "eat shit and die" expression, one that "just spit on us all some more," and an "evil" expression.[32] For Participant 22, McVeigh's expression was so defiant that a relaxation in his facial posture was the preeminent physical sign of his death; 22 could sense that he had passed "because the facial expression changed" where "he was so defiant until the end." Witnesses also stated that McVeigh's face registered pride or arrogance, describing it as "triumphant," a "fuck you all, I won" look, one that said "I did the right thing and I'm not sorry" or "I'm willing to die for my idea." Ironically, witnesses further described McVeigh's expression as registering absence, explaining that it was blank ("nothing"), unremorseful ("no remorse"), uncaring ("didn't give a flip," "didn't care") and free of suffering ("you're not hurting me," "no sign of discomfort," "showed no pain").

Interpreting McVeigh's gaze as communicative certainly had interpersonal consequences from survivors, from angering them to disappointing them to hurting them further or, in a more positive direction, enabling forgiveness. Participant 25 stated in a media interview following the execution that "What I was hoping for, and I'm sure most of us were, we could see some kind of, maybe, 'I'm sorry.' You know, something like that. We didn't get anything from his face" (Associated Press, 2001). Similarly Participant 15 stated, "he died like he didn't care and I cried because of that, because he did not care." Participant 5 stated in a media interview following the execution that "He got the final word ... I thought I would feel something more satisfying" (Bryant, 2001). This perception was echoed by Jay Sawyer, a nonparticipant closed-circuit witness whose mother was murdered in the bombing, who stated in a media interview, "[w]ithout saying anything he got the final word, absolutely. His teeth were clenched, just like when he was first arrested. His teeth were clenched, his lips were pursed and just a blank stare. It was the same today" (Bryant). But according to Participant 21, confronting McVeigh face to face is what enabled 21 to have an intensely spiritual experience in which 21 forgave McVeigh.[33]

It is immediately apparent that perceptions of McVeigh as defiant are confined to remote witnesses who saw McVeigh's face throughout the execution procedure. Surprisingly, live witnesses who viewed the execution in Terre Haute did not perceive either that McVeigh was attempting to communicate with witnesses or what he was attempting to communicate. Participant 25 stated that McVeigh "glared" into the victim witness room, "trying to figure out who was who, who was in there and where we were standing at," but 25 did not interpret anything significant in McVeigh's expression other than confusion. In a media interview immediately following the execution, Participant 25 had stated, "we didn't get anything from his face. His facial expressions were just about as calm as they could be" (CNN Live Event, 2001). Participant 29 also recalled McVeigh's prolonged gaze into the victim witness window, but other than characterizing that look as being akin to a "glare," 29 did not know whether McVeigh was "trying to give us [live witnesses] something." Live witnesses may have wished for more communicative interaction; survivor Anthony Scott, another live execution witness, stated in a media interview immediately following the execution that "I wish that there might have been eye to eye contact, but he couldn't see us" (CNN Live Event). Participant 25's disappointment was also evident: "I was hoping to look at this man, but it didn't work guys. So we went with what we felt like going in" (CNN Live Event). This communicative ambiguity may have made it difficult for live witnesses to categorize McVeigh's emotional state at the moment of his execution. As Participant 25 stated in a media interview, "I mean he's not a monster, guys. I mean not when you're looking at him in the face. I mean he's just a regular human being. But, you know, there's no facial expressions on him whatsoever so there was no way of knowing just exactly what he is and how he is."

Still other closed circuit witnesses revealed in media interviews or statements that McVeigh exhibited signs of fear. Survivor Calvin Moser stated, "To me, he had the look of, 'I'm not in control of this. As much as I've criticized the government, the government has me'" (Horne, 2001). Oneta Johnson, a family member, stated that "He looked up and stared at us, but I saw his jaw quiver" (Horne).

Witnesses, whether live or closed circuit, wanted to respond communicatively in turn to McVeigh's gaze.[34] Significantly, the one closed circuit witness who stated that it was not meaningful that McVeigh could not actually see other witnesses believed that only "someone who has a lot of vengeance would want that." Strikingly, two of the live witnesses brought in small photographs of their murdered loved ones and held the photographs up against the glass during the execution. Participant 29 brought a photograph of 29's murdered sibling. While entering the witnessing room in Terra Haute, Participant 29 was in the front row, and placed it up to the glass; Participant 29 described how another witness did the same thing with a photograph of a murdered child.[35] When asked whether it was as if 29's sibling were witnessing the execution, Participant 29 replied "Yeah, that's why I did it. Symbolically I felt that way, yeah."

6.3. Dimensions of Silence

Silence has a multitude of meanings. It may be "a sign of someone's power or control over others, or it may be a sign of a person's weakness and submission," it may be "a state in which one gains knowledge, or it may be a state of idle ignorance or unlearning" (Jaworski, 1993, p. 69). "Affection, reverence, attention, hesitation, and other states and emotions are ordinarily and naturally communicated through silence" (Jaworski, p. 38). Jaworski (p. 85) states that silence is a "highly ambiguous" form of communication as "it does not manifest any particular assumptions in a strong way" and so "is more open for the audience to speculate about which assumption(s) the communicator had in mind to make manifest or more manifest in his or her use of silence." Therefore, we must reject a simplistic view of silence as merely a counter to speech, an absence defined as such because it is bereft of verbal presence. Under such an impoverished perspective, "humans are metaphorically conceptualized as machines, and the constant 'humming' of the machine is regarded as a sign of its proper functioning," but when the humming ceases and silence reigns, "the (human) machine is perceived as if it no longer work[s] well" (Jaworski, p. 46). Under this perspective, wording equates to working. However, silence does "retain the illocutionary force of speech ... it is fully capable of actualizing the common speech acts of apologizing, refusing, complaining, questioning, etc.," and "it is through this potential that silence can have positive or negative social consequences: cohesive or devisive ... informative and revelational" (Sobkowiak, 1997, p. 46). Jaworski (p. 46) posits instead a conceptualization of silence that does not treat it as a "negative phenomenon with respect to speech" but locates both silence and speech "on a communicative continuum of forms ... from most to least verbal."

We are interested here in the communicative dimensions of silence. Therefore, it is a clear prerequisite that, for silence to be communicative, it must be somehow communicatively significant, invested with meaning. Jaworksi (1993, p. 34) posited that one person only interprets another's silence when there is an interactional expectation, when "the communication process is expected or perceived to be taking place," when one person intends to communicate something to another. He then exemplified "noncommuni-cative" silence by a hypothetical situation where two strangers pass on the street without intending to interact with one another; the lack of intent to communicate means that the silence is not socially meaningful. This seems a strange notion, for as researchers, we would contest that this silence does have communicative meaning regardless of the intentions of these two strangers. In Jaworski's eyes, then, meaningfulness is constructed from the perspective of the interaction participant and not an external observer. This conception of communicative silence thus presupposes communicative engagement or the expectation for such engagement.

When silence is meaningful, then, it may assume social functions. One researcher has identified five functions of silence: a linkage function, where "silence may bond two (or more) people or it may separate them"; an affecting function, where "silence may heal (over time) or wound"; a revelation function, where "silence may make something known to a person ... or it may hide information from others"; a judgmental function, where "silence may signal assent and favor or it may signal dissent and disfavor"; and an activating function, where "silence may signal deep thoughtfulness ... or it may signal mental inactivity" (Jaworski, 1993, p. 67).

Within the interactional context of the McVeigh execution, there are three primary contexts of silence: that of the witnesses, that of McVeigh himself, and execution as a means of imposing silence upon McVeigh.

6.3.1. Witnesses' Own Silence

At the FAA Center in Oklahoma City, the remote site to which McVeigh's execution was broadcast via closed circuit television, what talking there was took place before the execution began. Three of the five remote witnesses spoke of the execution as something of a reunion or social gathering, a description aided by the fact that juice, coffee, and fruit were provided in the kitchen in the back part of the viewing room.[36]

The social dimensions of collectively witnessing the execution were especially apparent for live witnesses, some of whom traveled to Terra Haute together, and all of whom had dinner together the evening before the execution and breakfast the morning of the execution. Participant 29 knew many of the other live witnesses: "when I got there, this was the first time I had met [witness] and [witness]'s a little bit of a character and of course [witness] was there and I knew, I knew a couple of others which was given – you only have 10 people, that I knew about half of us was really weird. So we had a nice sense of camaraderie right off the bat." Participant 29 and other witnesses shared a similar attitude toward many aspects of the proceedings, including viewing in a humorous light the many preachers and mental health professionals present at a dinner with the warden the evening before the execution: "you know we were all like – we were in a pretty good mood given you know what – maybe we hadn't thought about what we're getting ready to do, the gravity of it but anyway it's just – we were ... I think the people I was close to there kind of felt the same way.... Anyway, we made a joke of it." According to Participant 29, the "good mood" of witnesses persisted through the execution itself: "I think there was one person and this was not even until we were in the room that one person seemed you know to be very solemn about it ... you know we were just kind of I don't want to say joking and certainly not laughing but it was not a somber experience in that room."

Closed circuit witnesses describe the atmosphere in the witness room in Oklahoma City as being very different that the atmosphere in Terre Haute. Despite the interactions between witnesses, an air of nervous anticipation was palpable. Participant 5's spouse stated that closed circuit witnesses were "milling around" "really restless" and "on edge" before the execution began because "their anticipation was kinda getting to them." Participant 21 stated that different witnesses awaited the execution in differing frames of mind: "The mood in there. There were some that were just, somber like me just, you know, there were some that were like, I remember one, one woman go, 'This is a great day for an execution.' I mean, you know, you had every feeling in there." Participant 22 stated that "Everybody was nervous. I think. I mean it appeared to me that everybody I talked to was pretty nervous. One girl just passed out. She just, she just was too overwhelmed. She stayed though. She got better." Participant 28 described there being "all kind of nervous talk, kind of chitchatting."

During the remote broadcast of the execution itself, witnesses were silent; Participants 7 and 15 states that they were "very quiet," and 7 stated that there was no audible crying. Participant 5's spouse was allowed to describe to 5 what was going on during the closed circuit execution even though "everybody else was cautioned to be quiet, be orderly ... they didn't want any outbursts or no, ah, they didn't want any kind of clapping or yelling or loud crying or anything like that," and so Participant 5's spouse described events in a "real low tone." Participant 21 stated that things were "Very quiet, I was amazed, when he actually died. It was silent... . I really expected some people to, to have an outburst, you know, clap or something. It was very silent." In Terra Haute, however, according to Participant 25, there was some talking in the execution chamber as some of the female witnesses who had brought photographs made comments: "Probably the women made comments about this is my husband or this is my brother or what.... With photographs." Participant 29 also stated that one of the witnesses was speaking during the execution: "I mean [witness] was 'hey you son of a bitch over here, look at this picture.' You know yelling at him."

After the execution, 7 stated that there was an attitude of "okay it's done, let's move on." This is precisely how live witnesses described the execution; as Participant 25 stated, "when it was over with, you know, they said, 'It's over, it's done.'" In Oklahoma City, there was an air of quiet afterwards according to Participant 28: "everyone kind of just got up, made their way out, went and got in the cars."

If we accept Jaworski's proposition that silence and speech are two ends of a communicative spectrum, it is easy to understand that, like speech, silence can be "situation specific," depending on "the practical conventions of the event itself" (Jaworski, 1993, p. 22). Such events may actually be interactions structured through silence.[37] It thus appears that the closed circuit viewing of McVeigh's execution was structured for witnesses through silence, while the live viewing was either structured to a much lesser degree through silence or, more likely, was not structured at all through silence. These statements causes us to question the nature of the "silence" that characterized the remote and live witnessing experiences. It is abundantly clear that, in the live witness room, there was no felt need for reverent silence, as is observed at funerals (Sobkowiak, 1997, p. 48). In such somber ceremonies, silence mediates status transitions; through "the reduction of the amount of ceremonial talk – reserved to very few high-ranking participants – the community's silence manifests its unity with the absolute" (Enninger, 1987, p. 292).[38] Instead, feelings of relief were celebrated through noise.

In view of the rather obvious somber silence one would expect would characterize execution witnessing, it initially seems surprising that live witnesses report that there was less silence in the witnessing room at Terra Haute than closed circuit witnesses report in the remote witnessing room in Oklahoma City. After all, one might think that the strictures in the prison environment would impose silence upon the act of witnessing in Terra Haute. This would suggest that the farther one gets from the event, the looser the controls over speech and silence during the act of witnessing become. Clearly, participants' remarks support the opposite of this observation. An explanation may be found, however, by switching the focus from how far removed witnesses are from the witnessed event to whether the target of witness' communicative actions is within communicative range. Thus, it is more likely that the converse is true: that closed circuit witnesses in Oklahoma City had little reason to break silence because McVeigh, the target of any communicative efforts they would have made, was literally remote, appearing through a mediated image. It was the live witnesses standing in a room removed from McVeigh by only one wall who stood in communicative proximity to McVeigh. This change in focus was provoked by a conversation I had with a colleague concerning the college graduation of his daughter.[39]

6.3.2. Witness Perceptions of McVeigh's Silence

Witnesses elect to view executions for many reasons, prominent among them being the longing for some sign of repentance or suffering from the condemned – an apology, an acknowledgment of the pain and suffering endured by those reclaiming their lives after a capital crime. Thus, witnesses subject the condemned's behavior to intense scrutiny, searching for a communicational opening, some sign of interactional engagement. McVeigh did not make any statement, remorseful or otherwise, at the warden's request for last words. However, copies of his final written statement, a copy of the poem "Invictus" by William Ernest Henley, were distributed at least to media officials, since media sources reported receiving copies of the statement whereas no witnesses recall having received one.

After the execution, McVeigh's appellate attorney Robert Nigh, who had visited with McVeigh prior to the execution, addressed the media to explain why his client had not made a final statement, stating "To the victims of Oklahoma City, I say that I am sorry, that I could not successfully help Tim to express words of reconciliation that he did not perceive to be dishonest" (Associated Press, 2001). Thus, Nigh connected McVeigh's silence to an unbending insistence that his actions were justified.

Whereas some execution witnesses wanted McVeigh to say something instead of remaining silent, other witnesses were fearful that McVeigh would use the opportunity to hurt survivors and family members further. Participant 5 just wanted McVeigh to say something instead of remaining silent: "I'd liked for him to say something.... . I don't know. I just liked for him to say something." Witnesses' hope for a remorseful statement was dimmed by the perception that it wasn't in his nature to apologize, perhaps because McVeigh had never seemed to regret the bombing. Thus, witnesses wanted an apology yet either did not expect one or would not have believed McVeigh if he had apologized. Participant 5 was not surprised when McVeigh did not make a remorseful statement, and stated that "I think it'd have been important if he'd apologized, but I don't, I don't think he'd meant it if he did apologize. And he didn't mean it even if he you know, no, no apology was really in that man as far as I could tell." Participant 5's spouse who narrated the execution for 5 would have been surprised if an apology had been forthcoming: "It didn't surprise me that he was silent. I really, it would have surprised me if he would have just said anything." Participant 22 acknowledged a "ridiculous" hope for an apology.[40]

Participant 7 is the only execution witness who was angered by McVeigh's silence, particularly given his prior commitment to his "movement," but also was not surprised that McVeigh chose to remain silent in view of his military training, acknowledging that McVeigh's behaviors were constructed by past life experiences.[41]

Two live witnesses, Participants 25 and 29, did not care whether or not McVeigh apologized. Though Participant 25 wanted McVeigh to finally reveal "what had happened and why he did it," 25 states that an apology was unimportant because McVeigh would not have meant it and because remorse was unexpected: "I feel like in my own mind that if this man apologized I think it would have been phony. And so I didn't really expect him to say anything like it." Participant 29 states similarly that an apology was unexpected: "I knew he would never would so I never really thought about it. I- I- given his personality it was not even- that's not even an option."

Two execution witnesses were relieved that McVeigh was silent, in view of other, more harmful communicative choices he could have made. Participant 21 did not only expect an apology, but expected McVeigh to make a statement with the intent to cause further harm.[42] Participant 28 would have appreciated an explanation of "why" McVeigh carried out the bombing, or a statement of remorse, but preferred McVeigh's silence to a hurtful statement.[43] Participant 28 also was concerned that McVeigh would gasp for breath as Participant 28's father had done at his own death, and felt peace because McVeigh's death was more peaceful.[44]

In communicative interactions, the refusal to speak can be troubling and potentially toxic; "one's failure to say something that is expected in a given moment by the other party can be interpreted as a sign of hostility or dumbness" (Jaworski, 1993, p. 25). In hostile situations colored by anger and violence, where silence is usually thought to be the antithesis of noisy rage, silence can be a weapon, and "silent treatment of the opponent may be even more powerful than uttering the harshest of words and drives many people crazy" (Jaworski, p. 49). Hence the power of the adage "turn the other cheek." How much more painful can silence as a weapon be when there is no future opportunity for the one who wields it to reestablish communication and contact? When delivered in response to an offer or invitation, "silence is the extreme manifestation of indirectness" and, consequently, a strong form of disengagement, if not disregard (Tannen, 1985, p. 97). It is also a "highly face-threatening act" (Brown & Levinson, 1987). Here, silence embodies rejection – of the offer, and potentially of the offeror as well.

When this request to speak/refusal to speak pattern plays out in the context of an execution, the condemned only has a very limited attempt to respond, and to refuse this invitation to give "last words" is to remain silent forever, barring a last minute reprieve. The scripted regimentation of an execution protocol provides an opportunity for the warden to invite the "condemned" to utter any last words (U.S. Department of Justice, 2001).

This very request/refusal pattern played itself out in the McVeigh execution. Thus, one of the obvious manifestations of a condemned body's taboo status is that the condemned becomes silenced through the order-bearing protocol of the execution, speaking only when he is bidden, just as other taboo bodies do when subject to the strictures of other ceremonies, in giving vows, taking oaths, and delivering eulogies (Jaworski, 1993, p. 198).

In the point-counterpoint pattern of offer and refusal, McVeigh's silence was in effect his response; his reaction to the warden's request for "last words" immediately before the process of lethal injection began. McVeigh's particular responsive intent in remaining silent is largely irrelevant simply because numerous witnesses found his silence to be so meaningful. Eighteen participants desired some statement from McVeigh relating to his motivations, the "truth" behind the bombing, remorse, divine reconciliation, or admission of guilt; however, most of these participants commented that they did not expect McVeigh to be so forthcoming. Yet, witnesses still interpreted McVeigh's silence as pregnant with defiant meaning.

McVeigh's execution, as a ceremony involving change in status, posed a threat that had to be mediated through protocol and formulaics. But McVeigh's silence itself posed an additional threat since he did not oblige witnesses with a verbal response. Additional insight can be gained into the communicative, threatening nature of McVeigh's silence by applying the principles of Brown and Levinson's Politeness Theory. Brown and Levinson follow Goffman's conception of "face," defined as "the public self-image that every person wants to claim (Sifianou, 1997, p. 66). Face is both "positive" and "negative," where positive face refers to "the desire to be liked, appreciated and approved of by selected others," and negative face "expresses the desire to be free from imposition" (Sifianou, p. 66). In every interaction, "it is in the mutual interest of both participants in an interaction to attend to each other's face" (Sifianou, p. 66). According to Brown and Levinson, almost all "verbal activities" – which as the previous discussion shows would include silence – "entail a threat to either the positive or negative aspect of face of the addressee and/or the speaker, and are thus face-threatening acts (FTAs)" (Sifianou, p. 66). The extent of the threat is not intrinsic to the verbal act but is dependent upon "the social distance between the interactants, the relative power differential between them, and the intrinsic weight of the imposition entailed by the particular act" (Sifianou, p. 66). A speaker will determine which verbal act to make depending on this social calculus of threat.

Brown and Levinson propose five major "strategies" or choices for managing FTAs (Fig. 1).

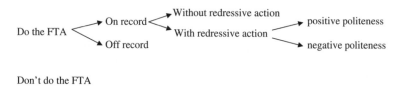

Fig. 1.   Five Strategies for Managing FTAs.

Speakers proceed through a communicative "calculus" when determining what interactive route to take.[45]

Witness responses suggest that McVeigh's decision to remain silent in response to the request for "last words" was interpreted as an FTA within the calculus of Politeness Theory – preserving his own face by not apologizing or otherwise undercutting his anti-government creed, a decision that also did not save witnesses' face. McVeigh at times was even credited with a desire to threaten witnesses' face further. In essence, he was either perceived to be not concerned with politeness, or thought to be deliberately impolite. Witnesses ascribed McVeigh's choice to a conscious decision, crediting him with the choice to perform the FTA. Thus, McVeigh's silence was perceived as a strategic verbal act – demonstrating that silence and speech are part of the same communicative continuum, and silence is then a species of linguistic act. The strategic nature of silence explains the presence of its social consequences. As Sifianou states, in encounters where the participants have unequal status, "the superior's status may indicate domination, whereas the inferior's silence may indicate subordination" (Sifianou, 1997, p. 68). It is the interaction of silence and volubility which determines the reading of the behavior (Sifianou, p. 68). Even when witnesses do not read McVeigh's silence in conjunction with his handwritten final statement, they perceive that McVeigh's strategy did not involve negative politeness – an unwillingness to burden witnesses by introducing an interactive potential into the event. Such silence was not perceived as having a rapport benefit, implicating "shared mutual knowledge" and "solidarity and common ground," but a dividing quality, emphasizing unequal or imperfect knowledge and a disparate perspective (Sifianou, p. 72).

Having examined more precisely the threatening dynamics of McVeigh's silence, we can thus return to the silencing of the condemned's taboo body. The notion that a body is silenced implies that there is an authoritative agent which silences – an entity that can be responded to. Therefore, McVeigh's silence, connected to his anti-government creed, was perceived by witnesses as both a linguistic response and an ideological response – if indeed the two can be separated – or perhaps more appropriately, a linguistic response dictating a social and ideological orientation. This perception sheds additional light on why witnesses were not surprised by McVeigh's silence. In analyzing the silenced status of other organizational bodies such as dominated sociopolitical groups and political opponents whose position is potentially or actually threatened, that group often chooses not to engage in genuine dialogue with the superordinate structure, instead questioning that structure's authority by not responding, and remaining silent. Thus, witnesses may have thought that McVeigh utilized this strategy in responding to the "last words" request through silence. Alternatively, an oppressed group may respond by speaking on its own terms or in its own context, breaking its silence by "choosing media of communication that are not controlled by the power group" (Jaworski, 1993, p. 131). Witnesses were also aware that McVeigh pursued these strategies as well, pursuing a response in other contexts free of state protocols. First, McVeigh collaborated in the publication of *American Terrorist: Timothy McVeigh & the Oklahoma City Bombing*, an account in which McVeigh classified the bombing as an act of war, angering untold numbers of family members and survivors who took issue with his casual "collateral damage" treatment of victims, particularly children, killed in the Oklahoma City Bombing (Michel & Herbeck, 2001). McVeigh also did an interview on "60 Minutes" which further angered survivors and family members. A possible third context of which many witnesses do not appear to be aware is his final statement distributed to media witnesses after his death.

6.3.3. McVeigh's Death as Imposing Silence

A third dimension of silence in Timothy McVeigh's execution was the fact that McVeigh himself was now permanently silenced, an absence instead of a communicative presence. A living Timothy McVeigh – both in the sense of McVeigh himself as a communicative presence, and the construction of McVeigh by continued media coverage – served simultaneously as a potential to "jab" victims (as Participant 21 described it), as a reminder of the bombing, and as a reminder of injustice, as those who he had murdered were no longer alive to speak. In addition, there was a fear that McVeigh could somehow influence others through media communications, and a weariness of continuously hearing the defendants' names in the press; as Participant 1, a nonwitness, stated of Nichols: "to think he's still influencing people every day in the media I am *tired* of seeing his name appear in the Oklahoma newspaper and it still appears in there every few months."

Execution was perceived by 10 pro-death penalty participants as the only way to effectively silence an offender; as Participant 24 stated, "You know, after someone is executed you are completely finished with every battle you have to fight in that arena. No more McVeigh battles to fight. Don't have to worry about what's gonna come out in the newspaper that he said to some reporter somewhere."

Eighteen nonwitnesses and witnesses experienced relief that there was silence following the execution. However, participants characterized this silence very differently depending on whether they were for or against the death penalty. All participants who opposed the death penalty spoke of this relief in terms of a cessation of media activity, whereas all participants who were for the death penalty stated that it was an end to McVeigh's actual presence – *his* silence, not that of the media – that was the crucial factor. This suggests that participants who supported the death penalty felt that their relationship with McVeigh as para-social enemy was somehow more threatening.

Both nonwitnesses and witnesses who supported the death penalty expressed relief from McVeigh's death. Participant 1, a nonwitness survivor, stated, "when those people are executed and you know they're *gone*, there, there is a change for the people that were victims of that crime. It's gotta be better. It was for me." Most participants who were for the death penalty specifically connected this relief to either McVeigh's ability to no longer speak with the intent to harm others or his ability to incidentally harm others in speaking. In these statements, survivors and family members were positioned as being affected by communications from the offender(s), and were thus accorded a quasi-participant status in these interchanges. Participants also acknowledged that McVeigh was the *subject* and not the *origin* of media coverage was also problematic and hurtful; as Participant 24, a nonwitness survivor, remarked, "[a]nd part of that [the inability to entirely leave behind the emotional entanglement with offenders] without blaming the media, part of that was the media because… every time you write a story, every time you, you know, question what happened or who was involved and those kind of things, those lesions were always there period." Similarly, 16 was thankful that "I don't hear his name constantly for the rest of my life."

Nonwitnesses who supported the death penalty also experienced relief that McVeigh was silenced. Describing her relief after the execution, Participant 8, a nonwitness whose best friend was killed in the bombing, stated that "It's still death but yeah there was that relief. We don't have to hear his crap anymore. He can't he can't hurt us. He's gone. He got what he deserved.... You know he can't write no books any more, he can't grant no interviews...." Participant 8 would have felt differently had McVeigh remained alive, with the potential to keep speaking: "I think that would have been harder because he would've, you would've heard things. Every now and then I'm sure he would've wrote something or talked to a reporter or you know it would have been in your face for life." For that reason, Participant 8 only could forgive McVeigh "[w]hen his mouth was shut." Participant 12, a critically injured survivor and nonwitness, felt a physical relief from McVeigh's silence: "But the interesting thing to me is that uh when, when McVeigh was killed I felt a huge sense of relief.... I think physically it was a major uh benefit to me, and uh I think spiritually um he's not making headlines, no one is reading his letters in the newspaper, like the bomber the clinic, abortion clinic bomber." Speaking about a recent statement that Nichols had released from prison, Participant 12 compared Nichols to the infamous murderer Charles Manson, stating "he [Nichols] should be dead, he shouldn't be capable of speaking, and I knew that this was something that could happen because Manson is alive. And he's still impacting people and...and that shouldn't happen, and that can't happen for McVeigh, he's gone." Participant 12 stated that life imprisonment should mean an inability to communicate with others: "to me, life imprisonment would be cruel and unusual punishment, because they should not see another living human being, they should not be able to communicate with another human being." Participant 12 connected an offender's ability to communicate with the ability to impact victims and survivors: "I don't care what they do, it's what they say, if they can impact, affect have any type of bearing on any other human being, it's wrong. And if they're dead, they can't do that."

Execution witnesses who supported the death penalty also focused on McVeigh as a communicative agent in expressing relief in the aftermath of his execution. Participant 15, a survivor and closed circuit witness, spoke in terms of silencing McVeigh: "I don't have to listen to his mouth ever again, ever .... That's what I wanted. You know I wanted someone to silence him because all he did was hurt people still and he got his kicks out of it and there was nothing." For Participant 25, McVeigh's willingness to use the media to continue to inflict harm on family members and survivors was one reason why 25 felt McVeigh needed to be executed, in contrast to Nichols, whose quiet prison presence met that 25 could "live with" his continued existence.[46]

Similarly, Participant 28, a family member and closed circuit witness, found the execution meaningful in terms of the silence of McVeigh: "I wanted him to be silenced and I saw him being silenced."[47] Finally, for

Participant 29, a live witness, the execution ended McVeigh's presence: "I felt a real peace ... because I'm not carrying him in my head. He's gone. He's out of my head now. And that's more room for [29's sibling]. To think I have to share room with that son of a bitch with such a nice guy like my [sibling]. That sucks."

Participant 21, one of the few who expressed no opinion on the death penalty, also explained the sense of relief after the execution in terms of terminating McVeigh's potential as a communicative agent: "Um the jabbing is what I am very happy has stopped ... . Because that was a very, very painful when he came out and said the children were collateral damage and it was like, that was so hard on the families."

Participants who were against the death penalty, on the other hand, described their sense of relief as emanating from the termination of media coverage of McVeigh, and not the death of McVeigh in itself. Participant 3, a survivor and nonwitness, noted that "I just wanted the media to quit talking about it [the execution]... . I just wanted some return to, as much return to normalcy as I could have." But Participant 3 stated that, while cessation of media coverage was an improvement, coverage would have "died down" if McVeigh had been given life imprisonment, as it had with respect to Nichols. 11 also stated that it was media coverage was kept 11 on edge.[48] Participant 19, a survivor and nonwitness, specifically attributed a sense of relief following the execution to media coverage instead of McVeigh's presence.[49]

7. CONCLUSION

This inquiry is but the first step towards researching the perceptions which murder victims' family members form towards legal proceedings, including execution, as well as the psychological and mnemetic effects that attendance and participation in legal proceedings has upon reconstruction and recovery. More research is needed to determine more precisely the effects of perpetrator media images upon families' perceptions of those perpetrators, as well as on the permutations and limitations of the victim–offender relationship. Finally, McVeigh is an atypical perpetrator, and the Oklahoma City bombing is most definitely an atypical murder case in terms of mass victimage and intensity of media coverage, and so additional research is needed to address what occurs in less-publicized murders with fewer victims.

Nonetheless, this research into the collective formation of memory and resolution of the cultural trauma of the Oklahoma City bombing through social group membership and legal proceedings offers a glimpse into the mechanisms by which "justice" is expanded and status as "justice" stakeholders is extended to victims' families and survivors in addition to legal actors. The expansion has two dimensions. First the status of "victim" no longer is granted only to the dead body of the murder victim whose wounds and markings serve as objective "evidence" at the murder trial, but now encompasses as well the murder victims' family members and all the subjectivity of their suffering. The living make more demands than the dead, but speak with the weight of the grave in their rhetoric. Prosecutory proceedings for McVeigh and Nichols were rife with instances where victims asserted their right to move out of the legal periphery – the right to be allowed to attend the presentation of evidence despite being slated to give victim impact testimony, the right to attend the trial after venue was moved from Oklahoma City to Denver, the right to witness the execution despite a witness room with a capacity of 10 witnesses. Second, the concept of penal "justice" itself has been enlarged from what is privately owed to the perpetrator in recognition of his individual free will and capacity for responsibility to include as well that which is publicly owed to the victims' family in recognition for their loss and suffering. As part of this expansion from privatized punishment to public reckonings, demands for justice have increasingly been for *witnessed* justice. These developments serve to problematize concepts such as accountability and vengeance, rendering them more complex than merely prosecuting and obtaining a conviction.

The implications of this case study are sundry. Just as the social construction of victims and justice alters, so must the responsibilities of the State incorporate these constructions into its judicial operations. No longer may the State just arrest and prosecute; now it must recognize the victims' suffering and compensate for their losses as well. Evolving constructions of victimhood demand that law be progressive in its aims, expanding its focus so that "[i]t is no longer about individuals and their responsibilities, about crime and punishment," but increasingly about "public responsibility and public solidarity, about risks of life and collective support" (Giesen, 2004, p. 66). In this way, law – as a collective institution – "not only defines the imperfection of the social order but takes responsibility also for its repair; it not only assesses the harm inflicted to victims but also carries the burden of its healing" (Giesen, p. 66). Law's foundations, then, are no longer rooted in individual responsibility but collective accountability, "engender[ing] a turn from retaliatory justice to public responses to suffering" (Giesen, p. 66). Gradually, then, law is stepping into the shoes of cultural redefinition, albeit at times unwillingly.

NOTES

1. Contact letters and postage were provided to an officer of the Murrah Federal Building Survivor's Association, who then addressed and mailed the letters to association members.

2. For additional information, see the writings of Kammen (1995, pp. 245–261) and Schwartz (1996, pp. 908–927).

3. Traumatic change that is cultural "may reverberate in the area of affirmed values and norms, patterns and rules, expectations and roles, accepted ideas and beliefs, narrative forms and symbolic meanings, definitions of situations and frames of discourse" (Sztompka, 2004, p. 161).

4. As Halbwachs notes, "when a judge or attorney enters the court building, he does not feel himself excluded or separated from the groups in the midst of which he spends the rest of his day... . Their actual presence is in fact unnecessary to allow him to continue to think and to behave — even when he is at a distance from them – as a member of these groups" (Halbwachs, 1992[1941], p. 142).

5. "Even as the court seeks to delimit its professional tasks, to reject any role as history teacher or scholar, it cannot quite contain itself from proclaiming the trial's 'educational significance' and 'educational value'" (Osiel, 1999, p. 82).

6. For Halbwachs, collective frameworks are not "constructed after the fact by the combination of individual recollections" but are the "instruments used by the collective memory to reconstruct an image of the past which is in accordance, in each epoch, with the predominant thoughts of the society" (Halbwachs, 1992[1941], p. 40).

7. According to Irwin-Zarecka, although the very presence of a "community of memory bonded by traumatic experience" in a broader collective such as a nation-state may "be enough to secure remembrance or redefine collective identity," more often, there will be a transition from "unspoken bonding to outspoken (and frequently institutionalized) activity that the community of memory acquires public resonance ... but others, especially as the years go by, find it essential to record their experience, to create memorial markers for those who had died, to talk to the young, to join groups or associations" (Irwin-Zarecka, 1994, p. 51).

8. Title I of the Act substantially amended federal habeas corpus law (as it applies to both state and federal prisoners whether on death row or imprisoned for a term of years) by (a) barring federal habeas reconsideration of most legal and factual issues ruled upon by state courts; creating a general one year statute of limitations and a six month statute of limitation in capital cases, and requiring the approval of an appellate court for repetitious habeas petitions.

9. Of the participant population, 6 were members of the habeas group, and 17 were members of the memorial task force.

10. According to Rando, complicated mourning arises from the nature of a homicidal death – its suddenness, violence, trauma, and horror, and preventability – as well as survivors' feelings of anger, guilt, self-blame, and shattered assumptions (Rando, 1993).

11. The "just world hypothesis" posits that "individuals have a need to believe that they live in a world where people generally get what they deserve" in order to "confront his physical and social environment as through they were stable and orderly" and "commit himself to the pursuit of long-range goals or even to the socially regulated behavior of day-to-day life" (Lerner & Miller, 1978, p. 1030).

12. "Major bereavement is not calm, appraising, and rational. It is instead at once a physical, emotional, and symbolic process that is built around a bewildering cacophony of intense sensations that suffuses fields of experience" (Rock, 1998, p. 40).

13. Again, the term "participants" is used to refer to interviewees, and not to group participants who did not participate in the research project.

14. Not only do survivors feel a "loss of interest in the world without the loved one," but they also feel isolated from the "experience of frustration felt by others with the bereaved person's continued suffering", to the extent that this isolation interferes with natural healing processes (Shear et al., 2006, p. 327).

15. As Rock (1998, p. 101) notes, "in their fervour and sense of urgency, in their anger and bewilderment, most survivors could have had no patience with anything but a simple and certain morality, and they turned to unambiguous schemes that would subdue doubt, establish firm boundaries between order and disorder, expel confusion, and point to directions for action." Reconstructed moral schemas can sometimes have archetypal or mythic proportions; Rock notes, "it was as if on occasion survivors were recapitulating the plot of some very ancient myth, moral disorder turning to order, flux to structure... (Rock, p. 101).

16. "Survivors thereby sought information, a restoration of control, and an end to the marginality which magnified their feelings of powerlessness and kept them apart from important sources of understanding" (Rock, 1998, p. 99).

17. Eleven participants were willing to meet with McVeigh, 12 did not want to meet with McVeigh, and 4 were unsure whether or not they would have been willing to take this step.

18. Emblematic of these comments are the remarks of Participant 25: "McVeigh ... was defiant... . He would speak out to the media. He would tell the families to grow up... . And everything that he did was doing nothing but hurting the family members here in Oklahoma. So the only way for us to have any kind of peace was to execute this man."

19. Participants 19 and 24 also made similar statements. Nineteen reflected, "if he wouldn't have been writing people and calling people and giving interviews and making pronouncements and so on, you know, it'd be a lot easier to live with him, being in prison for the rest of his life." 24 stated, "I have always felt like that if, if McVeigh and Nichols for example had access to the family members, survivors, through the media, through books, through whatever purposes they had that it would always just be keep digging at us, sticking that knife and twisting."

20. Analyzing the para-social relationships that viewers of television news form with newscasters, Levy notes, "[e]ven though this affective tie is completely the subjective invention of the audience, para-socially interactive viewers believe it is genuine and they interpret the behavior of the news personae as reciprocating this 'real' bond." (Levy, 1979, p. 185).

21. In the wake of "Crocodile Hunter" Steve Irwin's sudden death on August 31, 2006 from a stingray barb embedded in his chest, this popular figure was publicly mourned, as reported by one CNN story on the intense coverage of Irwin's death and public mourning that featured a media expert who directly attributed the phenomenon to the strong para-social relationships Irwin fostered in audiences:

"Every now and then a TV star has the ability to transcend the electronic barrier of what a television is and really feel like they're one of the family..." (Williams, 2006).

22. See, for example, Ambady, Hallahan, and Conner (1999) and Ambady and Rosenthal (1993).

23. Participants 15 and 29 made similar statements. Participant 29, a live execution witness, noted, "I'd say leaning towards more like a glare like you know boy – I can't give him credit for anything. You know, the guy ... has never had much of a look in his eye. Even when I listen to like that 60 Minutes interview." Similarly, Participant 15, a closed-circuit execution witness, stated, "Yes, very cold. He was the whole time. Any time you ever saw him on TV."

24. Five participants commented on McVeigh's failure to display emotion. Participant 2 stated that he "was always just sitting there expressionless, never showed any remorse. Never showed any emotion. He was just like a statue there." Participant 24 remarked, "there was absolutely no remorse whatsoever ... no emotion whatsoever uh no I mean you just really couldn't read from his expressions whether anything bothered him or not." Participant 28 noted that "he never showed anything.... It was – so what, people die ... even if he'd said something whether you could have trusted that what he was saying was honest or ... I mean just because he was so stoic throughout the trial and he always had the same look on his face." Participant 29 recalled that "McVeigh was just automaton almost. Just so – didn't move. Nothing. Just stony. Like I said, no like – wasn't even a human being." Finally, Participant 8 stated "he started looking around the room. And I remember he met ... met me eye to eye ... I just went white and I had to turn around ... it's like someone had just taken my breath away ... I said it was like looking at the devil eye to eye. It was just a horrible, horrible feeling."

25. Participant 28 stated "[t]hat [change of venue proceeding] was the first time I saw McVeigh you know, face to face that is, from here to the door.... And I remember when they drove in, he was ... he was just waving at people and talking to them. And I was like ... and I thought, he was really smiling. And I thought, oh my gosh..." Participant 8 recalled that "Tim was just like I'm enjoying myself. Propped his feet up on the chair in front of him." Finally, Participant 16 noted that "McVeigh would walk into the courtroom laughing, and joking, and sneering, and looking at the victims, you know. And he was just carrying on and laughing like he was just having a good old time until the jury and the judge would come in..."

26. Participant 22 remarked,

[i]t was interesting watching him in the courtroom. The things he paid attention to were anyone who was testifying about that had bomb knowledge, uh, how they're built and what works, what doesn't work. Oh, he was very interested in that testimony and any rescue workers. He was interested in that because he wanted to know the damage he'd done. And victims. He wanted to know how much he had hurt everybody.

Similarly, Participant 25 stated, "He watched a lot of the jurists, I mean the people testifying. He got involved in a lot of it. When they brought out parts and they was talking about the telephones and the chemicals, he looked like he was really interested in to it more than Nichols was."

27. Although McVeigh terminated his appeals of his own accord and asked that an execution date be set, this did not seem to affect participants' perceptions that he was defiant until the moment of his death, other than fueling participants' perceptions that McVeigh did so as an act of defiance and was attempting to establish himself as a martyr. No participant commented on the ironic fact that when McVeigh dropped his appeals he opted for an outcome that was desired by numerous family members and survivors, ultimately aligning his interests with theirs. Similarly, no participants remarked that McVeigh's willingness to die was a factor affecting any satisfaction or relief they might have felt following the execution.

28. In a conversation with one state victim advocate who witnesses executions with victims' families and who wished to remain anonymous, the advocate described that the victim viewing room was positioned at the foot of the gurney, which was flat and not inclined. During the execution of an obese offender, victims complained that they were not able to see past the offender's girth to his face. Afterwards, the head of the gurney was positioned at a sloping angle to allow witnesses to see the offender's face at all times.

29. Participants 7 and 22 also felt that McVeigh was aware of witnesses' presence. 7 states,

> you almost, you could see him almost like visibly like he's looking at each person in there. Specifically making specific attention of the fact that he's looking at each person in there.... . There being, ah, in Indiana, where he is. It's almost like he's looking at each family member or whoever's there.... . His eyes could move, I don't recall him picking up his head. Uh, I just remember he's laying and it's like, so he might have tilted it a little bit, um, I don't recall him actually picking up his head, but you could see him you know – You could tell what he was doing.

Participant 22 believes that McVeigh was conscious of the camera suspended above him: "Oh, yeah, he knew. He knew. He was very aware of it. No doubt."

30. Fisek and Ofshe found that half of groups comprised of students undifferentiated in status characteristics such as sex, race, and age formed a stable status order within the first minute of interaction (Fisek & Ofshe, 1970). In addition, Rosa and Mazur (1979) were able to predict students' rankings in similar groups moderately well by observing eye contact behavior during the first 15 seconds of interaction.

31. See Moore and Gilliland, 1921; Thayer, 1969; Exline, Ellyson, and Long, 1975; Ellsworth, 1975; Ellsworth and Langer, 1976; Liebow, 1967; Fromme and Beam, 1974.

32. The impression of "evil" was also echoed by closed-circuit witness Gloria Buck, who stated in a media interview that "It was almost like the devil was inside him, looking at us" (Horne, 2001).

33. Participant 21 stated,

> I am still not looking at him and he kind of raised up and I think was glaring into the camera, and all of sudden it's like, you know because I have this faith ... when I was there viewing him and watching him, it was like, all of sudden he came to me, ... I started to thinking of him as Timothy McVeigh, the soul and not Timothy McVeigh, the man and I started praying for him that this is his last chance, this is his last breath and I prayed for him and it just like overtook me.... . Um, I was able to let it go, I guess

to me that was the true forgiveness, not to oh yeah Timothy you could be my best buddy
type forgiveness. So it's forgiveness in different stages... . To me this was a true
forgiveness letting it go.

34. Participant 7 noted, "[I wish McVeigh could have seen me] Just so that he
could see that I'm not a monster. That we are not monsters, we're just people too.
You know and all we did was go to work that day. That's it." Participant 28 stated,
"I would like for him to look at my face and know the pain that I knew he's caused.
And to see, you know, to see my daughter and to know that you know, you killed my
daughter and her baby. You killed them." Finally, Participant 25 remarked,
"I wanted to see him when he was in the chair, like that, and I wanted him to see me.
Because I wanted him to know that no matter what he did or didn't do, we were
going to survive this thing and we would be better afterwards."
35. Participant 29 recalled that she and another execution witness pressed pictures
of their lost relatives up against the glass:

> I got in the front row and [witness] and I had both had a picture. Because both our guys
> were [same name] ... . She had her [name]'s picture and we put them right up to the
> window. Not that he could see it. It was more symbolic and we had to do it very
> discreetly because we had guards behind us. But yeah, stuck a picture up there so
> [sibling's name] could watch it happen.

36. Participant 7 recalled, "it was almost like just a little social gathering before
a meeting." Participant 15 stated, "you got to see people you hadn't seen because
I quit going to survivor's meetings and ... there weren't any meetings to plan the
memorial and so it's really sad that something like that you had to see those people
again because it was the execution but it was nice seeing them again." Finally,
Participant 21 noted,

> it had been a long while since a lot of us had been together and we all were there for one
> purpose. We were all there ... we were able to talk and laugh and share things that have
> gone on with our families because I mean we're like a whole community ... it was like ...
> even with the memorial, the anniversary, it's almost like a, a family reunion.

37. Jaworksi (p. 19) posits that meditation and walking are two such activities.
38. In instances of ceremonial spectacle, silence ensures that listening ears do not
overtax listening eyes with respect to the visual focus of the event: the body to be
buried, the life lost, the couple being joined, the infant being dedicated. Silence also
contextualizes these events, infusing them with a peaceful, proprietary, respectful,
reflective, and solemn character. Indeed, we speak of such rituals being
"solemnized." Silence may mark or facilitate moments of transcendence; "it is in
silence that [church] members experience 'the presence of God' and are able to 'listen'
to what it is that God wishes to communicate to them" (Szuchewycz, 1997, p. 241).
39. I am indebted to Bill Bowers for providing this insight. Graduation day
temperatures soared to 90 degrees, and there was limited shade for attendees,

prompting college officials to open a remote witnessing location featuring a big screen in the campus chapel. Attendees in the chapel, including my colleague, could see everything of note – individual graduates receiving degrees, the enthusiastic cheering of the live spectators. However, when the loved ones of remote witnesses received their degrees, remote witnesses did not cheer or clap; what my colleague referred to as a "sheepish few" clapped, but did so half-heartedly and stopped their clapping very soon. There seemed to be little purpose in either communicating in the absence of the communicative participant, particularly in view of the code of silent witnessing that was imposed, producing the differences in communicative activity in the closed circuit location in Oklahoma City and the witness room in Terra Haute.

40. 22 stated,

I think also many of us who attended the execution were, you just can't help but have this hope even though you know its ridiculous and that's not going to happen you still have that hope you'll say something that is remotely remorseful. And, uh, you know, it didn't happen. He was very very defiant until the last instant.

41. As Participant 7 explained,

Well, it ticked me off ... I thought if you're so um, behind your movement, whatever his movement was, then why don't you speak about it to the end? You know, if you truly believe what you did was the right thing to do, why don't you talk about it to the very end? ... I think it just goes back to military training. You just keep your mouth shut and say nothing unless asked and even then maybe say nothing.

42. Participant 21 stated,

I felt going in there that he was going to say something that would anger everybody. I didn't expect him to confess or ask for forgiveness. I was more concerned that he was going to say something that had angered everybody. He had that book that was written and it was seem like every time he turned around, he was doing some thing to jab at us and it was just very painful because he could sit there behind those bars and get us three squares a day and everything and not have all these worries and, and he kept jabbing at us in his own little way and we didn't get that with Nichols.

43. Participant 28 remarked, "I didn't want him to say anything except why he did it or that he was sorry that he did it. I would have liked for him to have said something like that. But if he was going to be ugly ... I did not want it. More than anything, I probably just wanted him to be quiet."

44. Participant 28 recalled,

My dad struggled for every breath. It was horrible, it was horrible to hear him. And I was afraid. That was the one thing I was afraid of, because my Dad was the only person I'd ever seen die. And so I was afraid that I was going to hear the same sounds. So maybe that gave me a little peace, because he just went to sleep and I didn't hear all that.

45. This calculus can be described as follows:

The first decision a speaker has to make is whether to perform the act or remain silent. He or she has to weigh two conflicting desires very carefully: the desire to avoid or minimize the loss of face against the desire to communicate the face-threatening act and achieve his or her goal. When the risk of loss of face is judged as extremely high, most speakers will seek to avoid the threat.... If the speaker decides to perform the face-threatening act, there are various ways of doing so. The speaker may decide to perform the act baldly on record, without redressive action.... Redressive action means action which counterbalances the potential face threat; it is achieved by using additional linguistic elements and/or structural elaboration.... Such direct utterances ... are normally considered to be least polite since they pay no attention to face considerations ... . The last major alternative is for a speaker to go off record, i.e. to use a vague, ambiguous or indirect utterance (Sifianou, pp. 66–67).

46. Participant 25 stated,

McVeigh, even though he knew that he was getting the death sentence, he was defiant all the way up to the point where it actually happened, okay? He would speak out to the media. He would tell the families to grow up, it's collateral damage that we killed your kids, you know. And everything that he did was doing nothing but hurting the family members here in Oklahoma. So the only way for us to have any kind of peace was to execute this man. Now on Nichols, Nichols is a little different because since he's been tried and convicted, you don't hear about him. And so even though he was ninety percent involved ... I can live with him being in prison for the rest of his life, for the simple reason that he is not defiant and he's not going out and getting on the news and so forth and trying to hurt the family members.

47. Participant 28's full statement was

Seeing it through and to know that he really was silenced. That he really is dead. I saw him die. It can't be any of this – we saw President Kennedy on a yacht or we saw ... you know, Elvis Presley working at Burger King or whatever, you know. I mean you hear all this crap. And I mean I know I saw him die and I know he is silenced. And that is what I wanted.

48. Participant 11 remarked, "I just felt like, it was kept stirring up, stirred up, stirred up, stirred up and just - all the time and ... there was still Terry Nichols to deal with, that all the media and everything, it just – that kept me toned up ... it was constant – constantly bringing everything up again."
49. Participant 19 noted,

it's not so much that he is or isn't alive, it's that, his ... access to media ... if he wouldn't have been writing people and calling people and giving interviews and making pronouncements and so on, you know, it'd be a lot easier to live with him, being in prison for the rest of his life ... all the media packed up like you know what we are free, they will not ever come back in this manner again ever ... you will not ever get any more pronouncements from McVeigh on anything.

ACKNOWLEDGMENTS

The author would like to thank Martha Minow, William J. Bowers, Barbie Zelizer, and Edward Linenthal for their invaluable comments on earlier drafts of this project.

REFERENCES

Alexander, J. (2003). Introduction: The meanings of (social) life: On the origins of a cultural sociology. In: J. Alexander (Ed.), *The meanings of social life: A cultural sociology*. New York, NY: Oxford University Press.

Ambady, N., Hallahan, M., & Conner, B. (1999). Accuracy of judgments of sexual orientation from thin slices of behavior. *Journal of Personality and Social Psychology, 77*(3), 538–547.

Ambady, N., & Rosenthal, R. (1993). Half a minute: Predicting teacher evaluations from thin slices of nonverbal behavior and physical attractiveness. *Journal of Personality and Social Psychology, 64*, 431–441.

Argyle, M. (1988). *Bodily communication* (2nd ed.). New York: Methuen & Co.

Argyle, M., & Cook, M. (1976). *Gaze and mutual gaze*. Cambridge, UK: Cambridge University Press.

Associated Press. (June 12, 2001). McVeigh shows no remorse at execution. CourtTV. Retrieved August 14, 2007, from the World Wide Web: http://www.courttv.com/news/mcveigh_special/0612_noremorse_ap.html

Beccaria, C. (1963[1764]). *On Crimes and punishments* (Henry Paolucci, Trans.). Englewood Cliffs, NJ: Prentice Hall.

Bessler, J. (1997). *Death in the dark: Midnight executions in America*. Boston, MA: Northeastern University Press.

Blair, C. (2006). Communication as collective memory. In: G. J. Shepherd, J. St. John & T. Striphas (Eds), *Communication as...: Perspectives on theory* (pp. 51–59). Thousand Oaks, CA: Sage.

Bochner, A. P. (1989). Interpersonal communication. In: E. Barnouw (Ed.), *International encyclopedia of communications*. New York, NY: Oxford University Press.

Brown, P., & Levinson, S. (1987). *Politeness: Some universals in language usage*. Cambridge, UK: Cambridge UP.

Bryant, N. (June 11, 2001). Pain remains for McVeigh victims. *BBC News*. Retrieved August 14, 2007, from the World Wide Web: http://news.bbc.co.uk/1/hi/world/americas/1383171.stm

Burgoon, J. K., & Hoobler, G. D. (2002). Nonverbal signals. In: M. L. Knapp & J. A. Daly (Eds), *Handbook of interpersonal communication* (3rd ed., pp. 240–299). Thousand Oaks, CA: Sage Publications.

CNN Breaking News. (June 6, 2001). Judge denies stay of execution for McVeigh, appeal expected. Transcript retrieved August 14, 2007, from the World Wide Web: http://transcripts.cnn.com/TRANSCRIPTS/0106/06/bn.03.html

CNN Live Event. (June 11, 2001). Family members witness [sic] to McVeigh execution recount their experience. Transcript retrieved August 14, 2007, from the World Wide Web: http://transcripts.cnn.com/TRANSCRIPTS/0106/11/se.08.html

Douglas, L. (2001). *The Memory of judgment: Making law and history in the trials of the holocaust.* New Haven, CT: Yale University Press.

Eliot, G. (2003). *Middlemarch.* New York, NY: New American Library.

Ellsworth, P. (1975). Direct gaze as a social stimulus: The example of aggression. In: P. Pliner, L. Krames & T. Alloway (Eds), *Nonverbal communication of aggression.* Norwell, MA: Kluwer Academic Publishers.

Ellsworth, P., & Langer, E. J. (1976). Staring and approach: An interpretation of the stare as a nonspecific activator. *Journal of Personality and Social Psychology, 33,* 117–122.

Enninger, W. (1987). What Interactants Do With Non-Talk Across Cultures. In: K. Knapp, W. Enninger & A. Knapp Potthoff (Eds), *Analyzing intercultural communication.* The Hague: Mouton de Gruyter.

Exline, R., Ellyson, S., & Long, B. (1975). Visual behavior as an aspect of power role relationships. In: P. Pliner, L. Krames & T. Alloway (Eds), *Nonverbal communication of aggression.* Norwell, MA: Kluwer Academic Publishers.

Fisek, M., & Ofshe, R. (1970). The process of status evolution. *Sociometry, 33,* 327–346.

Fromme, D., & Beam, D. (1974). Dominance and sex differences in non-verbal responses to differential eye contact. *Journal of Research in Personality, 8,* 76–87.

Garland, D. (1990). *Punishment and Modern Society.* Chicago, IL: University of Chicago Press.

Giddens, A. (1991). *Modernity and self identity: Self and society in the late modern age.* Stanford, CA: Stanford University Press.

Giesen, B. (2004). *Triumph and trauma.* Boulder, Co: Paradigm Publishers.

Halbwachs, M. (1992 [1941]). On Collective Memory (Lewis A. Coser, Trans.). Chicago, IL: University of Chicago Press.

Handlin, S. (2001) Profile of a mass murderer: Who is Timothy McVeigh? CourtTV. Retrieved August 14, 2007, from the World Wide Web: http://www.courttv.com/news/mcveigh_special/profile_ctv.html

Holmes, O.W. (1881). *The Common Law.* Publisher Unknown.

Horne, T. (June 12, 2001). Viewers struck by look in McVeigh's eyes [Electronic Version]. *The Indianapolis Star.* Retrieved August 14, 2007, from the World Wide Web: http://www2.indystar.com/library/factfiles/crime/national/1995/oklahoma_city_bombing/stories/2001_0612b.html

Horton, D., & Wohl, R. (1956). Mass communication and para-social interaction: Observation on intimacy at a distance. *Psychiatry, 19*(3), 215–229.

House Resolution 924, 105th Congress (1997).

Irwin-Zarecka, I. (1994). *Frames of remembrance: The dynamics of collective memory.* New Brunswick, NJ: Transaction Publishers.

Jaworski, A. (1993). *The Power of silence: Social and pragmatic perspectives.* London, UK: Sage Publications.

Kammen, M. (1995). Review of frames of remembrance: The dynamics of collective memory by I. Irwin-Zarecka. *Historical Theory, 34*(3), 245–261.

Kendon, A. (1967). Some functions of gaze direction in social interaction. *Acta Psychologica*, *26*, 1–47.

Le Goff, J. (1992). *History and memory* (S. Rendall & E. Claman, Trans.). New York, NY: Columbia University Press.

Lerner, M. J., & Miller, D. T. (1978). Just world research and the attribution process: Looking back and ahead. *Psychological Bulletin*, *85*, 1030–1051.

Levy, M. (1979). Watching TV news as para-social interaction. In: G. Gumpert & R. Cathcart (Eds), *Inter/Media: Interpersonal communication in a media world* (2nd ed., pp. 177–187). New York, NY: Oxford University Press.

Liebow, E. (1967). *Talley's Corner: A Study of Negro Streetcorner men*. Boston, MA: Little, Brown & Co.

Lifton, R. J., & Mitchell, G. (2000). *Who Owns Death? Capital Punishment, the American Conscience, and the End of Executions*. New York, NY: HarperCollins.

Linenthal, E. (2001). *The Unfinished bombing: Oklahoma City in American memory*. New York: Oxford University Press.

Mazur, A., Rosa, E., Faupel, M., Heller, J., Leen, R., & Thurman, B. (1980). Physiological aspects of communication via mutual gaze. *American Journal of Sociology*, *86*(1), 50–74.

Meyrowitz, J. (1979). Television and interpersonal behavior: Codes of perception and response. In: Gumpert, G. & Cathcart, R. (Eds), *Inter/Media: Interpersonal communication in a media world* (2nd ed., pp. 56–76). New York, NY: Oxford University Press.

Michel, L., & Herbeck, D. (2001). *American terrorist: Timothy McVeigh and the Oklahoma city bombing*. New York: Harper.

Moore, H., & Gilliland, A. (1921). The measurement of aggressiveness. *Journal of Applied Psychology*, *5*, 97–118.

Olick, K., & Robbins, J. (1998). Social memory studies: From "collective memory" to the historical study of mnemonic practices. *Annual Review of Sociology*, *24*, 105–140.

Osiel, M. (1999). *Mass Atrocity, Collective Memory, and the Law*. New Brunswick, NJ: Transaction Publishers.

Rando, T. (1993). *Treatment of complicated mourning*. Champaign, IL: Research Press.

Rock, P. (1998). *After homicide: Practical and political responses to bereavement*. New York, NY: Oxford University Press.

Romano, L. (June 12, 2001). McVeigh is executed: Bomber is 1st federal prisoner put to death since 1963, Washington Post, p. A01.

Rosa, E., & Mazur, A. (1979). Incipient status in small groups. *Social Forces*, *58*, 18–37.

Sarat, A. (2001). *When the state kills: Capital punishment and the American condition*. Princeton, NJ: Princeton University Press.

Schwartz, B. (1996). Memory as a cultural system: Abraham Lincoln in World War II. *American Sociological Review*, *61*(5), 908–927.

Senate Resolution 735, 104th Congress (1996).

Sharp, S. F. (2005). *Hidden victims: The effects of the death penalty on families of the accused*. New Brunswick, NJ: Rutgers University Press.

Shear, M. K., Zuckoff, A., Melhem, N., & Gorscak, B. J. (2006). The syndrome of traumatic grief and its treatment. In: L. A. Schein, H. I. Spitz, G. M. Burlingame, P. R. Muskin & S. Vargo (Eds), *Psychological effects of catastrophic disasters: Group approaches to treatment* (pp. 287–334). Binghamton, NY: Haworth Press.

Sifianou, M. (1997). Silence and politeness. In: A. Jaworski (Ed.), *Silence: Interdisciplinary Perspectives* (pp. 63–84). New York: Mouton de Gruyter.

Sitterle, K., & Gurwitch, R. (1999). The terrorist bombing in Oklahoma City. In: E. S. Zimmer & M. B. Williams (Eds), *When a community weeps: Case studies in group survivorship*. Philadelphia, PA: Taylor & Francis.

Smelser, N. (2004). Psychological trauma and cultural trauma. In: J. C. Alexander, R. Eyerman, B. Giesen, N. J. Smelser & P. Sztompka (Eds), *Cultural trauma and collective identity* (pp. 31–59). Berkeley, CA: University of California Press.

Smith, B. J., Sanford, F., & Goldman, M. (1977). Norm violations, sex, and the 'blank stare'. *Journal of Social Psychology, 103*, 49–55.

Sobkowiak, W. (1997). Silence and markedness theory. In: A. Jaworski (Ed.), *Silence: Interdisciplinary perspectives* (pp. 39–62). New York: Mouton de Gruyter.

Sztompka, P. (2004). The Trauma of Social Change: A Case of Postcommunist Societies. In: J. C. Alexander, R. Eyerman, B. Giesen, N. J. Smelser & P. Sztompka (Eds), *Cultural trauma and collective identity* (pp. 155–195). Berkeley, CA: University of California Press.

Szuchewycz, B. (1997). Silence in ritual communication. In: A. Jaworski (Ed.), *Silence: Interdisciplinary perspectives* (pp. 239–260). New York: Mouton de Gruyter.

Tannen, D. (1985). Silence: Anything but. In: D. Tannen & M. Saville-Troike (Eds), *Perspectives on silence* (pp. 21–30). Norwood, NJ: Ablex.

Thayer, S. (1969). The effect of interpersonal looking duration in dominance judgments. *Journal of Social Psychology, 79*, 285–286.

U.S. Department of Justice. (2001). 2001 Bureau of Prisons Execution Protocol. Retrieved August 14, 2007, from the World Wide Web: http://www.thesmokinggun.com/archive/bopprotocol24.html

Wattenberg, M. S., Unger, W. S., Foy, D. W., & Glynn, S. M. (2006). Present-centered supportive group therapy for trauma survivors. In: L. A. Schein, H. I. Spitz, G. M. Burlingame, P. R. Muskin & S. Vargo (Eds), *Psychological effects of catastrophic disasters: Group approaches to treatment* (pp. 505–580). Binghamton, NY: Haworth Press.

Williams, D. (September 6, 2006). Irwin's death strikes a chord. CNN News. Retrieved August 14, 2007, from the World Wide Web: http://www.cnn.com/2006/SHOWBIZ/TV/09/06/irwin.outpouring/index.html

APPENDIX. PARTICIPANT CHARACTERISTICS

Participant No.	Sex	Status	Interviewed	Viewed Execution	Attended Trial	Testified at a Legal Proc.	Opinion on DP B/F	Opinion on DP After	Misc. Info
1	M	S	6/24/2005	N	Y – all	N	For	For	
2	F	S	6/24/2005	N	Y – 2/3 days	Y	Against	Against	
3	M	S	6/24/2005	N	N	N	Against	Against	
4		RESCUE							Not Included in Analysis
5	M	S	7/2/2005	Y	Y	N	For	For	
6	F	S	7/3/2005	N	Y – 1 day	N	Against	Against	
7	F	S	7/5/2005	Y	Y	Y	For	For	
8	F	FM	7/5/2005	N	Y	N	For	For	
9	F	S	7/5/2005	N	Y – 1 day	N	No opinion	For	
10	F	FM	7/6/2005	N	Y, extensively	Y	For	For	
11	F	S	7/9/2005	N	Y	N	Against	Against	
12	M	S	7/9/2005	N, but would have liked to	Y	Y	Against	For	Critically injured
13		RESCUE							Not Included in Analysis
14	F	FM	7/16/2005	N	N	N	For	For	
15	F	S	7/16/2005	Y	Y – 40 hours	N	For	For	
16	F	S	7/17/2005	N	Y	N	For	For	
17	M	FM	7/17/2005	N	Y	Y	Against	For, then Against	
18	M	S	7/24/2005	N	N	N	For	For	Does not live in Oklahoma

APPENDIX. (*Continued*)

Participant No.	Sex	Status	Interviewed	Viewed Execution	Attended Trial	Testified at a Legal Proc.	Opinion on DP B/F	Opinion on DP After	Misc. Info
19	F	S	9/29/2005	N	Y	Y	For	Come to be more against	
20	M	S	9/29/2005	N	N	N	For	For	
21	F	S	9/30/2005	Y	Y	Y	No opinion, on fence	No opinion, on fence	
22	F	FM	9/30/2005	Y	Y	Y	For	For	
23	M	S	10/2/2005	N	Y	Y	Against	Against	
24	M	S	11/2/2005	N	Y only as witness	Y	For	For	
25	M	FM	4/29/2006	Y – Live	Y – 1 week Denver, 40-45% in OKC	N	N	Case-by-case	
26	F	S	4/29/2006	N	Y – 2 weeks	N	For	Case-by-case, now more against	
27	F	S	4/29/2006	N	Y – 3 days	N	For	Against	
28	F	FM	4/30/2006	Y – Live	Y, 1 week Denver, 2–3 days/week OKC	Y	For	For	
29	F	FM	5/22/2006	Y – Live	Y – 1 week for each of 3 trials	Y	Case-by-case	Case-by-case	

POWER, POLITICS, AND PENALITY: PUNITIVENESS AS BACKLASH IN AMERICAN DEMOCRACIES

Katherine Beckett and Angelina Godoy

ABSTRACT

Across the Americas, public discussions of crime and penal practices have become increasingly punitive even as political struggles have resulted in a broad shift toward Constitutional democracy. In this chapter, we suggest that the spread of tough anti-crime talk and practice is, paradoxically, a response to efforts to expand and deepen democracy. Punitive crime talk is useful to political actors seeking to limit formal and social citizenship rights for several reasons. First, it ostensibly targets problematic behavior rather than particular social groups, and thus appears to be consistent with democratic norms. At the same time, crime talk often acquires coded meanings that enable those who mobilize it to tap into inter-group hostility, anxieties, and fear. In addition, the emphasis on the threat of crime and disorder offers those seeking to limit democratic expansion a way to legitimate truncated visions of the rights and entitlements of citizenship. Tough anti-crime rhetoric often resonates with those who have experienced or fear the loss of symbolic and/or material benefits as a result of democratic reform. In short, the broad shift toward hyper-penality is, at least in part, a consequence of struggles over political democracy, citizenship and governance across the Americas.

Studies in Law, Politics, and Society, Volume 45, 139–173
ISSN: 1059-4337/doi:10.1016/S1059-4337(08)45004-4

INTRODUCTION

Many scholars have noted Latin America's relatively recent and dramatic (re)turn to liberal democratic rule (Agüero & Stark, 1998; Brysk, 2000; Diamond, 1999; Farer, 1995; Karl, 1990; O'Donnell, 1993, 2004; O'Donnell & Schmitter, 1986). As a recent United Nations Development Programme report declared, "The 18 Latin American countries[1] ... today fulfill the basic requirements of a democratic regime; of these only three lived under democratic regimes 25 years ago" (UNDP, 2004). The return to constitutional democracy across much of Latin America in the last 25 years marks a watershed moment. Not only did this shift (re)establish universal suffrage as the basis for government but, perhaps more significantly for our purposes here, the revival of constitutional democracy was accompanied by unprecedented efforts to include historically disempowered groups, including women, racial and ethnic minorities, and the poor in the political process. These efforts have taken various forms, and vary greatly in their effectiveness, but have included the official recognition of indigenous languages, cultures, and legal practices, and the creation of state agencies to uphold human rights, redistribute land, or otherwise redress historic iniquities.[2]

In the United States, too, recent decades witnessed a significant effort to broaden and deepen democracy, and in particular to extend voting rights to previously excluded groups. Although the 15th Amendment prohibited the denial of the right to vote on the basis of race, the state courts nonetheless allowed southern states to impose poll taxes, literacy tests, grandfather clauses, and other devices in order to effectively disenfranchise many African-Americans. It was not until the 1960s, as a result of the civil rights movement, that these and other forms of democratic exclusion were finally, though not entirely, swept away.[3]

Of course, the definition of democracy is hotly contested. While the bulk of the academic literature accepts the Schumpterian notion of free and fair elections with universal suffrage as constitutive of democracy, it is widely recognized that democracy varies in quality and depth. In so-called "low-intensity" or "thin" democracies, formal rights are largely recognized but political participation remains limited by both legal and extra-legal factors, and the state's obligation to ensure basic social and political rights is minimal (see especially O'Donnell, 1993). By contrast, "deep" democracy is characterized by full participation, especially of women and minorities, in the political process; high levels of confidence in public institutions, particularly among the historically disadvantaged; and the institutionalization of the state's obligation to ensure the basic social and political rights of those occupying positions of marginality (see Schedler, 1998; Shifter, 1997). Democratization, then, is not an end-point nor a single scale along which countries can be easily measured, but a set of complex processes involving multiple facets of state–society relations that have been and continue to be the subject of intense political contestation.

While the return of some form of constitutional democracy across Latin America and the eradication of most formal barriers to political participation in the United States have not meant the establishment of "deep" democracy across the hemisphere, this development is nonetheless highly significant. Paradoxically, though, political struggles for democratization have been accompanied by increasingly strident calls for tough anti-crime measures. Indeed, anti-crime rhetoric and practices have become increasingly harsh across the Americas. Incarceration rates rose most dramatically in the United States, reaching an astounding 751 per 100,000 residents by the end of 2006 (International Centre for Prison Studies, n.d.).[4] But the use of prisons has also increased in all but one Latin American country in recent years[5] (see Table 1; see also Human Rights Watch World Report, 2005; The Economist, 2004a, 2004b; Ungar, 2003; Walmsley, 2001). As the figures shown in Table 1 illustrate, there is significant variation in incarceration rates and the degree to which they have increased across Latin America. Yet the general trend is quite clear: imprisonment rates rose by an average of 62% over the past decade.

Although important, incarceration rates are only one measure of the trend toward harsher penal rhetoric and practice we highlight here. In some countries, such as Guatemala, heightened punitiveness finds expression instead in the advocacy of more aggressive policing practices (both legal and extralegal) rather than in prison expansion. Indeed, "zero tolerance" policing is increasingly popular in both North and South American cities (de Palma, 2002; Harcourt, 2001; Herbert, 2001; Smith, 2001; Wacquant, 2003a). Similarly, despite recent controversies surrounding the administration of the death penalty in the United States, calls for the reinstatement and/or application of capital punishment are abundant across Latin America (Cevallos, 2004; Sarat, 2002; Sheridan, 1998). At the rhetorical level, Latin American candidates for electoral office frequently jostle for position as the toughest on crime, sometimes echoing (and augmenting) professions of toughness from their U.S. counterparts. Not infrequently, these politicians are joined by members of murder victims' families calling for zero-tolerance policing, longer sentences for a range of offenses, and an expanded or expedited use of the death penalty.[6] For example, in

Table 1. Change in Latin American Incarceration Rates, 1992–2005.

Country	1992/1993	2005–2008	Percent Change (%)
Argentina	63	154	144.4
Belize	310	460	48.4
Bolivia	71	82	15.5
Brazil	74	219	195.9
Chile	155	279	80.0
Columbia	100	134	34.0
Costa Rica	105	181	72.4
El Salvador	99	174	75.8
Ecuador	74	94	27.0
French Guiana	241	365	51.5
Guyana	174	260	49.4
Guatemala	56	57	1.8
Honduras	110	161	46.4
Mexico	98	198	102.0
Nicaragua	85	114	34.1
Panama	178	337	89.3
Paraguay	60	96	60.0
Peru	71	139	95.8
Suriname	308	356	15.6
Uruguay	97	193	99.0
Venezuela	111	77	−30.6

Notes: Data are compiled by the International Centre for Prison Studies, King's College, University of London and are available at http://www.prisonstudies.org/. Most recent figures are shown here, and were accessed on May 7, 2008.

Argentina's 2003 Presidential elections, candidate Enrique Venturino ran on a platform summarized by the slogan "Law, Order, and Steel Fist." Not to be outdone by the incumbent's declaration of support for zero tolerance, Venturino called for "triple zero tolerance" (Venturino, 2003). In Chile, during the fall 2005 presidential campaign, candidate Joaquín Lavín called for a "three strikes you're out" law (Dammert, 2005), to which his socialist opponent, current President Michelle Bachelet, responding by advocating a "one strike you're out" policy (Toro, 2005).

Nor are politicians the only ones preoccupied with penality. Across Latin America, apparently punitive crime-talk abounds, among citizens (Caldeira, 2000) as well as in official discourse (Chevigny, 2003). Opinion polls indicate that crime and insecurity often top the list of public concerns in many Latin American countries[7] (Chevigny, 2003; Dammert, 2001; Dammert & Malone,

2003), as was the case in the United States in the 1980s and 1990s (Beckett, 1997; Garland, 2001).

This broad shift is, of course, complex and variable; although the contours of a trend can be discerned, there are undoubtedly exceptions to it and contradictions within the general pattern. In the United States, for example, there are signs that the broad trend toward hyper-penality has created significant fiscal pressures for state and local governments; this fiscal strain has created opportunities for those seeking to relax some of the most draconian anti-crime policies. Although we focus on the broad shift toward hyper-penality, we recognize that penal practices vary significantly across borders and even within the same jurisdiction. Similarly, in focusing on the trend toward "hyper-penality," we admittedly sidestep the many differences between and among cases in the Americas and run the risk of obscuring penal developments that may be expressions of something other than punitiveness. Moreover, because we do not analyze each country's historical and cultural specificities, we are unable to explain the very particular outcomes in each locale and the many significant ways in which penal practices and rhetoric diverge (Melossi, 2001).

Nonetheless, we contend that a general shift toward what Loic Wacquant calls "hyper-penality," Latin American observers dub "mano dura" (the iron fist), and what we refer to as "punitiveness" in anti-crime rhetoric and penal practice is underway. In addition, we seek to explain the apparently paradoxical coincidence of somewhat successful movements for democratization and the ascendance of tough and exclusionary crime talk and practice across the hemisphere.

By "punitive," we mean anti-crime practices and policies that seek to intensify the pain associated with punishment by intensifying its severity and/or duration, and by increasing its application (see Matthews, 2005). Examples include the passage of "three strikes" laws, mandatory minimum sentencing policies, incarceration under deliberately harsh conditions, efforts to increase the application of the death penalty, tolerance of police brutality or extralegal violence against suspected criminals, and the relaxation of due process standards. We also treat political rhetoric that dehumanizes those associated with crime and calls for an expansion of the state's coercive apparatus as an indicator of the broad shift toward punitiveness. Although the effects of this kind of rhetoric on criminal justice institutions and penal practices are variable and complex, our case studies suggest that tough anti-crime rhetoric often has important political and symbolic consequences.

Ironically, many of the countries in which "hyper-penality" is most evident have also experienced significant and in many ways successful efforts to democratize and expand citizenship rights during the period under investigation. A few cases, explored more fully later in the chapter, illustrate the coincidence of democratization and the shift toward "mano dura" across the Americas.

Brazil. Even as Brazil has become a global champion of human rights and a regional pillar of democratic development, it has launched in its marginal settlements what Loic Wacquant calls "a veritable dictatorship over the poor" (2003, p. 200). By most accounts, the practices of police violence have intensified since the return to constitutional democracy in the late 1980s. Today, they enjoy widespread tolerance among a populace riven by fear of crime (Caldeira, 2000; Wacquant, 2003; Zaluar, 2000). In one March 2005 incident, 29 people were shot dead in the shantytown of Baixada Fluminense by a roving death squad believed to consist of members of Rio's military police force. As of December 2005, no one had been charged in connection with this incident, the largest massacre in Rio's history. As Amnesty International (2005) reported, "Death squad killings are a routine and daily occurrence in the Baixada Fluminense, and this massacre is only distinguished from other killings because of the unusually high number of victims."

Nor is the state response to perceived criminality limited to extralegal tactics. Policing is so overtly targeted against residents of the shantytowns that, according to Amnesty International, Rio's military police have set up a permanent training camp in one *favela*. In these raids, collective search and arrest warrants are sometimes used to justify indiscriminate actions against entire communities (Amnesty International, 2005). As a result, in part, of the imposition of harsher sentences for lesser crimes (Amnesty International, 2002; Rolim, 2006) and the indiscriminate sweeps of marginal areas (Amnesty International, 2005), the incarceration rate has increased by more than 200% since 1992 (see Table 1). According to Marcos Rolim, Brazil's prison population is growing by approximately 42,000 inmates per year (2006, p. 16). Not only are more Brazilians winding up behind bars, but many are subjected to increasingly harsh treatment while there: overcrowding has produced prison conditions declared "subhuman" by the U.N. Special Rapporteur on Torture (Amnesty International, 2002), and recent reforms have given the authorities greater ability to hold prisoners in solitary confinement, among other things (Rolim, 2006).[8]

Guatemala. In Guatemala, the 1996 signing of the Peace Accords heralded the end to the country's 36-year civil war and committed the country to a host of sweeping reforms intended to redress historic inequities and usher in a pluricultural, multiethnic democracy characterized by the widespread participation of previously marginalized groups. In this context, state anti-crime practices have taken a sharply punitive turn, including the expansion of the death penalty (Human Rights Watch, 1999), the construction of maximum-security prisons[9] and the militarization of domestic policing. Guatemala has also followed its neighbors in instituting harsh anti-gang legislation. Dubbed "Plan Clean Sweep" (Plan Escoba) and "Plan Vacuum Cleaner" (Plan Aspiradora) – deliberate allusions to trash removal – Guatemalan crime control policies are characterized by sweeps through low-income areas and the detention of youths based on their appearance[10] (La Hora, 2003). Nor has the end to the war meant an end to the violence. On the contrary, contemporary homicide rates are higher than those that existed during the final years of the conflict. In this context, vigilantism and efforts at "social cleansing" have resurfaced (Godoy, 2006): "Eliminate rabies by killing the dogs that carry the disease," read leaflets left on bodies of supposed "criminals" found shot through the head near the city of Quetzaltenango (Debusmann, 2006).

The United States. In the United States, too, tough "crime-talk" (Sasson, 1995) and the adoption of punitive anti-crime policies followed on the heels of the civil rights movement and the extension of citizenship rights and legal equality to formerly excluded groups, particularly African-Americans. Indeed, the social movements responsible for this expansion and deepening of democracy triggered a backlash that has dominated U.S. politics over the past several decades (Edsall & Edsall, 1991; Omi & Winant, 1986).

Since the 1960s, professions of the need to get tough on crime have been a staple of national political discourse, and members of the public have become more likely to express support for punitive policies such as the death penalty and "three-strike" sentencing laws (Beckett, 1997; Garland, 2001; Simon, 2007). Lawmakers (local, state, and federal) have broadened definitions of crime, intensified law enforcement efforts, lengthened prison sentences, and restored capital punishment (Beckett & Sasson, 2004; Garland, 2001; Mauer, 1999; Simon, 1997, 2007; Tonry, 1995). More recently, "broken windows" policing – often referred to as "zero tolerance" – has become increasingly popular among police officials and officers (Fagan & Davies, 2000; Harcourt, 2001; Herbert, 2001; Wacquant, 2003), and the persistent problem of police brutality appears to have worsened in this context (Harcourt, 2001; see also Amnesty International, 1996; Human Rights Watch, 1998).[11] At the same time, an increase in the number of "deportable" offenses and intensified INS surveillance means that record numbers of immigrants are being detained and deported (Dow, 2004; Welch, 2002). As a result of these and other developments, the U.S. criminal justice system has expanded dramatically.[12]

In this chapter, we explore the paradoxical coincidence of at least partially successful struggles for democratization and the shift toward more punitive anti-crime rhetoric and practice across the Americas. There are, of course, significant differences between the Latin American cases discussed above and developments in the United States. One of the most noteworthy of these is the fact that the United States now boasts the highest incarceration rate in the world (Sentencing Project, 2004b). Another is the widespread tolerance in Brazil and Guatemala for extralegal violence against crime – vigilantism – committed by private forces or off-duty members of the security forces. In the United States, such acts of "social cleansing" are rare, and although police brutality is well-documented, the frequency and openness of extra-legal responses to perceived wrongdoers are far greater in Latin America.[13] Rates of crime also vary significantly: both Brazil and Guatemala (and indeed, many, but not all, Latin American countries) have experienced rapid increases in crime, while crime rates have dropped in the United States over the past two decades.

Despite these and other differences, a broad shift toward "mano dura" is discernible across the Americas. Although many researchers have examined trends in criminal justice policy in the United States and, increasingly, in Western Europe, few have endeavored to explain the emergent similarities between North and South America. In this chapter, we adopt a transnational perspective, one that spans the global North and South and foregrounds the relationship between democratization and hyper-penality.[14] Given limited space, we illustrate our thesis with examples drawn from the largest economies of South, Central, and North America (Brazil, Guatemala, and the United States), although we believe signs of the same trend may be discerned in other countries as well.[15] Our chapter is intended to be suggestive rather than conclusive; clearly, careful empirical research in multiple contexts is needed to more completely assess the applicability of our argument and to further "unpack" the political processes that appear to fuel punitiveness in the context of struggles over democratization.

The chapter is structured around two main goals. The first of these is to consider whether and how the social forces identified as important by researchers whose work focuses on the global North shed light on recent developments in Latin America. We therefore begin by examining existing explanations for the trend toward hyper-penality, most of which have emerged on the basis of U.S.-West European comparisons and therefore have somewhat limited applicability to our analysis. However, our review of this literature identifies two main inter-related dynamics that do span the North-South divide: the acceleration of globalization and intensification of its ontological effects, and the rise of neoliberalism. These developments, then, are, along with democratization, quite plausibly related to the emergence of hyper-penal rhetoric and practice in the Americas. At the same time, we argue, none of these social forces and processes can, in of themselves, explain the political ascendance of punitive crime talk and policy *and* the popularity of this rhetoric and practice with many members of the public.

Our second section focuses draws on three American cases to identify the more proximate cause of the shift toward mano dura. Our analysis indicates that political struggles over democracy have triggered a backlash against democratization, one that is often couched in terms of, and legitimated through, a rhetorical emphasis on the threat of crime-particularly crime that is symbolically and rhetorically linked to the social groups making claims upon the state. This rhetorical strategy has, in turn, led to the adoption of the various punitive anti-crime practices described previously, although the institutional expressions of this political discourse vary according to local conditions and circumstances. Furthermore, we suggest that the expansion of the rights of citizenship may help to explain the popularity of punitive anti-crime talk among important sectors of the public: this rhetoric resonates with members of social groups who have incurred, or fear incurring, material or symbolic losses as a result of democratization. Our conclusion summarizes this argument and considers its theoretical and empirical implications.

EXPLAINING HYPER-PENALITY

Many analysts have offered accounts of a broad convergence around tough anti-crime rhetoric and practice in the global North.[16] In what follows, we consider these alternative accounts and piece together insights from them that shape our analysis of democratization and the emergence of hyper-penality in three American countries.

The Role of Crime

According to one school of thought, the broad shift toward hyper-penality is, in part, a function of increases in criminal behavior (see Garland, 2001; Young, 1999). Despite the intuitive appeal of this account, the existence of cases in which these appear to have been concomitant trends, and the severity of the crime problem in some Latin American countries, crime rates alone cannot explain rising punitiveness across the Americas. In the United States, for example, rates of incarceration and criminal justice supervision continue to rise even as crime rates plummeted for nearly two decades (Beckett & Sasson 2004; Manza & Uggen, 2006).[17] Similarly, as Fig. 1 shows, changes in incarceration rates in Latin America do not necessarily correspond to changes in crime rates, at least as measured by levels of homicide. In Mexico and Colombia, for example, homicide rates dropped in

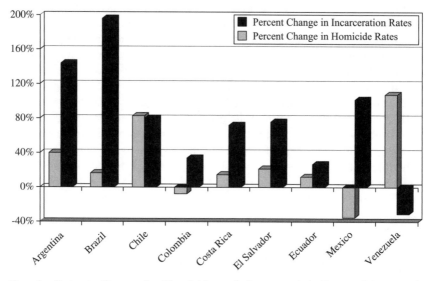

Fig. 1. Percent Change in Homicide and Incarceration Rates, Select Latin American Countries, 1992/3-2005/8. *Notes:* Incarceration data were taken from the International Centre for Prison Studies, King's College, University of London and are available at http://www.prisonstudies.org/. Homicide data were taken from Pan American Health Organization, Area of Health Analysis and Information Systems, PAHO Regional Mortality Database (2004) revision (2005). Recent homicide data for Guatemala are not available

recent years, yet the rate of incarceration rose significantly. Nor does hyper-penality correspond to absolute homicide rates. For example, calls for law and order abound and incarceration rates have increased in Chile and Costa Rica, where rates of homicide are among the lowest in the hemisphere.[18] In short, the worsening or severity of the crime problem cannot, in and of itself, explain the trend toward increased punitiveness, though it may be a factor in some countries.

The Role of Policy Export

Another possibility is that the United States has "exported" its policies to other countries, and that this policy transfer accounts for any convergences in penal rhetoric and practices. Newburn (2002) and Newburn and Jones (2005) have shown, for example, how U.S. innovations in crime policy and controversies around crime have shaped penal rhetoric and, to a lesser extent, practice in the United Kingdom. Similarly, Wacquant (2003a) stresses the role of U.S. "experts" in the export of "made in the USA" anti-crime policies, particularly zero-tolerance policing. Yet while policy transfer has undoubtedly occurred, it cannot account for broad convergences in anti-crime rhetoric and practice. As Newburn (2002) and Newburn and Jones (2005) emphasize, the process by which criminal justice policies are imported, rejected, or modified requires explanation. And although the United States employs both threats and incentives to encourage adoption of specific penal approaches in Latin American countries (particularly toward terrorism and drug trafficking),[19] the breadth of policy changes underway in Latin America and the popularity of crime talk among both politicians and the public suggest that indigenous dynamics are also fueling the trend toward hyper-penality. Our goal is to shed light on these internal dynamics that render the policies and practices exported by U.S. security consulting firms and think tanks attractive to Latin American officials.

The Cultural Underpinnings of Hyper-Penality

Another body of scholarship suggests that recent changes in crime talk and policy are a manifestation of shifting cultural sensibilities, attributable, according to some, to late modern social conditions (see, e.g., Garland, 2000, 2001; Young, 1999). David Garland's (2001) *The Culture of Control* provides the best known and most comprehensive argument of this sort.

Garland argues that the transformation of the U.S. and U.K. "crime control fields" reflects the changing nature of "cultural sensibilities" – structures of feeling and ways of thinking and talking – about crime, order, and security under conditions of late modernity. Specifically, Garland suggests that the social, economic, and cultural relations characteristic of late modernity engender novel risks, insecurities and control problems, all of which undermine support for the penal-welfare state and increase support for "tough" responses to crime. Garland identifies several dimensions of late modern social organization that, he maintains, have contributed the worsening of "control problems" and engendered diffuse anxiety and fear: the modernizing dynamic of capitalist production and market exchange, the entrance of growing numbers of women into the workforce, changes in social ecology and demography (especially suburbanization and the increasing separation of home and work), the spread of electronic media, especially television, and the democratization of social and cultural life (2001, pp. 78–89). Together, he suggests, these manifestations of late modernity increased criminal behavior, weakened the state's response to crime and disorder, and gave rise to what Garland (following Giddens (1990) refers to as widespread and diffuse "ontological insecurity."

This perspective, though compelling, provides little leverage on the Latin American cases we examine here. Garland defines late modernity as "the specific social arrangements and conditions" … "that emerged in America, Britain, and elsewhere in *the developed world* in the last third of the 20th century" (2001, p. ix). His arguments are thus largely inapplicable to the countries of the global South, where the experience of late modernity has been quite different.[20] More profoundly, however, the emergence of analogous "crime control fields" in Latin American countries characterized by very different experiences suggests that something other than the Northern experience of late modernity is afoot. Although we agree that the emergence of a hyper-punitive "crime control field" can only be fully understood by taking into account the socio-cultural landscape in which it emerges, the emphasis on the Northern experience of "late modernity" does not provide analytic leverage for analyses of penal developments in the global south, and the northern experience of "late modernity" can not account for the broad trend toward mano dura underway across much of Latin America.

Other scholars have suggested that an acceleration of the processes associated with globalization has had ontological and cultural consequences that may be related to the rise of punitiveness. In his deeply influential book *The Consequences of Modernity* (1990), Anthony Giddens highlights the destabilizing ontological effects of globalization as it is experienced at the local level. Specifically, Giddens argues that globalization separates people from local frameworks, practices and norms such that every aspect of behavior and identity is subject to "reflexive choice." This increase in reflexivity/choice means that less is "given" or "fixed," a development that, in turns, fuels widespread and diffuse "ontological insecurity." Although Giddens does not explicitly link this development to an analysis of penal trends, the implication is that widespread and diffuse insecurity may fuel support for tough crime-talk and policy.

Giddens' contention that globalization causes deep and diffuse insecurity is also the foundation of a recent exploration of crime-talk among residents of a small, middle English town (Girling, Loader, & Sparks, 2000). For these authors, the key central theoretical and substantive issue is globalization's impact on people's relation to places and on how they think and talk about crime. In contrast to those who argue that place is of diminishing importance in an increasingly global era, Girling et al. (2001) suggest that place awareness is quite pronounced, although it "tends to be relational and comparative" (p. 11). Growing awareness of other places (and the problematic people who inhabit them), they suggest, figures centrally in people's assessment of and reactions to local crime problems. Indeed, as they point out, much "crime-talk" is about the protection of places against incursion from outsiders. Thus, for Girling et al., the heightened awareness of other places wrought by globalization fundamentally alters one's relationship to the place in which one resides, and therefore has the potential to enhance anxiety about order and security.

This argument is amply demonstrated in Girling et al.'s analysis of a small town in Middle England, and we strongly suspect that it has wider empirical applicability. However, as these authors note, there is reason to suspect that the ontological insecurities associated with globalization do not necessarily or automatically express themselves as demands for punitive anti-crime politics. Indeed, as Girling et al. (2000) emphasize, there is significant variation in the extent to which punitive policies are accepted by members of the public.[21] In short, even if globalization does generate or intensify diffuse feelings of insecurity, these anxieties do not necessarily express themselves as demands for harsh state responses to criminals.

Angelina Godoy's work (2006) among highland Mayan communities in Guatemala yields similar insights. In recent years, many of these communities have engaged in "lynchings" – the execution of suspected criminals at the hands of mobs, often invoked in political discourse as the ultimate example of popular punitive sentiment. Yet most of Godoy's respondents expressed a yearning for greater control and autonomy more than a specific desire to impose harsher punishment on offenders. Although political actors have seized on popular frustrations to propose ever-harsher sanctions for ever-more minor offenses, most of Godoy's respondents remained deeply skeptical about any such state initiatives.

Taken together, these detailed and intensive analyses of popular sensibilities provide reason to suspect that globalization may intensify concerns about change, order and disorder. Yet they also suggest that popular support for harsh penal practices and policies is sometimes ambivalent or even non-existent; the ontological consequences of globalization do not automatically express themselves as demands for "mano dura." While diffuse anxieties about change, disorder, and the incursion of "the other" may well be intensified by globalization, and may, under some circumstances, fuel support for mano dura, the processes by which these translations do or do not occur require explication.

Neoliberal Capitalism and Hyper-Penality

The fact that the trend toward hyper-penality in the United States, Western Europe, and Latin America has occurred alongside the ascendance of neoliberal, global capitalism has not escaped notice. Even before it assumed its neoliberal form, capitalism generated social dynamics that often fueled concern about change and increased support for cracking down on criminals. As Dario Melossi (2001) argues, the flow of people across local and national boundaries – a phenomenon that is clearly linked to capitalist dynamics – often triggers fear and support for punitive action. As Melossi argues, migrants have long been associated with crime in the minds of settled peoples and frequently fuel punitive reactions among those populations.

Indeed, there is much evidence that the recent intensification of the "push" and "pull" factors that shape transnational migration has strengthened fears about crime, order and security in many destination countries (Angel-Ajani, 2003; Calavita, 2001; Hall, Critcher, Jefferson, Clarke, & Roberts, 1978; Melossi, 2001, 2003; Van Swaaningen, 2005). Tyler and Boeckmann's (1997) study of support for three-strikes legislation and other "tough" responses to crime provides evidence that immigration fuels triggers anxiety and support for punitive anti-crime policies in the United States as well.[22] And although research on the links between immigration and crime-talk has largely been situated in the global North, both rural-urban and transnational migration are ongoing around the globe, where concerns about the erosion of local communities and their norms are often strikingly similar to expressions discussed by other scholars working in Northern contexts (Godoy, 2004; Goldin, 1999; Goldstein, 2004). In short, it appears that the internal and transnational migrations associated with global capitalism (and other factors) may fuel both fear about and punitive responses to crime.

This body of scholarship thus provides compelling evidence that concerns about migration frequently fuel support for punitive anti-crime rhetoric and policy. And yet hyper-penal rhetoric and practices can emerge in the absence of significant controversy around migration, or in cases such as Guatemala, countries where out-migration is the primary trend. Thus, while, transnational migration is often a crucial source of concern about crime and disorder, especially in the global North, popular attitudes and penal policies may become more punitive in the absence of immigration.

A related body of scholarship attributes the rise of hyper-penality to the recent ascendance of neoliberal governance, that is, national and transnational policies that limit state responsibility for the provision of social welfare, facilitate private economic transactions, and favor corporate interests and established hierarchies of wealth.[23] Insofar as neoliberalism is ascendant across the globe, its rise has the potential to account for the broad shift toward hyper-penality across the Americas.

Perhaps the best known and most powerful articulation of the relationship between penal developments and neoliberalism is found in the work of Loic Wacquant. Wacquant argues that the growth of penal populations in "advanced" societies is a consequence of the replacement of the welfare apparatus with the penal system as the "instrument for managing social insecurity and containing the social disorders created at the bottom of the class structure by neoliberal policies of economic deregulation and social-welfare retrenchment" (Wacquant, 2001, p. 401). For Wacquant, then, the "penalization of poverty" is "designed to manage the effects of neo-liberal policies at the lower end of the social structure of advanced societies" (p. 401) and is therefore the functional and necessary counterpart to neoliberal social policies. At a practical level, the penal state manages and contains "disorders spawned by the deregulation of the economy, the desocialization of wage labor, and the relative and absolute immiseration of large sections of the urban proletariat" (2003, p. 200). From this perspective, the deregulation of the economy is necessarily accompanied by hyper-penality, as elites seek to manage the social consequences of rising inequality caused by neoliberalism. Wacquant also argues that symbolically, get-tough policies dramatize political elites' "new-found commitment to slay the monster of urban crime and because they readily fit the negative stereotypes of the poor who are everywhere portrayed as the main source of street deviance and violence" (2003, p. 198).

Urban geographers and sociologists working from a political-economic perspective offer a similar account of the relationship between intensified urban policing efforts and neoliberalism. These scholars stress the simultaneous emergence of "fortress cities," punitive anti-crime policies and neoliberalism. For example, Mike Davis (1992) argues that in neoliberal cities such as Los Angeles,

> the defense of luxury life-styles is translated into a proliferation of new repressions in space and movement, undergirded by the ubiquitous "armed response." This obsession with physical security systems, and, collaterally, with the architectural policing of social boundaries, has become a zeitgeist of urban restructuring, a master narrative in the emerging built environment movement of the 1990s. (p. 223)

Critics such as Davis argue that architectural and policing techniques are used to "contain" the socially undesirable in one area of the city and to enhance and protect the social insulation of the middle and upper classes who seek to "revitalize" the city (see also Caldeira, 2000; Lynch, 2001). From this perspective, the transformation of the global economy explains the need for aesthetically pleasing urban landscapes and the immense popularity of zero tolerance policing among urban elites. The increased mobility of industry and finance associated with deindustrialization and deregulation has led many cities to attempt to create the most hospitable environment for investors and to aggressively promote tourism and retail operations (Christopherson, 1994; Gibson, 2003; Mitchell, 2003; Parenti, 1999). Particularly in cities that depend on tourists and shoppers for their economic well-being, the "environment" on city streets has become the subject of much official attention. In this context, municipal governments often engage in what Timothy Gibson (2003) calls "projects of reassurance": efforts to counter widespread images of cities as sites of decay and danger with sanitized images of urban consumer (and investment) utopias. The appeal of broken windows policing to urban developers and city officials is, from this perspective, clear: broken windows policing promises to facilitate the "revitalization" of urban downtowns.

In short, this body of scholarship suggests that the implementation of neoliberal social policies necessitates hyper-penal practices at both the national and local levels. Whether by "disciplining" the disruptive elements of the working class through incarceration or by creating urban, "bourgeois playgrounds," hyper-punitive policies are, from this perspective, functionally integral to global neo-liberalism. This argument is consistent with, and finds support in, studies that document a correlation between low levels of welfare spending and social democratic policies, on the one hand, and a high degree of reliance upon incarceration on the other (see Beckett & Western, 1999; Cavadino & Dignan, 2006; Sutton, 2004). This perspective also offers a compelling account of the attractions of zero tolerance policing and other expressions of hyper-punitiveness to political elites across the hemisphere. Indeed, in the global South, efforts to reassure potential investors play out not only in municipal, but also national, politics, as resource-poor governments compete to attract the foreign investment necessary to bolster ailing national economies. In the South, it is not primarily the image of the blighted inner city that political actors must counter to reassure skittish employers and investors, but rather the specter of "third world lawlessness," where tourists or executives are vulnerable to kidnappings or extortion and the local political environment is prone to populist uprisings that might impact property laws.[24,25]

At the same time, the *processes* by which neoliberalism generates "tough" responses to crime require further explication. The argument that neoliberalism *necessitates* hyper-penality in order to manage and contain the "disorders spawned by the deregulation of the economy, the desocialization of wage labor, and the relative and absolute immiseration of large sections of the urban proletariat" (Wacquant, 2003, p. 200) does not shed light on the process by which crime-related problems assume political ascendance, nor does it account for popular receptivity to calls to get tough on crime. In addition, this argument overstates the extent to which hyper-punitive policies and practices reduce social conflict and ameliorate the effects of neoliberalism: it is not clear that "tough" penal policies actually manage the social disruptions caused by neoliberalism other than sometimes achieving "containment" and spatial segregation at the local level. Indeed, Wacquant himself emphasizes that the implementation of hyper-penality in Brazil and other Latin American countries "promises to produce a social catastrophe of historic proportions" (2003, p. 197). The adoption of these policies cannot be explained in terms of a function they do not serve.

Finally, this account leaves unexplained the persistence of the punitive shift even as several South American countries challenge the model of global neoliberalism.[26] And as will be illustrated in the following discussion of our three cases, the mobilization of punitive anti-crime talk in response to struggles for democracy predates the rise of neoliberalism.

In sum, scholars seeking to explain the broad convergence around "tough" anti-crime rhetoric and practice have identified a number of plausible explanations of this trend across the United States and Western Europe. While some of these accounts are inapplicable in the global South, several factors – policy transfer, globalization, and neoliberalism – do span the North-South divide and are undoubtedly influential in both hemispheres. Yet the process by which manu dura has emerged and been legitimated across the Americas requires further explication. Political dynamics are the crucial medium through which concerns about crime and disorder are named, framed, and channeled; popular perceptions of these issues and policy options do not spring "naturally" from some element of the globalized or neoliberal social condition. In addition, a comprehensive account of the hemispheric trend should explain *both* popular sources of support for mano dura and its popularity among political and economic elites. Finally, we note that none of the existing literatures foregrounds struggles over democracy and citizenship, on the one hand, and penal trends on the other. Although we agree that globalization and the rise of neoliberalism are important and consequential developments, the case histories presented below suggest that opponents of democratic expansion have employed punitive crime talk, harsh criminal laws, and tough penal practices to limit claims to political and economic rights long before either of these trends were ascendant (see also Adamson, 1983; Hay, 1992; Manza & Uggen, 2006; Wacquant, 2003b).

DEMOCRATIZATION, NEOLIBERALISM, AND HYPER-PENALITY IN THE AMERICAS

Despite the existence of compelling accounts of the trend toward hyper-penality, we believe a more process-oriented analysis has the potential to shed light on how and why calls for mano dura have become common across the hemisphere. In the following discussion of our three American cases, we pay close attention to the context in which tough crime talk and practices were adopted in three countries characterized by intense political struggles over democracy. We seek to identify the ways in which expressions of mano dura have been rhetorically and politically useful to those seeking to limit the deepening of democracy and the extension of the citizenship rights. In what follows, we draw on our own research and the work of others to illustrate how these processes played out in Brazil, Guatemala, and the

United States – the largest economies of South, Central, and North America, respectively.

Democracy and Penality in Brazil, Guatemala, and the United States

Across Latin America, the discourse of law and order has repeatedly been invoked to justify or maintain restrictions on democratic rights. In fact, as Greg Grandin (2004) suggests, the rise and fall of dictatorships throughout the 20th century can be understood as the result of inter-institutional struggle over democracy and social reform; it was precisely in reaction to the democratization that occurred mid-century that elite forces mobilized the military to seize executive power in the name of order.[27] By branding political opponents as "criminals" and "agitators," right-wing dictatorships legitimated their political project as the "defense of democracy" even as they went about dismantling the building blocks of democracy itself. The branding of leftists, reformers, even aid workers or clergy who ministered to the poor as "criminals" was a key component of state terror.

These processes are quite evident in Brazil. From 1964 to 1966 in Brazil, a nationwide Operação Limpeza (Cleanup Campaign) was conducted under the leadership of the military's appointed president, General Castelo Branco. That campaign sought to eliminate leftists from government employment as part of an effort at "moral rehabilitation" (Huggins, Haritos-Fatouros, & Zimbardo, 2002, p. 64). The cleanup led to massive arrests in broad sweeps that took as many as 50,000 people into police custody in the first three months of the dictatorship alone (Huggins et al., 2002, p. 64). The police, as Huggins et al. (2002) show in a recent inquiry into police training during this period, were trained to view proponents of democracy, leftists, and those associated with human rights or social justice, as "criminals." The rhetoric of law and order was thus mobilized in an attempt to protect elite privileges from democratization and socioeconomic reforms.

In Guatemala, too, the 1954 coup against reformist Jacobo Arbenz was followed by a series of sweeps in which democrats and reformists were dubbed criminals and "agitators" were rounded up and, often, killed. As the testimony to the UN-sponsored truth commission later revealed, militarized police meted out brutal "justice" not only to guerrilla supporters and leftists (including nuns, literacy workers, and others involved in delivery of basic services to the poor) but also petty criminals, including neighborhood drunks (Godoy, 2006).[28] In the early 1980s, the media were banned from using words such as "guerrillas"; only the terms "terrorists," "subversives," and "criminal gangs (*bandas delincuentes*)" were permissible (Black, Jamail, & Chinchilla, 1984, p. 126). The attempt to define those opposed to authoritarian rule as criminals was clearly at attempt to delegitimate their political cause.

The return to constitutional democracy across Latin America after the Cold War made possible the exercise of some rights first granted at mid-century. Newly minted Constitutions recognized previously marginalized groups such as the indigenous; Peace Accords committed states to substantive socioeconomic reforms; and new state dependencies were created to tackle historic imbalances (in land distribution, e.g.) (see Jonas, 2000, Pearce, 1998). Yet for some members of elite classes, the deepening of democracy opened yet again the possibility for social and economic change – and again represented a threat to their entrenched privilege. As Paul Chevigny notes, in this context, "the pressures to draw upon the fear of crime for political advantage are enormous" (2003, p. 83), particularly when politicians face new electorates adversely affected by the policies they have put in place.

The temptation to use crime-talk to shore up elite privilege and reverse democratic gains is evident in the trend toward what Chevigny (2003) calls "the populism of fear." In Sao Paulo, Brazil, for example, rightist politicians (and segments of the general public) blamed rising rates of crime on post-dictatorship attempts to rein in police violence[29] (Chevigny, 2003). Recent political campaigns further illustrate the centrality of crime-talk to efforts to limit democratization. For example, Luiz Antonio Fluery Filho, governor of Sao Paulo in the late 1980s insisted that police violence was targeted not against the poor, but against criminal "low-lifes" (Chevigny, 2003, pp. 87–88). Despite widespread suspicion of the police as corrupt, many Brazilians express support for extralegal police violence, particularly against the predominantly poor and dark-skinned residents of shantytowns so associated with criminality in the popular imagination (Caldeira, 2000; Holston & Caldeira, 1998). As Caldeira (2000, p. 51) suggests,

The increase in violent crime since the mid-1980s obviously adds insecurity to already intensified anxieties over economic uncertainty, inflation, unemployment, social movements, and political transformation. Discussions about fear of crime reveal the anguish produced when social relations can no longer be decoded and controlled according to old criteria. Although there are certainly many positive aspects to the disintegration of old power relations in Brazil, it is also clear that many social groups have reacted negatively to the enlargement of the political arena and the expansion of rights. These groups have found in the issue of crime a way of articulating their opposition.

In Guatemala, too, discussions of crime control have dominated national elections since the late 1990s, and in recent years, candidates for office have struggled to outdo one another in assuring the public that they are "tough on crime" (The Economist, 2004a, 2004b). Widespread concern about rising crime rates has provided a window for conservative politicians to call for the reversal of democratic "permissiveness," suggesting that "moral decay" rather than poverty lies at the root of today's crime wave (Godoy, 2006). The 1999 referendum on the Peace Accords provides one telling example. In the referendum, citizens were called to the polls to vote on a package of legislation necessary to implement the specific socioeconomic reforms in the Accords. The legislation included a prohibition on military involvement in domestic policing, as well as recognition of indigenous languages and legal practices as legitimate in a multicultural society. In the lead-up to the vote, conservatives emphasized that the implementation of such reforms would lead to "special rights" for the indigenous. The referendum failed, condemning the Peace Accords to non-implementation (Carey, 2004). In place of the extension of socio-economic rights – themselves a vehicle for addressing crime in a society gripped by high rates of poverty and unemployment – conservative forces have offered increasingly punitive crime policies, including militarized sweeps through poor neighborhoods, longer sentences, and an extended death penalty (Godoy, 2006).

In short, the rhetoric and politics of law and order were mobilized in mid-20th century Latin America and again in more recent decades as conservatives struggled to limit democratic expansion. In more recent years, newly democratized states have enabled their security forces to police class and ethnic boundaries in the name of safety and stability. While mounting crime talk is undoubtedly fueled by real increases in crime in some countries, including Guatemala, it is deftly translated into support for hyper-punitiveness through an elite discourse that interprets crime as caused by democratic expansion and moral decay (rather than by poverty or social exclusion). In this way, conservatives seek to legitimate the de facto and even de jure denial of key democratic rights. As a result of the ascendance of this discursive framework, resources have been redirected from social reforms to crime-fighting efforts, gutting recent democratizing moves of their transformative potential.

In the United States, too, political elites seeking to reverse democracy's expansion have emphasized crime and punishment in an attempt to legitimate their political goals. In the 1950s and 1960s, the civil rights movement sought to extend democratic rights, including the right to vote, to previously excluded groups. As in many Latin American countries, this and related movements for democratization triggered a vigorous backlash, one that has dominated U.S. politics ever since (Edsall & Edsall, 1991). Although no concerted effort has been made to eliminate the formal rights that were extended as a result of civil rights activism, the post-civil rights era has been dominated by conservative political actors seeking to ensure that the extension of these formal rights does not involve the reallocation of financial resources or institutional opportunities.

As in Latin America, this political project involved significant reliance upon crime-talk. This dynamic became evident in the wake of the Supreme Court's 1954 Brown versus Board of Education decision, as civil rights activists across the South used civil disobedience in an attempt to force reluctant Southern states to desegregate public facilities. Southern governors and law enforcement officials seeking to shore up support for Southern states' right to segregate characterized its tactics as "criminal" and suggested that the rise of the civil rights movement was indicative of the breakdown of "law and order." Crime rhetoric became prominent in political discourse as southern officials called for a crackdown on the "hoodlums," "agitators," "street mobs," and "lawbreakers" who challenged segregation and black disenfranchisement (see Beckett, 1997; Caplan, 1973; Cronin, Cronin, & Milakovich, 1981).

This rhetoric was subsequently mobilized by conservative electoral politicians opposed to both the extension of civil rights and Kennedy's "war on poverty" programs (Beckett, 1997; Katz, 1989). In 1964, candidate Goldwater campaigned largely on a "law and order" theme that blended an emphasis on the threat of street crime and a vision of government that emphasized its role in maintaining a "free" economy as well as "law and order."

> Tonight there is violence in our streets, corruption in our highest offices, aimlessness among our youth, anxiety among our elderly... Security from domestic violence, no less that from foreign aggression, is the most elementary form and fundamental purpose of any government, and a government that cannot fulfill this purpose is one that cannot command the loyalty of its citizens. History shows us that nothing prepares the way for tyranny than the failure of public officials to keep the streets safe from bullies and marauders. We Republicans seek a government that attends to its fiscal climate, encouraging a free and a competitive economy and enforcing law and order.[30]

Although Goldwater's bid for the presidency was unsuccessful, this kind of rhetoric was mobilized by conservative opponents of the civil and welfare rights movements over the several next decades. The rhetorical emphasis on the dangers of street crime and disorder was quite useful to those seeking to reconstruct the public image of the poor and newly enfranchised as dangerous outsiders in order to limit democratic expansion and deepening. As Michael Katz (1989, pp. 185–186) suggests, "when the poor seemed menacing they became the underclass."

Thus, although superficially about crime, the conservative framing of the crime problem may be understood as a response to the civil rights and welfare movements, and was a component of a much larger contest over state policy (see Beckett, 1997; Hall et al., 1978; Katz, 1989; Melossi, 1993). This connection is made quite explicit in conservative rhetoric on the issue, as in this quote from Governor Reagan.

> *Here in the richest nation in the world, where more crime is committed than in any other nation, we are told that the answer to this problem is to reduce our poverty. This isn't the answer ... Government's function is to protect society from the criminal, not the other way around.*" (quoted in Beckett, 1997, emphasis added)

Over the years, even many liberal lawmakers came to support tough anti-crime talk and policy. The results of this political convergence are well known, and include the adoption of policies that have resulted in an unprecedented experiment in mass incarceration.

In sum, the extension of democratic rights that occurred in mid-20th century in many American countries provoked a significant backlash among conservatives apparently concerned about the destabilizing effects of new promises of inclusion. In this context, opponents of the deepening of democracy increasingly invoked the language of crime and punishment. Several factors help to explain the appeal of tough anti-crime rhetoric to political elites opposed to the deepening of democracy. First, because punitive crime-talk ostensibly targets problematic behavior rather than particular social groups, it appears to be universalistic rather than particularistic, and thus meshes well with the norm of formal equality that is the hallmark of liberal democracy. At the same time, punitive crime talk often has "coded" meanings that enable those who mobilize it to tap into inter-group hostility or fear. As a result, punitive crime-talk may provide a "legitimate" means of stigmatizing the very groups who seek to broaden and deepen democracy; discussions of crime are often a veiled yet emotionally powerful way of discrediting those who struggle to obtain a piece of the political pie.[31] In addition, the emphasis on the threat of crime and disorder offers conservatives a way to legitimate truncated visions of the rights and entitlements of citizenship. By emphasizing the threat of crime and the governments' obligation to buttress security (narrowly defined), the rhetoric of crime and punishment provides conservatives with an opportunity to legitimate a thin version of democracy.

This language has not been imposed from above in authoritarian fashion, but often resonates with many members of the citizenry. Punitive rhetoric may tap into latent and diffuse anxieties about migration, globalization, inequality and social change, as other scholars have contended. In addition, we suggest, this rhetoric resonates with members of social groups who have incurred, or fear incurring, material or symbolic losses as a result of democratization. In the United States, for example, the rhetoric of law and order has been especially popular among members of social groups who enjoyed some privilege under the previous system, many of whom have come to believe that the newly franchised pose a real and significant threat to their security and well-being. Specifically, white working class voters who abandoned their traditional political allegiance to the Democratic Party in the post-civil rights era did so largely in response to their perception that in supporting the Civil Rights Act and war on poverty programs, the Democrats were catering to "special interests" (i.e., blacks) (Edsall & Edsall, 1991; Omi & Winant, 1986). As Bobo (2007) has shown, it is racial resentment – that is the fear of the loss of resources, privilege and status – that fuels support for punitive anti-crime policies. Indeed, those most opposed to social and racial reform were also most receptive to calls for law and order (Beckett, 1997).[32] In short, popular support for tough crime talk and policy may reflect concern about the state's shifting allegiances, as important rights protections mandate greater attention and rights to disempowered groups. This dynamic also helps to explain the symbolic potency and popular appeal of hyper-punitive rhetoric and policies.

CONCLUSION

Across the Americas, efforts to broaden and deepen democracy have been met with political opposition that emphasizes the threat of crime, links newly empowered "others" to this threat to security, and seeks to limit or reverse the expansion of citizenship rights. It is the *rhetoric* and symbolic dimensions of crime and punishment that are of primary utility to those seeking to limit democracy; the policies and practices that flow from that rhetoric vary and are, in many ways, the unintended consequences of the discursive emphasis on the dangers posed by those making claims to citizenship rights. By labeling the newly or precariously enfranchised "criminals" and their political demands as "special interests," conservatives have endeavored to justify their repression; by highlighting the immediate threat of crime and criminality, these same political actors have sought to legitimate a more truncated vision of government and limit the rights of citizenship. Hyper-punitive policies and rhetoric are not necessarily functional in the sense of managing the social disruptions associated with the adoption of neoliberal social policies, but they have played a crucial political and ideological role in efforts to limit democracy's expansion and, in the recent period, the rise of neoliberalism.

How can we explain the popularity of hyper-penality in the context of democratization? In some places, high crime rates undoubtedly enhance support for hyper-punitive responses. Other factors identified in the broader literature – diffuse anxieties related to global flux and change, concerns about migration and mobility, and the insecurities associated with neoliberalism – may also be relevant. We suggest an additional factor as well: concerns about democratization itself may underpin support for mano dura. The fact that previously excluded groups obtain, with democratization, some role in civic and political life means that other members of the public – even those who are not part of the "elite"– may fear of losing even minimal privileges and become receptive to the argument that state is now overly beholden to so-called "special interests." In this context, the pain associated with the loss of race or class-based privileges or the adoption of neoliberal social policies (and, in Northern countries, deindustrialization) may plausibly be attributed to state policies that grant some benefit to newly empowered groups. We leave the question of whether or not this argument can be applied to other cases, particularly those in Western European countries, to scholars with more expertise in those regions of the world. But the fact that crime has been politicized by European conservatives who also seek to limit migration from the global South could plausibly be seen as evidence that, there too, the desire to limit access to citizenship rights may find expression in calls for law and order.

In the cases discussed here – Brazil, Guatemala, and the United States – conservative efforts to legitimate a thin version of democracy were largely successful, punitive crime talk became ascendant, and hyper-penal policies and practices have been institutionalized. Yet we are hopeful that this outcome is not inevitable (see also Wacquant, 2001). Although, as our cases suggest, punitive crime talk is often useful to those seeking to limit democratic rights and legitimate a narrow definition of the rights of citizenship, we do not wish to imply that the outcome of these political struggles is pre-determined. Indeed, our primary critique of alternative accounts of the broad trend toward hyper-penality is that these accounts place too little emphasis on the inherently unpredictable role of political contestation and struggle.

In many ways, the broad trend toward "mano dura" across the Americas reflects broader trends in governance in democratic societies more than it does on anything specific about crime per se. Democracy is now most threatened by the imposition of neoliberal social policies and tough anti-crime policies than by the repeal of formal political rights. Although democratic rights have not been repealed de jure in North or South America, tough anti-crime rhetoric and the thin vision of democracy it legitimates has allowed them to be undercut de facto. Political and social rights continue to exist on chapter, but have little substantive effect; societies remain formally democratic and egalitarian, but real inequality has become all the more entrenched. Ironically, punitive anti-crime policies are likely to exacerbate rather than manage the effects of this inequality over time. Their utility thus lies not in their practical effects, but primarily in the discursive and ideological frameworks through which they have been legitimated.

NOTES

1. The 18 nations examined include: Argentina, Bolivia, Brazil, Chile, Colombia, Costa Rica, Dominican Republic, Ecuador, El Salvador, Guatemala, Honduras, México, Nicaragua, Panama, Paraguay, Peru, Uruguay, and Venezuela. Cuba, of course, remains the exception to this regional trend.

2. Many of these new institutions and laws have had very limited practical effects, though a thorough examination of why lies beyond the scope of this chapter. Still, their creation at the urging of reform-oriented social movements, and the open discussion of these problems after decades (or as regards indigenous peoples, centuries) of official silence is in itself a significant democratizing move.

3. As Manza and Uggen (2006) point out, felony disenfranchisement statutes remain on the books in many states, and constitute the last significant barrier to universal suffrage in the United States.

4. These data are available online at http://www.prisonstudies.org/

5. In Venezuela, rates of incarceration have declined, although conditions of detention have deteriorated significantly (see Birkbeck & Perez-Santiago, 2004; Human Rights Watch, 1997).

6. See, for example, Human Rights Watch World Report, 2005; The Economist, 2004a, 2004b, p. 53.

7. Latinobarómetro provides a comprehensive source of public opinion data on issues relating to democracy and public policy, including citizen security. Beginning in 1995, annual surveys were administered across the region; crime consistently ranks high on the list of most important problems, but there are significant variations by country and across time. The database can be consulted at www.latinobarómetro.org

8. Rolim also notes that recent reforms passed by the left-leaning Lula administration extended the maximum length of time during which a prisoner could be held in isolation from 30 days to 720 days (2006, p. 17).

9. The construction of these high security units is underway, and leads us to suspect that incarceration rates, though still comparatively low, will likely increase significantly in the near future.

10. In Guatemala, the physical characteristics associated with criminality are not linked to ethnic identity per se, but rather to the stylistic markers of imputed gang membership. Across Central America, the use of tattoos is often presumed to indicate gang activity and can, in and of itself, serve as grounds for arrest.

11. Prior to the widespread adoption of broken windows policing, researchers estimated that between 1% and 5% of police encounters with criminal suspects involved the excessive use of force; blacks and Latinos were far more likely than whites to report such experiences (Walker, Spohn, & DeLone, 1996). The implementation of broken windows/zero tolerance policing appears to have worsened this problem. In New York City, for example, allegations of police misconduct increased by 68% in the first three years after the implementation of "quality of life" policing and remained comparatively high in the late 1990s (Harcourt, 2001, pp. 167–168).

12. Blacks and Latinos have been disproportionately affected by these developments: the black rate of incarceration, for example, is approximately seven times higher than the rate for non-Hispanic whites (Sentencing Project, 2004a). Recent research suggests that 30% of black men born between 1965 and 1969 without a college education and nearly 60% percent of those who did not graduate from high school went to prison by 1999 (Pettit & Western, 2004).

13. For a detailed discussion of how police violence in Brazil differs from police violence in the United States, see Holston and Caldeira (1998).

14. A few other scholars have also explored the connection between democracy and penality, although in ways that differ somewhat from our approach. For example, Jonathan Simon (2000) explored how 18th century American democratic reformers imagined post-monarchical criminal law. Vanessa Barker (2006) explored the relationship between U.S. state governance regimes and penal outcomes. In an analysis that is more similar to ours, Jeff Manza and Chris Uggen (2006) investigate the relationship between the expansion of voting rights and the subsequent adoption of felony disenfranchisement statutes. Manza and Uggen's show that in the United States, the adoption of such statutes was triggered by the prior expansion of the franchise to formerly excluded groups, and that the strongest predictor of whether a state adopted such a statute in the post-Civil War era was the size of its non-white population. These findings indicate that periods of democratization tend to trigger undemocratic reactions, and are thus quite compatible with the argument presented here.

15. For example, in the aftermath of its 2001 economic crisis, Argentina has experienced a punitive backlash (see Dammert, 2001, Dammert & Malone, 2002). Similarly, scholars have documented similar trends in Colombia (see Carrión, 2004).

16. As Newburn and Jones (2005) argue, much of the convergence has occurred at the symbolic and rhetorical level. Although the implications of this convergence around "tough" anti-crime rhetoric for penal policy and practice vary, this rhetorical convergence often has important political consequences.

17. Nor is it clear that U.S. crime rates generally increased in the 1970s and 1980s. Most researchers have concluded that the increase in crime suggested by the FBI's Uniform Crime Reporting Program was largely a consequence of two main developments: members of the public became more likely to report their victimization to the police (McCord, 1997), and the police became more likely to record these reports and to share their records with the FBI (Boggess & Bound, 1993; O'Brien, 1996).

18. According to the Pan American Health Organization, the rate of homicide was 5.3 per 100,000 in Chile and 6.2 per 100,000 Costa Rica in 2002, yet these countries boasted some of the highest incarceration rates in Latin America. By comparison, the homicide rates for Colombia and El Salvador were reported to be 84.6 and 43.4 (respectively) that year (Pan American Health Organization, Area of Health Analysis and Information Systems, PAHO Regional Mortality Database, 2004 revision (2005)). These data are available online at http://www.paho.org/English/SHA/coredata/tabulator/newTabulator.htm

19. In recent decades, for example, U.S. government pressures to penalize coca growing in the Andes have led authorities to crack down on drug offenders with increased zeal (La mayoría de detenidos es por narcotráfico, 2005; A casi 20 años de la ley 1008 es necesario encarar ajustes, 2005). The establishment of U.S.-funded training institutes such as the recently approved International Law Enforcement Academy in El Salvador also serve as vectors for the transmission of policing styles and strategies. And even without incentives or pressure from the U.S. government, many municipal governments in the Americas have adopted tactics aimed at mirroring "zero tolerance" tactics made famous in New York City (Wacquant, 2003a). For a longer-term history of US involvement in Latin American policing, see Huggins, 1998.

20. The equation of late modernity with the social conditions of "advanced" societies is troubling for another reason as well: it presumes that development is a linear path that individual countries traverse in isolation. In fact, the very changes that are seen by Garland as constitutive of late modernity rely on connections to the global South and would not be possible without the concomitant transformation of Southern economies. The Southern countries that fuel migration and provide cheap labor and raw materials are thus no less "late modern"; to suggest they are somehow trapped in an earlier phase of development ignores the interdependent nature of global capitalism and reiterates long-discredited evolutionary thinking about "development."

21. In some cases, what appears to be popular support for punitive approaches to crime may be something else entirely. For example, Girling et al. found that most adults want a more visible police presence on the streets, not because they craved a tougher system of fighting crime, but because they believed the police have become part of a distant bureaucracy and were no longer responsive to local feelings and concerns. Residents' attachment to the English bobby thus reflected a longing for the service and guardianship roles traditionally attributed to the English police rather than a desire to "get tough" (2000, p. 124).

22. In particular, Tyler and Boeckmann (1997) found that Californians who believe that increasing diversity led to a decline in moral cohesion and social solidarity were most supportive of three strikes legislation and capital punishment,

and that concerns about immigration had more impact on these attitudes than did fear of crime. Interestingly, Tyler and Boeckmann found that this support was not primarily based on fear of crime, but rather the sense that if moral cohesion and social solidarity had been weakened, rehabilitative approaches to crime simply could not work.

23. Although proponents of neoliberalism characterize this approach as moving toward a "free" and "unregulated" market, neoliberalism is in fact made possible by massive domestic and international interventions in the economy.

24. Indeed, assessments of investment climate and risk – such as those provided by the World Economic Forum in its Global Competitiveness Report – pay specific attention to security concerns, rating countries as more competitive where these are believed to interfere less with economic transactions. These ratings, in turn, affect investor decision-making.

25. In this context, governments frequently promote a two-tiered justice system (Domingo, 1995) where harsh justice is promised, and sometimes delivered, for those criminals who target tourists, foreigners, or the business class, yet cases of petty crime against poor victims languish unattended in inefficient national justice systems.

26. Since roughly 2000, South American countries like Brazil, Venezuela, Bolivia, Argentina, Ecuador, and Uruguay have elected leftist administrations whose policies challenge the neoliberal model to varying degrees. Yet such shifts in official policy have not necessarily been accompanied by reduced punitiveness in criminal justice policy. In fact, states and societies are fractured, heterogeneous, and often contradictory. Without an analysis of the processes that produce specific policies, assertions of neoliberalism's inherent punitiveness may suggest too direct a relationship between these broad shifts.

27. In many Latin American countries, new constitutions were established in the middle of the 20th century that legalized labor unions and leftist parties, recognized rights of women and marginalized groups, and made possible land redistribution to peasants, among other important provisions (Grandin, 2004). These Constitutions clearly extended democratic rights, though de jure rather than de facto.

28. For more on torture in Guatemala, see Harbury (2005).

29. In Brazil, law enforcement is primarily the task of state governments, and as a result, it is in campaigns for state, rather than national, offices that "tough on crime" discourse is often most pronounced.

30. "Goldwater's Acceptance Speech to GOP Convention," *New York Times*, July 17, 1964, cited in Beckett (1997).

31. This does not mean that only those social groups who directly benefit from the expansion of democracy will be affected by the shift toward hyper-penality (although that has been largely the case in the United States). There may be some disjuncture between the newly democratized groups and the newly punished groups because, under conditions of formal equality, leaders emphasize behavior rather than status characteristics and because politicians who engage in punitive crime talk influence but do not control the enforcement and implementation of criminal law and sanctions.

32. Ironically, it was the success of the civil rights movement in discrediting more explicit expressions of racist sentiment that led politicians to attempt to appeal to the public with such "subliminally" racist messages (Omi & Winant, 1986).

ACKNOWLEDGMENTS

Thanks to the University of Washington's Law, Societies and Justice workshare group, including Gad Barzilai, Rachel Cichowski, Steve Herbert, Tuna Kuyucu, George Lovell, Jamie Mayerfeld, Michael McCann, Joel Migdal, and Naomi Murakawa, as well as several anonymous reviewers, for their helpful comments and suggestions.

REFERENCES

A casi 20 Años de la ley 1008 es necesario encarar ajustes. Santa Cruz de la Sierra, Bolivia. (September 11, 2005). www.eldeber.com.bo/anteriores/20050911/santacruz_5.html (accessed November 29, 2005).

Adamson, C. (1983). Toward a marxian penology: Captive criminal populations as economic threats and resources. *Social Problems, 31*, 435–458.

Agüero, F., & Stark, J. (Eds). (1998). *Fault lines of democracy in post-transition. Latin America*. Miami: North-South Center Press.

Amnesty International. (1996). United States of America: Police brutality and excessive force in the New York city police department. Available online at www.amnestyusa.org/refugee/ document.do?id = FB04232694797C248025690000692CB9 (accessed February 18, 2006).

Amnesty International. (2002). Subhuman: Torture, overcrowding, and brutalisation in minas gerais police stations. Available online at: web.amnesty.org/library/Index/ENGAMR 190032002?open&of = ENG-BRA (accessed February 24, 2006).

Amnesty International. (2005). *They come in shooting: Policing socially excluded communities*. London: Amnesty International.

Angel-Ajani, A. (2003). A question of dangerous races? *Punishment and Society, 5*(4), 433–448.

Barker, V. (2006). Politics of punishing: Building a state governance theory of American imprisonment variation. *Punishment and Society, 8*(1), 5–32.

Beckett, K. (1997). *Making crime pay: Law and order in contemporary American politics*. Oxford: Oxford University Press.

Beckett, K., & Sasson, T. (2004). *The politics of injustice: Crime and punishment in America* (2nd ed.). Beverly Hills, CA: Sage Publications.

Beckett, K., & Western, B. (1999). Governing social marginality: Welfare, incarceration and the transformation of state policy. *Punishment and Society, 3*, 43–59.

Birkbeck, C., & Perez-Santiago, N. (2004). La redención de la pena y el tiempo de la condena: estudio de una cárcel Venezolana. *Revista CENIPEC*. 23: 33–71. Available at < 150.185.136.100/scielo.php?script = sci_arttext&pid = S0798-920220040 00100002&lng = en&nrm = iso> (accessed July 14, 2006).

Black, G., Jamail, M., & Chinchilla, N. S. (1984). *Garrison Guatemala*. New York: Monthly Review Press.

Bobo L. (2007). Of punitiveness and prejudice: Racial attitudes and the popular demand for harsh crime policies. Paper presented at the University of Washington, May 15, 2007.

Boggess, S., & Bound, J. (1993) Did criminal activity increase during the 1980s? Comparisons across data sources. *National Bureau of Economic Research*, Working Paper no. 4431.

Brysk, A. (2000). Democratizing civil society in Latin America. *Journal of Democracy*, *11(3)*(July), 151–165.

Calavita, K. (2003). A 'reserve army of delinquents': The criminalization and economic punishment of immigrants in Spain. *Punishment and Society*, *5*(4), 399–414.

Caldeira, T. P. R. (2000). *City of walls: Crime, segregation, and citizenship in São Paulo*. Berkeley: University of California Press.

Caplan, G. (1973). Reflections on the nationalization of crime, 1964–8. *Law and the Social Order*, *17*, 583–638.

Carey, D., Jr. (2004). Maya perspectives on the 1999 referendum in Guatemala: Ethnic equality rejected? *Latin American Perspectives*, *31*(6), 69–95.

Carrión, M. F. (2004). "La inseguridad ciudadana en la comunidad andina," In: José Luis Rhi-Sausi (Ed.), *El Desarrollo Local en América Latina: Logros y desafíos para la cooperación europea*. (pp. 149–162). Caracas: Recal/CeSPI/Nueva Sociedad.

Cavadino, M., & Dignan, J. (2006). *Penal systems: A comparative approach*. London: Sage Publications.

Cevallos D. (2004). "The War on Gangs – to Stop Gang Wars," *Global Information Network*, (October 5, p. 1).

Chevigny, P. (2003). The populism of fear: Politics of crime in the Americas. *Punishment and Society*, *5*(1), 77–96.

Christopherson, S. (1994). The fortress city: Privatized spaces, consumer citizenship. In: Ash Amin (Ed.), *Post-Fordism* (Chapter 14, pp. 409–427). Cambridge, MA: Blackwell Publishers.

Cronin, T., Cronin, T., & Milakovich, M. (1981). *The U.S. versus crime in the streets*. Bloomington: Indiana University Press.

Dammert, L. (2001). Construyendo ciudades inseguras: temor y violencia en Argentina. EURE (Santiago). [online]. 27(82) [accessed 21 Febrero 2007]. <www.scielo.cl/scielo.php?script = sci_arttext&pid = S0250-71612001008200001&lng = es&nrm = iso>.

Dammert, L., & Javiera, D. (2005). Es la cárcel solución para la delincuencia? Observatorio No. 1, May 2005, Santiago: FLACSO Chile.

Dammert, L., & Malone, M. F. T. (2005). Inseguridad y temor en la Argentina: El impacto de la confianza en la policía y la corrupción sobre la percepción ciudadana del crimen. *Desarrollo Económico*, *42*(166), 285–301.

Dammert, L., & Malone, M. F. T. (2003). Fear of crime or fear of life? Public insecurities in Chile. *Bulletin of Latin American Research*, *22*(1), 79–101.

Davis, M. (1992). *City of Quartz: Excavating the future in Los Angeles*. New York: Vintage Books.

De Palma, A. (November 11, 2002). The Americas court a group that changed New York. *New York Times*.

Debusmann, B. (January 23, 2006). Social cleansing in Guatemala Guatemala City (Reuters).

Diamond, L. (1999). *Developing democracy: Toward consolidation*. Baltimore: Johns Hopkins University Press.

Domingo, V. P. (1995). Rule of law and judicial systems in the context of democratisation and economic liberalisation: A framework for comparison and analysis in Latin America. Documentos de Trabajo del Centro de Investigación y Docencia Económicas, División de Estudios Políticos, Número 25.

Dow, M. (2004). *American Gulag: Inside U.S. immigration prisons*. Berkeley: University of California Press.

Edsall, T. B., & Edsall, M. (1991). *Chain reaction: The impact of rights, race and taxes on American politics*. New York: Norton and Co.

Fagan, J., & Davies, G. (2000). Street stops and broken windows: Terry, race and disorder in New York city. *Fordham Urban Law Journal, 28*, 457.

Farer, T. (Ed.) (1995). *Beyond sovereignty: Collectively defending democracy in the Americas*. Baltimore: Johns Hopkins University Press.

Garland, D. (2000). The culture of high crime societies: Some preconditions of recent "law and order" policies. *British Journal of Criminology, 40*(3), 347–376.

Garland, D. (2001). *Cultures of control: Crime and social order in contemporary society*. Chicago: University of Chicago Press.

Gibson, T. A. (2003). *Securing the spectacular city: The politics of revitalization and homelessness in downtown Seattle*. New York: Rowman & Littlefield Publishers Inc.

Giddens, A. (1990). *The consequences of modernity*. Stanford, CA: Stanford University Press.

Girling, E., Loader, I., & Sparks, R. (2000). *Crime and social change in Middle England: Questions of order in an English town*. New York: Routledge.

Godoy, A. S. (2004). When 'justice' is criminal: Lynchings in contemporary Latin America. *Theory and Society, 33*, 621–651.

Godoy, A. S. (2006). *Popular injustice: Violence, community, and law in Latin America*. Palo Alto: Stanford University Press.

Goldin, L. R. (1999). Rural Guatemala in economic and social transition. In: W. M. Loker (Ed.), *Globalization and the rural poor in Latin America* (pp. 93–110). Lynne Rienner.

Goldstein, D. M. (2004). *The spectacular city: Violence and performance in urban Bolivia*. Durhan: Duke University Press.

Grandin, G. (2004). *The last colonial massacre: Latin America and the Cold War*. Chicago: University of Chicago Press.

Hall, S., Critcher, C., Jefferson, T., Clarke, J., & Roberts, B. (1978). *Policing the crisis: Mugging, the state and law and order*. New York: Holmes and Meier Publishers, Inc.

Harbury, J. (2005). *Truth, torture, and the American way: The history and consequences of US involvement in torture*. Boston: Beacon Press.

Harcourt, B. E. (2001). *Illusion of order: The false promise of broken windows policing*. Cambridge: Harvard University Press.

Hay, D. (1992). Time, inequality, and law's violence. In: A. Sarat & K. Thomas (Eds), *Law's violence* (pp. 141–175). Ann Arbor: The University of Michigan Press.

Herbert, S. (2001). Policing the contemporary city: Fixing broken windows or shoring up neo-liberalism? *Theoretical Criminology, 5*, 445.

Holston, J., & Caldeira, T. (1998). Democracy, law, and violence: Disjunctions of Brazilian citizenship. In: A. Felipe & S. Jeffrey (Eds), *Fault lines of democracy in post-transitional Latin America* (pp. 263–296). Miami, FL: North-South Center.

Huggins, M. K. (1998). *Political policing: The United States and Latin America*. Durham, NC: Duke University Press.

Huggins, M. K., Haritos-Fatouros, M., & Zimbardo, P. G. (2002). *Violence workers: Police torturers and murderers reconstruct Brazilian atrocities*. Berkeley: University of California Press.

Human Rights Watch. (1997). *Punishment before trial: Prison conditions in Venezuela*. New York: Human Rights Watch.

Human Rights Watch. (1998). Shielded from justice: Police brutality and accountability in the United States. Available online at www.hrw.org/reports98/police/toc.htm (accessed February 18, 2006).

Human Rights Watch. (1999). World Report. Human rights overview: Americas entry. www.hrw.org/worldreport99/americas/ (accessed February 24, 2006).

Human Rights Watch World Report. (2005). Human rights overview: Argentina entry. Available online at www.hrw.org/english/docs/2005/01/13/argent9844.htm (accessed February 18, 2006).

Jonas, S. (2000). *Of Centaurs and Doves: Guatemala's peace process*. Boulder, Colo.: Westview Press.

Karl, T. L. (1990). Dilemmas of democratization in Latin America. *Comparative Politics, 23*(1), 1–21.

Katz, M. (1989). *The undeserving poor: From the war on poverty to the war on welfare*. New York: Pantheon Books.

La Hora (no byline). La policía continúa plan "escoba." August 7, 2003. www.lahora.com.gt/03/08/07/paginas/nac_2.htm#n4 (accessed February 24, 2006).

La mayoría de detenidos es por narcotráfico. (June 30, 2005). Blanco y Negro: Periodismo Investigativo. Quito, Ecuador. www.hoy.com.ec/suplemen/blan356/byn.htm (accessed November 29, 2005).

Lynch, M. (2001). From the punitive city to the gated community: Security and segregation across the social and penal landscape. *U. Miami L. Rev., 56*, 89.

Manza, J., & Uggen, C. (2006). *Locked out: Felon disenfranchisement and American democracy*. New York: Oxford University Press.

Matthews, R. (2005). The myth of punitiveness. *Theoretical Criminology, 9*(2), 175–201.

Mauer, M. (1999). *Race to incarcerate*. New York: The New Press.

McCord, J. (1997). Placing violence in its context. In: J. McCord (Ed.), *Violence and childhood in the inner city*. Cambridge, MA: Cambridge University Press.

Melossi, D. (1993). Gazette of morality and social whip: Punishment, hegemony and the case of the USA, 1970–92. *Social and Legal Studies, 2*, 259–279.

Melossi, D. (2001). The cultural embeddedness of social control: Reflections on the comparison of Italian and North-American cultures concerning punishment. *Theoretical Criminology, 5*(4), 403–424.

Melossi, D. (2003). In a peaceful life: Migration and the crime of modernity in Europe/Italy. *Punishment and Society, 5*(4), 371–398.

Mitchell, D. (2003). *The right to the city: Social justice and the fight for public space*. New York: Guilford Press.

Newburn, T. (2002). Transatlantic crossings: Policy transfer and crime control in the USA and Britain. *Punishment and Society, 4*(2), 165–194.

Newburn, T., & Jones, T. (2005). Symbolic politics and penal populism: The long shadow of Willie Horton. *Crime, Media, and Culture, 1*(1), 72–87.

Omi, M., & Winant, H. (1986). *Racial formation in the United States*. New York: Routledge and Kegan Paul.

O'Brien, R. M. (1996). Police productivity and crime rates: 1973–1992. *Criminology, 34*, 2.

O'Donnell, G. (1993). On the state, democratization and some conceptual problems: A Latin American view with glances at some postcommunist countries. *World Development, 21*, 1355–1369.

O'Donnell, G. (2004). Why the rule of law matters. *Journal of Democracy, 15*(4), 32–46.

O'Donnell, G., & Schmitter, P. C. (1986). *Transitions from authoritarian rule: Tentative conclusions about uncertain democracies*. Baltimore: Johns Hopkins University Press.

Parenti, C. (1999). *Lockdown America: Police and prisons in the age of crisis*. New York: Verso Press.

Pearce, J. (1998). From civil war to "civil society": Has the end of the cold war brought peace to Central America? *International Affairs, 74*(3), 587–615.

Pettit, B., & Western, B. (2004). Mass imprisonment and the life course: Race and class inequality in U.S. incarceration. *American Sociological Review, 69*(2), 151–170.

Rolim, M. (2006). La seguridad como desafío moderno a los derechos humanos, paper presented at the conference "Institucionalidad pública en ámbito de la seguridad ciudadana: experiencias de gobierno en los países del Cono Sur", organized by the Friedrich Ebert Foundation (FES-Chile), in Santiago, Chile, July 20–21, 2006. Available online at http://www.nuso.org/upload/seguridad/rolim.pdf (accessed February 21, 2007).

Sarat, A. (2002). *When the state kills: Capital punishment and the American condition*. Princeton, NJ: Princeton University Press.

Sasson, T. (1995). *Crime talk: How citizen's construct a social problem*. New York: Aldine de Gruyter.

Schedler, A. (1998). What is democratic consolidation? *Journal of Democracy, 9*(2), 91–107.

Sentencing Project. (2004a). State rates of incarceration by race. Available online at http://www.sentencingproject.org/pdfs/racialdisparity.pdf (accessed February 18, 2006).

Sentencing Project. (2004b). New incarceration figures: Growth in population continues. Available online at www.sentencingproject.org/pdfs/1044.pdf (accessed August 1, 2006).

Sheridan, M. B. (August 29, 1998). Crime plagued Mexicans shift death penalty stance, *Los Angeles Times* p. 2.

Shifter, M. (1997). Tensions and trade-offs in Latin America. *Journal of Democracy, 8*(2), 114–128.

Simon, J. (1997). Governing through crime. In: L. Friedman & G. Fischer (Eds), *The crime conundrum: Essays on criminal justice*. Boulder, CO: Westview Press.

Simon, J. (2000). Megan's law: Crime and democracy in late modern America. *Law and Social Inquiry, 25*(3), 1111–1150.

Simon, J. (2007). *Governing through crime: How the war on crime transformed American democracy and created a culture of fear*. New York: Oxford University Press.

Smith, N. (2001). Global social cleansing: Postliberal revanchism and the export of zero tolerance. *Social Justice, 28*(3), 68–75.

Sutton, J. R. (2004). The political economy of imprisonment 1960–1990. *American Sociological Review, 69*, 170–189.

The Economist. (October 2, 2004a). The battle for safer streets, p. 53.

The Economist. (July 29, 2004b). Guatemala: Not enough police, but who wants the army back in charge again? Available online at www.economist.com/research/backgrounders/displaystory.cfm?story_id = 2968778 (accessed July 14, 2006).

Tonry, M. (1995). *Malign neglect: Race, crime, and punishment in America*. New York: Oxford University Press.

Toro, I. (2005). Bachelet presenta batería de medidas contra delincuencia y Lavín persiste en sus críticas. La Nación, October 14, 2005 (http://www.lanacion.cl/prontus_noticias/site/artic/20051013/pags/20051013212949.html).

Tyler, T. R., & Boeckmann, R. J. (1997). Three strikes and you're out, but why? The psychology of public support for punishing rule breakers. *Law and Society Review, 31*, 2.

United Nations Development Programme. (2004). La Democracia en América Latina: Hacia una democracia de ciudadanas y ciudadanos. New York: UNDP. Available online at http://www.undp.org/spanish/proddal/informeProddal.html. (accessed July 14, 2006).

Van Swaaningen, R. (2005). Public safety and the management of fear. *Theoretical Criminology, 9*(3), 289–305.

Venturino. (2003). Los carapintada quieren ser presidente. Clarín, March 13, 2003 (http://www.clarin.com/diario/2003/03/13p-00801.htm).

Wacquant, L. (2001). The advent of the penal state is not a destiny. *Social Justice, 28*(3), 81–88.

Wacquant, L. (2003a). Toward a dictatorship over the poor? Notes on the penalization of poverty in Brazil. *Punishment and Society, 5*(2), 197–205.

Wacquant, L. (2003b). America's New "peculiar institution": On the prison as surrogate ghetto. In: G. B. Thomas & S. Cohen (Eds), *Punishment and social control* (2nd ed., pp. 471–482). New York: Aldine de Gruyter.

Walker, S., Spohn, C., & DeLone, M. (1996). *The color of justice: Race, ethnicity, and crime in America*. Belmont: Wadsworth Pub Co.

Walmsley, R. (May 10, 2001). An overview of world imprisonment: Global prison populations, trends and solutions paper presented at the United Nations Programme Network Institutes Technical Assistance Workshop in Vienna, Austria.

Welch, M. (2002). *Detained: Immigration laws and the expanding I.N.S. jail complex.* Philadelphia: Temple University Press.

Young, J. (1999). Cannabilism and bulimia: Patterns of social control in late modernity. *Theoretical Criminology, 394*, 387–407.

Zaluar, A. (May 10, 2001). Perverse integration: Drug trafficking and youth in the Favelas of Rio de Janeiro. *Journal of International Affairs* Spring 2000, *53*(2), 653.

PART II:
LAWYERING FOR THE
PUBLIC GOOD?

LEGAL AID'S LOGICS

Grace Park and Randy Lippert

ABSTRACT

In the Canadian province of Ontario government-funded legal aid underwent significant change in the 1990s in ways that mirror the trajectory of other governmental programs typically referred to in the governmentality literature as a shift to neo-liberalism. Through an analysis of interviews with lawyers and programmatic texts closely linked to legal aid practices this chapter reveals that legal aid is shaped by neo-liberal and pastoral rationalities. The implications of these findings both for legal aid research and governmentality studies are discussed.

INTRODUCTION

In the 1990s the Canadian province of Ontario experienced dramatic changes in government-funded legal aid. The program underwent reductions in funding coupled with the creation of an arms-length body – Legal Aid Ontario (LAO) – to oversee its delivery. Drastically reducing state expenditures while establishing a new quasi-public organization that promises to govern legal aid's remnants "at a distance" (Rose & Miller, 1992) from the state seems to especially befit the new arrangements of rule evident across policy domains. Such mutations seem to mirror the trajectory of myriad governmental programs examined by governmentality scholars in

Studies in Law, Politics, and Society, Volume 45, 177–201
Copyright © 2008 by Emerald Group Publishing Limited
All rights of reproduction in any form reserved
ISSN: 1059-4337/doi:10.1016/S1059-4337(08)45005-6

recent years typically represented as reflecting the welfare state's end and neo-liberalism's arrival.

This chapter examines legal aid in Ontario with close attention paid to the governmental logics (or governmentalities) that constitute and shape it and whether these rationalities of rule defy neat categorization as neo-liberalism. Our key interest here is to discern whether and how certain governmentalities make LAO possible. To this end, we consider the rise of neo-liberalism first by briefly discussing legal aid's development in Ontario and then by exploring its contemporary presence in legal aid. We argue that legal aid is shaped by neo-liberalism but also pastoral rationality, and that an assumed wholesale shift to the former inevitably obscures legal aid's complexities. In this configuration, legal aid and its key target, the legal subject, is seen to be constituted in complex ways that include targeting lawyers' subjectivity as a site of overlap between these rationalities. Especially in revealing pastoral rationality's presence, these findings have significant ramifications for understanding contemporary legal aid and for governmentality studies.

GOVERNMENTALITY STUDIES

In the Foucaultian-inspired governmentality literature, programs are seen to address the myriad problems of government (Dean, 1999, p. 16). Programs attempt to "make the objects of government thinkable in such a way that their ills appear susceptible to diagnosis, prescription and cure by calculating and normalizing intervention" (Rose & Miller, 1992, p. 182). Governmentalities come to be translated into programs. Widely discussed in this growing body of empirical work is a shift from liberal welfare rationality – typically understood as welfare state arrangements – to neo-liberalism in various domains (see Dean, 1999; Rose, 1999). Neo-liberalism – sometimes called "advanced liberalism" in governmentality studies (see Rose, 1999) – refers to a broad set of changes that contrast with liberal welfarism at the level of moralities and language (Rose & Miller, 1992, p. 198) and which is introduced with new governmental technologies. Programs consistent with neo- (or advanced) liberalism are exemplified by strategies to create markets or to "marketize" existing relations of rule (Dean, 1999) as well as through a new reliance on audits (Rose, 1999). Particularly pertinent to legal aid are related attempts to govern domains through individual choice, entrepreneurship, and partnership

(Lippert, 1998; Rose & Miller, 1992, p. 199) and empowerment techniques that target citizens' conduct (Cruikshank, 1999; Kesby, 2005).

In this literature, liberal welfare rationality is typically deployed as neo-liberalism's self-evident foil and predecessor. Liberal welfarism (also called "social liberalism" (Rose, 1999)) is rarely investigated in context by governmentality scholars, but is used instead to broadly refer to what is commonly understood as the welfare state. Thus, liberal welfarism as a rationality is assumed to command much of the 20th Century during which it sought to establish security for the population "from the cradle to the grave" through public programs providing employment insurance, pensions, education, and welfare provision (Dean, 1999, p. 150). This logic advocates a mutual responsibilization of the state and individual, whereby the state is to provide the general means for the population's well-being and individuals are to conduct themselves as good citizens (Rose, 1999, p. 139). Liberal welfarism's key innovation is said to be "to link the fiscal, calculative and bureaucratic capacities of the apparatus of the state to the government of social life" (Rose & Miller, 1992, p. 192). Yet, by the late 1970s, as these accounts go, this rationality became problematized, with liberal welfarism increasingly viewed as exercising excessive control over private relations. This cohered with critiques of a Keynesian style economics that required extensive state involvement in the economy but which was deemed unable to deal with recurring inflation and recession. Where the welfare state was most advanced, "enclosures" (see Rose & Miller, 1992, p. 195), characterized by the professions' monopolistic control over – and a corresponding insatiable demand for – state-funded services, also came under attack. This is especially evident in relation to the medical profession and medical services (e.g., Rose & Miller, 1992, pp. 194–195) but also, as will be seen, in regard to lawyers and legal aid. Advanced (or neo-) liberalism is said to have arisen to replace such state intervention and "enclosures" with greater emphasis on governing through market freedom and breaking through 'enclosures' using new governmental technologies such as audits (Rose, 1999, p. 153).

To be sure, a few governmentality scholars – albeit varied in approach – have begun to question the assumption of this wholesale shift (Larner, 2000a, 2000b; Lippert, 1998, 2005; O'Malley, 2001, 2002). Even a leading advocate, Rose (1999), suggests analysts should "avoid thinking in terms of a simple succession" (p. 142). Thus, neo-liberalism may well have a presence alongside other rationalities in current domains, suggestive of a more nuanced narrative than the sutured storyline above. That said, empirical research that explores whether and how more than one governmental logic constitutes and shapes specific regimes of practices remains exceedingly uncommon. Indeed, governmentality work has consistently promoted neo-liberalism as the solitary dominant rationality, as a broad governmental "master category" (Rose, O'Malley, & Valverde, 2006). One result can be theoretical closure, precluding other rationalities from being recognized and therefore theorized (Lippert, 1998; O'Malley, 2001; O'Malley, Weir, & Shearing, 1997). O'Malley (2001) writes: "[T]he nature, pervasiveness and impact of other rationalities are virtually ignored, so that the representation of contemporary government becomes a process in which advanced liberalism ascends or unfolds unopposed, or has already advanced over previously existing mentalities of rule" (p. 18).

One neglected governmentality is pastoralism, a logic drawn directly from Foucault's later writings and lectures (e.g., Foucault, 1982). Tracing its origin to Christian institutions, and using corresponding metaphors, Foucault asserts that pastoralism requires that the shepherd must know all aspects of a sheep's actions, moral and immoral. Foucault (1982) notes that "this form of power cannot be exercised without knowing the inside of people's minds, without exploring their souls, without making them reveal their inner most secrets. It implies a knowledge of the conscience and an ability to direct it" (p. 783). Thus, an intimate knowledge of individuals is necessary to lead them to salvation. While initially centered on the afterlife, Foucault suggests this rationality increasingly came to seek salvation for the governed in this world via sufficient standards of living, social security, and by fomenting programs based on charity and volunteerism (Foucault, 1982; see also Dean, 1999). To be sure, pastoralism has been taken up by governmentalitists within practices as varied as managing alcoholism (Valverde, 1998), workplace organization (Bell & Taylor, 2003), and refugee resettlement (Lippert, 1998), but rarely systematically, or in relation to other governmentalities to any degree. Indeed, it is crucial to point out that Foucault never elaborated "liberal welfarism" as described above, but instead wrote that 20th Century welfare state arrangements were but one historical instance of pastoralism. We therefore suggest that what is referred to as "liberal welfarism" in the governmentality literature is better seen as an historical and loose coupling of liberalism and pastoralism, of governing through freedom and governing through need (see Lippert, 2005), more an unstable and antagonistic mix of elements (Dean, 1999, p. 150) and less a solid and coherent rationality of its own. Furthermore, we think this coupling has become virtually unhinged and that the neglected rationality of pastoralism – albeit alongside other rationalities including neo-liberalism – nevertheless may have purchase in contemporary domains, including legal aid.

PREVIOUS LEGAL AID RESEARCH

Governmentality studies of legal aid are non-existent. Most legal aid research in the Canadian context – and undoubtedly in other liberal democracies – tends to avoid reference to theory and is policy-oriented, evaluating structural and administrative advancements (see Brook, 1977; Hoehne, 1989) and cost efficiency in relation to eligibility (see Currie, 1999; Taman, 1976; Thornley, 1983; Tsoukalas & Roberts, 2002; Zemans, 1978; Zemans & Monahan, 1997).

More theoretically informed critical scholarship includes work like Chouinard (1989), a neo-Marxist account of legal aid development, which views the Canadian state's role as central and equivalent to class power and repression. Ignoring the role of historical discourses and an understanding of power as constitutive of governmental practices, this account appears as reductionist and a-historical as a result. Feminist legal scholars have also studied legal aid in Canada (see Addario, 1998; Beaman, 2002; Gavigan, 1999; Mossman, 1993, 1998). A key theme here is legal discourse's tendency to silence women's voices, block access to justice, and construct clients as a "generic, gender-neutral category of unfortunate souls" (Gavigan, 1999, p. 213). Existing services are shown to be inadequate in fulfilling women's needs and are characterized by a deeply entrenched gender bias (Addario, 1998; Mossman, 1993, 1998). Certificate coverage categories, for example, fail to reflect the reality of women's legal problems (Gavigan, 1999). While vital in revealing rampant gender inequality in this domain, exclusive focus on inadequate responses to women's needs risks neglecting how legal aid is constituted by broader governmental discourses in which such legal discourses form. Attention to the former would seem necessary to strategically confront inequities based on gender, class, and other dimensions. Thus, an investigation of the broader logics that shape legal aid is overdue.[1]

METHOD

Qualitative methods were used for this study. First, newspaper accounts, Hansard debates (the official record of the Ontario legislature), policy documents, and secondary accounts were examined to see how legal aid in Ontario has developed, with close attention paid to changes from 1993 to 2000 during which neo-liberalism is widely assumed to have arrived. Second, current LAO texts were analyzed for instantiations of neo-liberal and pastoral discourse.[2] This entailed looking for key signifiers invoking choice and the market (neo-liberal) and charity, salvation and need (pastoral). These LAO texts were chosen based on their direct application to legal aid provision – texts likely used by practitioners and legal subjects – which constituted a move away from the orthodox practice within governmentality studies of examining broad programmatic statements (e.g., White Papers, policy statements, preambles to enabling legislation, etc. – see Rose & Miller, 1992). The aim was to better access the rationalities at work.[3] Third, our textual analysis was complemented by examining oral discourses (Jorgensen & Phillips, 2002, p. 65; see also Holstein & Gubrium, 1995; Lippert, 2005; Stenson, 1999) via open-focused interviews – also an unconventional practice in governmentality circles – which provided flexibility to probe beyond initial responses to questions and proceed in a conversation-like manner (Berg, 2001, p. 80). Questions were broadly focused on LAO's purposes and challenges as well as interviewee's practices. In all, ten interviews were conducted, six with private lawyers with extensive experience with the certificate program in Ontario, and the remainder with a LAO Area Director, Area Office Administrator, Supervisory Duty Counsel and Criminal Duty Counsel.[4]

NEO-LIBERALISM'S ARRIVAL

In the 1920s legal aid in Ontario was provided on an ad hoc basis, contingent upon an individual lawyer's charity (Reilly, 1988). The legal provision of in forma pauperis – in which a judge had discretion to waive court fees – was the only formal legal assistance available to Ontarians (Zemans, 1978). In the 1930s, the Depression saw an increase of economic and social dislocation and a corresponding greater demand for legal aid. To respond, the Board of Control in Toronto requested the York County Law Association provide a lawyer on a voluntary basis to staff an office and provide free legal aid to welfare recipients (Reilly, 1988, p. 87). The Association's participation was to be contingent upon the Board adopting an organizational model in which possible recipients would receive a list of lawyers willing to provide free legal advice (Reilly, 1988, p. 87). For emergencies only, these terms of organization and eligibility nevertheless mark the beginning of what is usually called liberal welfarism in the governmentality literature but which we suggest is a historical coupling of two rationalities that includes an effort to govern through legal subjects' needs. In the 1940s, the legal profession in Ontario officially acknowledged that providing legal services to those in need was their responsibility. In part this was a response to the prevailing sense in public discourse that legal aid should be made permanent and that lawyers had a duty to Canadian society to ensure access to justice (Reilly, 1988). The responsibility for legal aid arrangements was thus placed on the Law Society of Upper Canada (LSUC). Among lawyers was a consensus that government intervention should be circumvented, and while seemingly at odds with increasing state intervention in other domains at the time, the LSUC's continued responsibility for legal aid was typical of other professions' efforts to maintain autonomy (see Rose & Miller, 1992). Thus, the *Law Society Amendment Act* passed in 1951 allowed the LSUC to regulate legal aid services via a new Ontario Legal Aid Plan (OLAP) that maintained the voluntary basis of legal aid provision. It was to encompass both civil and criminal proceedings for the financially eligible based on income, number of dependents, and a discretionary needs test (Ministry of the Attorney General, 1996).

By the 1960s it had become evident the existing voluntary system was inadequate to satisfy demand. The Attorney General of Ontario then established a Joint Committee to report on the existing OLAP. The 1965 report criticized the lack of comprehensive coverage and the expectation that lawyers provide free services in the absence of state funding (see Chouinard, 1985). The report suggested the administration of legal aid should continue to be the LSUC's responsibility due to their expertise in this realm. Significant here is that the Committee recommended legal aid be considered a right and no longer a charitable gift, and that lawyers therefore be paid to deliver legal aid in a uniform manner (Thornley, 1983). This was consistent with liberal welfare rationality that entails extension of state responsibility for the well-being of the citizenry in other domains, such as via the Canada Assistance Plan, *The Medical Care Act*, and provincial welfare legislation (Ministry of the Attorney General, 1996).

The Ontario government passed the *Legal Aid Act* in 1967. It allowed the LSUC to remain the administrator of legal aid. A certificate model was adopted such that no full-time lawyers would be employed to provide services (Taman, 1976; Thornley, 1983). Rather, these services would be funded by the province on an open-ended, demand-driven basis (Zemans, 1978). Despite these changes, the OLAP encountered fiscal pressures from an open-ended funding scheme. This highlights broader concerns about fiscal control and accountability that would ultimately inspire a formal review of legal aid that resonates with neo-liberalism's emergence. The Osler Task Force on Legal Aid established in 1974 recommended the LSUC be replaced as legal aid's governing body by a new non-profit corporation called Legal Aid Ontario. Significantly, the report elicits a profound lack of trust of lawyers to serve the public good.

> The public good must be the sole purpose of the Legal Aid Plan, whereas the Law Society is by statute the governing body of the legal profession and must be primarily concerned with its welfare ... It is impossible to perceive the direction of the Legal Aid Plan as being sufficiently single-minded if it is left in the hands of a Committee of the Law Society, reporting to Convocation, the governing body of that Society, both groups being composed overwhelmingly of lawyers. (Osler, 1974 as cited in Taman, 1976, p. 377)

This report also demonstrates an increasing motivation to breach the professional authority of lawyers in the province, to break through their imagined "enclosure" (see Rose & Miller, 1992), and effectively render them governable. While mechanisms to displace the LSUC would not be implemented for two decades this recommendation nonetheless marks the first time the role of the LSUC in legal aid is questioned consistent with a broader problematization of liberal welfare rationality.

In the 1980s the range of services offered through legal aid expanded to most traditional areas of law, including criminal, family, and civil proceedings. However, financial eligibility requirements whereby the principle of the ability to pay was replaced by a gross income test. Clients with financial commitments exceeding maximums were now assumed capable of paying for their own legal representation (Thornley, 1983). Seriously undermining the principle of the right to legal representation, this shift was legitimated by a concern to control OLAP costs (Thornley, 1983).

In the 1990s legal aid continued to face growing demand, among the conditions of possibility of which were an economic recession, the Supreme Court of Canada 1990 judgement (*R. v. Askov*, 1990) requiring that persons be brought to trial within a reasonable time, and the increased prosecution of spousal abuse and impaired driving cases (Lawson, 1998). The increased certificate program costs in particular led the provincial government in 1994 to pressure the LSUC to sign a four-year Memorandum of Understanding (MOU) that capped funding, resulting in significant alterations to program delivery (Lawson, 1998). The MOU limited coverage to those charges that could result in jail sentences, whereas past coverage had been linked to a criminal charge's potential harm to a person's livelihood. Financial eligibility criteria were further tightened (Lawson, 1998, pp. 253–254). In late 1995, LSUC's Convocation voted to cut certificates from 155,000 to 100,000. Rates of pay or tariff maximums were reduced by roughly 22% in the average case cost and block fees were replaced by prescribed hourly maximums (Lawson, 1998, p. 254). Broadly, services were prioritized and those deemed less essential were eliminated.

Efforts to make legal aid and the legal profession calculable, and thus governable, justified severe program funding reductions via the MOU. An Area Director describes the MOU's effects.

> I had just become an Area Director and it changed in the sense that my job used to be to say "Yes." Within two months of getting the job, my job was then to say "No. I can't issue [a certificate]." We had open-ended funding, we had open-ended certificates, we covered a lot of stuff and it ended. So, for example, in that MOU in order to meet the capped funding we had to claw back the type of criminal certificates we would issue. So we used to issue [certificates] for things like, if the conviction would affect the ability to get a job, go to school, and there were a couple of other factors. So you weren't going to jail, but [if] having a record would negatively impact you, we would issue a certificate. Now the only time [a certificate is issued] is a probability of going to jail. (Interview 1)

In practice this meant "a lot of unrepresented" clients and undoubtedly sometimes dire consequences. But the newly excluded clients of legal aid – while most directly harmed – were not the only persons detrimentally affected. For example, "a lot of secretaries [were] put out of work" and it was lawyers who "absorbed the loss" (Interview 2). Lawyers were subjected to more restrictive rules for billing hours in addition to the 22% reduction in tariffs and hourly maximums. An Area Director commented on the lasting impact of controlling costs and economic management of LAO.

> Especially in family and CFSA [Child and Family Services Act], we have very few lawyers who are willing to take on those cases, because they are very challenging, the clients are challenging, and we don't pay. And the court time [that] takes them away from their paying client is really intensive. So keeping lawyers taking certificates has been a big challenge. (Interview 1)

These efforts to reduce costs and ultimately deny some access to legal aid are neo-liberal in character. Clients with cases not covered by legal aid certificates or who were financially ineligible for services began to be provided with self-help guides to help navigate the system. As a duty counsel supervisor explained

> [I]n a less formal way, the counter staff at the family counter is part of this in that they hand out forms people need. If they come in saying "I want to apply for custody." Okay. "Here's all the forms you need, here are information guides." We've also developed some things to try and recognize that there's no stop gap. We have these *self-help checklists* that we've created that we can hand out to clients who don't qualify financially but we can say "Look, here's the forms you need, here's the *self-help checklist*." (Interview 4; emphasis added)

The term "self-help" invokes neo-liberal notions of the responsibilized client, empowered in their own knowledge to improve the quality of their lives by accessing justice. Following Cruikshank (1999), this form of empowerment – while perhaps well-intentioned – works through clients' subjectivities to reinforce neo-liberalism.

This restructuring led to discontent among lawyers, some of whom then refused to take certificates as a consequence. In September 1995, in response to a revolt against unpaid accounts and lengthy payment waiting times, Ontario's Attorney General's office released a statement dismissing lawyers' concerns.

> [T]he law society has to realize that it has reached the end of the road. The money promised by the former government is all that is available. "There is no question they're going to have to live within the memorandum of understanding. There is no more money for them." (Mittelstaedt, 1995, p. A9)

Yet, it is necessary to note that these modifications are less about conflict between a professional body and the state and more about conflict between rationalities of government, in particular, resistance to "enclosures" that develop within liberal welfare arrangements. As Dean (1999, p. 11) notes, rationalities work through desires, aspirations and beliefs that include professional ethics and standards thought to be best policed by professionals themselves.

The funding reduction is symptomatic of a broader shift toward accountability which was further seen in 1997 when another legal aid review sought to "remodel the system to make it fiscally responsible, efficient and accountable to government" (Makin, 1997, p. A1). Its mandate was to

> consider all legal aid programs in the province with the objective of identifying aspects that should be reduced, maintained or enhanced, including new ideas in the management and delivery of legal aid in order that the current and future legal needs of low income residents of Ontario can be met in the most effective and efficient way possible within the existing funding allocation. (Lawson, 1998, p. 259)

The review provided the final impetus for LAO's creation, as prescribed by the earlier Osler Report. The *Legal Aid Services Act* was passed in 1998 in an effort to breach legal expertise with audits. Control of legal aid was to move from LSUC to LAO, the latter of which was foreseen overseeing legal aid policy from hereon. As in other policy domains, legal aid would now be governed by a quasi-public body "at a distance" from the state. As well, LAO would provide legal services but also certificates to clients to take to lawyers of their choice. The lawyer would then authorize the certificate through LAO.[5] For lawyers to participate in legal aid, minimum experience and professional development requirements were to be met for assignment to criminal, family, or refugee law panels (see LAO, n.d.b, n.d.c, n.d.d, & n.d.l). Empanelled lawyers were to submit to LAO a summary of hours up to a set maximum to receive payment for services. Thus, these changes plainly targeted the conduct of lawyers as much as clients.

LAO requires clients to meet financial eligibility requirements based on income and asset assessment measured against standard allowances set in legislation (LAO, 1999). When a client fails to meet eligibility requirements, the Area Director can decide their capacity to pay (LAO, 2006a). In addition, the legal merit of a client's case is to be considered. In criminal matters, the Area Director makes merit determinations. In family or refugee matters, where legal merit is uncertain, the Area Director can issue a two-hour certificate for a lawyer to assess merit in an opinion letter. For criminal matters, opinion letters also can be authorized if a lawyer requests additional service beyond an existing certificate's allotment (LAO, 2006a).

Legal aid developments befit changes characteristic of a shift to neo-liberal rule. For example, LAO's broader purpose set out in the *Legal Aid Services Act* (Ontario, 1998)

> is to promote access to justice throughout Ontario for low-income individuals by means of, (a) providing consistently high quality legal aid services in a cost-effective and efficient manner to low-income individuals throughout Ontario; (b) encouraging and facilitating flexibility and innovation in the provision of legal aid services, while recognizing the private bar as the foundation for the provision of legal aid services in the areas of criminal law and family law ...; (c) identifying, assessing and recognizing the diverse legal needs of low-income individuals and of disadvantaged communities in Ontario; and (d) providing legal aid services to low-income individuals through a corporation that will operate independently from the Government of Ontario but within a framework of accountability to the Government of Ontario for the expenditure of public funds. (c. 26, s. 1)

Neo-liberalism is instantiated as "cost-effective" and "efficient," "operate independently," and "accountability." Other LAO texts similarly reveal instantiations of neo-liberal discourse. For instance, in the *Duty Counsel Manual* (LAO, 2002b) and the *Tariff and Billing Handbook* (LAO, 2002c) there are 7 instances of "choice," 12 of "accountability," 50 of "efficient/ effective," and 54 of "responsibility" thus illustrating the neo-liberal thrust of broader policy statements is also present in texts arguably closer to legal aid practice. Another noteworthy example of neo-liberalism's presence is the Post Payment Examination's (PPE) implementation in 2005 to "ensure accounts paid through Legal Aid Online are valid and properly billed"

(LAO, n.d.f). This key mutation eliminates the need to examine every lawyer-submitted account. Rather, randomly chosen accounts are to be reviewed to ensure accuracy. The rationale of the new examination policies is

> to *simplify and streamline* the way we do business to make it easier for lawyers to do legal aid work. In contrast to our previous investigations process, where we conducted detailed reviews of every account paid during a two-year period for a lawyer, post-payment examination will *randomly select individual accounts for examination.* Lawyers who bill frequently may expect that three or four accounts per year may be selected for examination. (LAO, n.d.f; emphasis added)

Simplification and streamlining are synonymous with neo-liberal efficiency and fiscal responsibility which displaces "internal logics of expertise" (Rose, 1999, p. 154). Lawyers are to closely account for their conduct indicative of a neo-liberal "regime of distrust" (Rose, 1999, p. 155). Lawyers can be further subjected to a detailed "targeted examination" should random examinations flag problems in their accounts.

> A targeted examination may be initiated where a random examination identified issues that *support an expanded scrutiny of accounts* paid to a lawyer, or where the nature and/ or extent of identified suggest that there are merits to conducting a review of additional accounts submitted by the lawyer and may include such factors such as: complaints; repeated pattern or errors or high incidence of errors; disparity in account information in comparison to a peer group; or high billing amounts. (LAO, n.d.h; emphasis added)

This is reflective of neo-liberal governance of the professions. A lawyer working with legal aid for five years echoes this "truth" of accountability as a means of justifying more rigorous measures to which lawyers must consent when doing legal aid work.

> There are certain parameters that you have which you have to work with if you are willing to accept a legal aid certificate. [The] first parameter is there's a limit on the hourly billing rate, the second parameter is that when a bill is rendered, there are *very careful controls that go into the process.* You have to account for every six minutes. And if the period of time that you are billing for, individual time on a bill exceeds half an hour ... you have to put down the times of day that the half hour covers. *And there's very good reasons for that and it comes out of abuses in legal aid in the past. So it's a safeguard. It's public money.* The third parameter within which you have to work is the payment cycles. So when you submit a bill you have to abide by whatever their turnaround is [when] paying an account. Part of the agreement I signed is to ... basically not sue legal aid if they chose not to pay one of my accounts. (Interview 5; emphasis added)

This control of the likely litigious in the new legal aid arrangements (i.e., lawyers), while on the surface about controlling "abuse," creates a means to govern the legal profession's "enclosure." Through audits lawyers are to be made responsible for their own governance. For instance, the PPE policy states:

> The detection of errors in a targeted examination may result in an investigation in circumstances where the nature and/or extent of errors identified suggest a significant *lack of care* in preparing the accounts, advertent errors, or other factors that suggest that merit exists for a closer scrutiny of the lawyer's accounts. (LAO, n.d.h; emphasis added)

This "lack of care" signals a lack of prudence on a lawyer's part, thus suggesting they are poor neo-liberal subjects.

Arbitrary discretion exercised by unaccountable experts and bureaucrats was a chief target of critiques of the welfare state. The solution to arbitrary discretion here was to apply more rules and laws to render legal aid decisions predictable. For example, we see the proliferation of manuals and policy guidelines in LAO that attempt to create a measure of accountability and limit discretion's scope. By curbing experts' power, "enclosures" are to cease being such (Rose, 1999, p. 142). The hierarchical structure of legal aid allows for accountability measures as well as ensuring that discretion is exercised by only a few. The *Area Office Policy Manual* requires Area Directors to exercise discretion conservatively and to "be prepared to justify their discretionary decision. It is a good practice to keep a memo on file or record and an Encounter Note to support the decision" (LAO, 2006a, p. 8.4). Yet, an analysis of texts reveals discretionary powers are not limited to the Area Director. Other legal professionals continue to influence legal aid. For instance, Area Directors unsure of merit can issue an opinion letter, as noted earlier, in which discretionary powers are handed off to lawyers whose opinion can determine a case. The *Area Office Policy Manual* supports this: "The critical part of the letter is generally the lawyer's position on the merits of the case or the client's position" (LAO, 2006a, p. 9.5). In addition, the duty counsel lawyers also exercise discretionary powers outside the legal aid mandate.

> In terms of qualifying for our service, we do a similar type of financial application but not as detailed ... . [I]f in the course of the interview with a client that you're about to help at court it becomes apparent that they are on assistance because they say so, in fact we don't even worry about administrating a financial eligibility test because we know that they qualify ... . And now generally speaking, having said that, *if someone is there and needs some summary kind of process-related advice that we can give in ten or fifteen minutes we will still help them.* (Interview 4)

These discretionary practices are not accounted for by reference to neo-liberalism and have several implications. First, individual lawyers still possess considerable power to determine whether a given client receives legal aid. Although LAO was created as a means to deal with LSUC's exclusive control of legal aid, the program remains heavily influenced by LSUC. In addition, Area Directors are to be selected from among members of the bar (LAO, 2006a). These elements reveal the incompleteness of neo-liberal attempts to puncture "enclosures" via employing managers or non-experts to oversee legal programs. Secondly, the client is imagined here quite differently from a neo-liberal subject. Determinations of merit for obtaining a lawyer (and hence deciding the clients' best interests) are made by lawyers, rather than the responsibilized, autonomous client. In fact, obtaining an opinion letter to verify merit assumes the client cannot make a prudent or responsible decision about whether it is worth seeking legal advice. The general merit test – "[W]ould a reasonable client of modest means choose to use his/her own money to fund the litigation?" (LAO, 2006a, p. 4.1) – no longer applies. These findings are not anomalies or the residue of past logics washed away by neo-liberalism's tide; they indicate the presence of other rationalities shaping legal aid.

Neo-liberal discourse is also found coupled with a discourse of rights. This is especially evident in two key LAO texts: *Duty Counsel Manual* (LAO, 2002b) and the *Tariff and Billing Handbook* (LAO, 2002c). Here there are some 49 instances of "rights" and 67 instances of "access." LAO manuals also note:

> The certificate and duty counsel programs are a form of public-private partnership in serving low-income individuals throughout Ontario. LASA obliges LAO to recognize the private bar "as the foundation of legal aid services in the areas of criminal and family law" – this maintains the fundamental *right* of choice of counsel for poor people. (LAO, 2002b; emphasis added)

Similarly, a client brochure states, "You have the rights to the best service possible, whether you are on legal aid or paying out of your own pocket" (LAO, n.d.m, Your Lawyer's Job section, para. 3). An image of the legal client as a rights bearing subject is produced. Social rights that seek to guarantee equal access to services are intimately linked to liberal welfare rationality. While never achieving universal entitlement, here rights are contingent upon an individual's actions to earn them, more of a good that can be given or taken away, which of course contrasts with the human rights ideal (Lightman & Riches, 2000). Constituting subjectivities in this way lends itself to neo-liberal governance and responsibilization. For instance, *You and Your Lawyer* (LAO, n.d.m), a legal aid brochure, instructs clients to engage in responsible conduct when communicating with a lawyer.

Your time with your lawyer may be limited and costing you money so use your time carefully. Every phone call with your lawyer is using up time. If you are on a legal aid certificate, understand that the lawyer is only allowed to spend so much time on your case. Be prepared for your meetings with your lawyers. Write down your questions before you go ... Don't expect to see your lawyer without an appointment. Your lawyer is very busy and may not be in the office all the time. Call ahead if you can't keep an appointment and don't forget to schedule another one. Keep a file or envelope with all your papers in it and bring it to every meeting with your lawyer. Read all the materials that your lawyer gives you. Bring a notebook with you to each meeting so you can make notes of what your lawyers says. (LAO, n.d.m, Preparing for Your Meeting section, para. 1)

This indicates how legal aid clients are to be efficient with lawyers' time. Lawyers and administrators often expressed in interviews a sense of frustration with clients who evoked (an older sense of) rights. For example, a family lawyer stated:

[M]ost of the people, and this is going to sound judgemental, stereotypical; they are not grateful for the support they are given. They do not recognize that I don't work for free. Somebody's paying me. And indirectly, they're paying me, every time they buy something in the store and it goes to provincial sales tax. But because it does not come directly out of their pockets, they don't recognize that they're publicly funded and that it is a limited resource. They can be the most demanding clients; they can be the least grateful clients. Because they have no vested interest, they have no stake in the process. And if I would propose a change to legal aid, it would be that. Have them have some kind of a stake in the process. Let it have some meaning for them, [an understanding] that someone is making sacrifices for them, be it through the taxes, be it through the lawyers who accept the legal aid certificates. Somebody else is making a sacrifice for you and you better well appreciate it. And most of them do not have any appreciation for that. (Interview 5)

Here responsibility that comes with pursuing rights is deemed to be avoided by clients; their subjectivities are assumed to be constituted via unconditional entitlement based solely on need that is consonant with liberal welfarism. But notice "making sacrifices" here, which raises the possibility of the presence of a pastoral rationality in legal aid that requires a closer look.

PASTORALISM

Thus far this chapter has discussed neo-liberalism's arrival in the legal aid domain. In what follows we argue that pastoral rationality overlaps with neo-liberalism and that the two logics at certain points are mutually constitutive. An analytically separate governmental discourse, first and foremost, pastoralism is about sacrificial caring for the needs of the governed. The term "judi*care*," widely used to refer to certificate arrangements, itself hints at pastoral power's continued presence. The examination of LAO texts similarly reveal pastoralism's place in what is a new configuration. The client is governed based on the notion that the lawyer can provide for their "salvation" and guidance. To achieve "salvation," the client must let the lawyer know their "deepest secrets" (Foucault, 1982). In the widely distributed brochure, *You and Your Lawyer*, subjects are instructed.

> Tell your lawyer as much as possible about your legal problem even though you may feel uncomfortable or embarrassed. Your lawyer understands this and is not there to judge you. *Lawyers need to know all the facts so that they can help you.* Answer the lawyer's questions completely and truthfully. Be clear with the lawyer about what you expect. If the lawyer knows exactly what you want, he or she will be able to help you better. (LAO, n.d.m, The First Meeting section, para. 1; emphasis added)

It further states:

> Your lawyer may not always tell you what you want to hear or be able to fix every problem, but he or she is the best person to advise you about what to do. Even though your friends may have had a problem like yours, your case is probably different. (LAO, n.d.m, What to Expect section, para. 1)

The image of needy clients is reproduced in the broader context of a needs-based system. Part of LAO's mandate is "assessing and recognizing the diverse legal needs of low-income individuals and disadvantaged communities" (LAO, 2006a, p. 1.1). Imagining the client as needy legitimates the obligation of lawyers to provide guidance, thus creating a space where pastoral discourse flourishes. Furthermore, neo-liberalism's emphasis on individual responsibility and enterprise is not fully present, a situation that coaxes pastoral power to pick up the slack. While LAO's mandate includes assurance of equality through choice, there is recognition among some lawyers that clients are incapable of making good choices: "For people who are say, from the [United] States, or who really don't hang with the criminal crowd, they're given the [lawyer] list and they just [say], oh that looks like a nice name" (Interview 2). In part, the brochure *You and Your Lawyer* (LAO, n.d.m) was created to confront this imagined deficiency in the client's ability to choose.

> The lawyer you choose should be sensitive to your needs, so make sure you are completely comfortable with the lawyer you choose. Think about the kind of lawyer you would like to work with. Do you prefer a man or a woman? You should try to find a lawyer who has experience with your kind of legal problem. It may also be a good idea to

get a lawyer who speaks your language and who will *help you understand your choices.*
Ask the legal aid office [for] ... a list of lawyers who deal with cases like yours. (LAO,
n.d.m, Finding the Lawyer for You section, para. 2)

Encouragement to obey your lawyer is premised on individuals' capacity to
choose the best lawyer the first time around. As the brochure, *Can I Get a
Legal Aid Certificate* (LAO, n.d.a) states: "Make sure you are comfortable
with the lawyer you choose. It is unlikely that you will be allowed to change
lawyers" (How do I Find a Lawyer? section, para. 2). From there, as a
criminal lawyer suggested, it is only the lawyer who has the capacity to
discern the client's "best interest."

I've had people switch from me. And sometimes it will be a complete breakdown... .
And I'm not just going to do what the client wants me to do if it's improper or *if it's not
in his best interest because that's what he wants to do. Especially if it's not in his best
interest* ... . (Interview 9; emphasis added)

Clients and lawyers are imagined in ways consistent with pastoral power.
For example, the *Tariff and Billing Handbook* (LAO, 2002c) states:

If you feel that the client needs services that the certificate does not cover, request an
amendment from the Area Director in a timely fashion before performing any services. If
you wait until after the services are complete, the Area Director may require evidence of
the client's continuing eligibility to add services to the certificate that were not previously
authorized. The Area Director may not approve the additional services pursuant to legal
aid policies. *If the client does not attend at the Area Director's office to prove continuing
eligibility, or cannot be located, your requested amendment might not be granted.* (LAO,
2002c, pp. 1–5; emphasis added)

Here the special position of lawyers in gaining intimate knowledge of clients
is consistent with pastoral power and from a neo-liberal perspective is used
as a mechanism of governing the client on the basis of a discovered absence
and decline of need. Regarding a change in a client's financial circumstances,
lawyers are advised as follows:

Clients might tell you that their financial circumstances have changed, or you might
discover it yourself. In either case, you must notify the area director. You must also
notify the Area Director if you find any of the following: the client may have
misrepresented his or her circumstances in applying for legal aid; the client failed to
make full disclosure at the time of applying for legal aid; and anything that indicates that
the client may no longer be entitled to the certificate. (LAO, 2002c, p. 1.8)

This reveals another point of overlap between neo-liberal and pastoral
rationalities.

Pastoral rationality seeks to create an ideal lawyer as the metaphorical
shepherd possessing an ethical willingness to give (Dean, 1999, p. 96). For

example, in the brochure for potential legal aid lawyers entitled, *Legal Aid and You Partners in Justice* (LAO, n.d.e): "Legal aid work offers significant benefits to new lawyers. It provides an opportunity to contribute toward improving Ontario's justice system by helping some of our society's most disadvantaged people" (p. 3). The brochure profiles lawyers' legal aid experiences.

> "Legal aid makes it possible to represent people who would not otherwise have access to a lawyer," he says. "Immigration can be a very big deal. In some cases, it can be life or death." Helping new Canadians is a particularly rewarding part of his work says Michael. "You can help them stay in Canada – they wouldn't have had a shot if you hadn't been there." (LAO, n.d.e, p. 3)

This resonates with the imagined shepherd whereby "pastoral power enlists persons 'to do something'" (Lippert, 2005, p. 114). This cultivation of the willingness to give legitimates sacrifices made by shepherds who oversee and care for the flock. One administrator commented that only "special" lawyers are willing to provide criminal and family law services through a certificate.

> Quite frankly, family [law] is seen as sort of the – how do I put this eloquently? – criminal and family are the low class law. Family is not attractive to most people. Why would you want to do that stuff? And I think it does take a special person but that's why not everyone does it … there's a hierarchy that commercial, corporate commercials lawyers would see themselves as far more important and far more influential and that may be. In terms of their direct interaction with the public and especially low income [clients], they don't have any of that … and I say this to * all the time. I was never good at the business side of it because, you know, she's sitting across the desk from me and she has $200. She either buys groceries or she pays me. Often times, she bought the groceries. (Interview 4)

As noted, this ethos dates to legal aid's beginnings, in which the inception of a permanent program was legitimated by LSUC acknowledgement of responsibility. A criminal lawyer noted:

> Well you know obviously people in jail or whatever, you're not going to just let them [pauses] – it's essentially the government taking advantage of us feeling bad for people in jail and you know we're going to take care of them, and we're not going to get paid for it. (Interview 2)

Referring to the intimate knowledge of legal aid recipients so characteristic of pastoral rationality, another criminal lawyer approached a denial of recipients' client status when contrasted with "cash clients."

> So I've got lots of clients that I've acted for, for years and years. So I know them, I know their parents, I know their kids. *I know everything about them. So to me, they are almost like friends, as opposed to clients.* And very often the cash clients are people that you

might represent one time, who are not likely to be charged again and again. So it's not as close a relationship sometimes. (Interview 9; emphasis added)

Legal certificates along with per diem duty counsel lawyers remain a LAO component. Remuneration for certificates is not equivalent to fees stemming from "a cash paying client" (Interview 5). In response to MOU-related (neo-liberal) program reforms, a lawyer acknowledged his sacrifice.

But you know it's hard for you. I've got a couple hundred clients, there's no way I can say, well because you know I'm getting less money now, I'm not going to represent you. You ... have a relationship with these people, and what it came down to is we're the ones who, I can't say suffered but, we're the ones who *absorbed the loss*. (Interview 2; emphasis added)

While this discourse of sacrifice is evident, it cannot be denied that elements of neo-liberalism remain whereby legal aid becomes a "lifestyle choice" for new lawyers. Thus, *Legal Aid and Your Partners in Justice* states: "Legal aid is also an excellent way to make professional contact and gain courtroom experience, and for many lawyers, the flexibility of legal aid work is an attractive career and lifestyle choice" ([37]LAO, n.d.e, p. 3). This sentiment was echoed in all interviews with lawyers who accepted certificates and was highlighted by a criminal lawyer.

Especially when you are young [and] you're starting off it's a good way to make some money and get some experience ... . When you're young your practice is essentially 80–90 percent legal aid ... . It puts food on the table. There's no way as a young lawyer you are going to make a go of it without legal aid clients. (Interview 2)

It is lawyer's subjectivity, then, where pastoralism and neo-liberalism can be seen to overlap. Neither rationality fully supplants the other here. Rather, legal aid work in these moments is at once sacrificial and a rational career choice.[6]

CONCLUSIONS

The foregoing illustrates that legal aid's governmental logics are complicated and overlapping, manifesting themselves in varied ways and that neo-liberalism is not the only rationality relevant to this domain. The historical coupling of liberalism and pastoralism may well have become unhinged but what remains is a configuration more complex than the onset of neo-liberalism. We do not deny neo-liberalism's presence and deleterious effects, especially on disadvantaged clients' access to justice, but we suggest this focus obscures a more complex picture whereby neo-liberalism is seen to variously complement and conflict with other rationalities at certain points of articulation. Such inter-discursivity within legal aid suggests future governmentality studies should seek to determine what rationalities are present in a specific realm and how they articulate with one another. We wish to encourage this alternative view of a research program that seeks more than mapping neo-liberalism's inevitable march to dominance. This may require paying closer attention to operations manuals and interviews with practitioners which was essential to discovering this legal aid program's complexity. Staying within the governmentality orthodoxy of analyzing broad policy texts can overlook rationalities, effectively creating theoretical coherency and consensus where it does not exist.

Future research should consider potential rationalities that inform legal aid programs. By assuming neo-liberalism is the overarching rationality, the certificate program is seen as preoccupied with reproducing a responsible client who actively chooses the right lawyer, recounting testimonials in strictly legalistic terms, and becoming cost-conscious. Yet, if pastoralism has purchase as a sometimes overlapping but nevertheless distinct rationality, as this study suggests, how the ethos of the desire to give among lawyers is made possible and historical shifts in that ethos also become worthy of study. If Ontario is any example, legal aid always has been based upon pastoralism to some degree; state involvement, fiscal concerns, and neo-liberal mutations came later. One among several possible endeavors is to explore how and to what extent the ethical cultivation of the desire to give has been historically produced within legal education. This also implies an alternative potential point of intervention to alleviate inequality within legal aid. Feminist studies have examined how women's access to legal aid is systematically hindered and existing services reflect a gender bias but exclusive attention to neo-liberalism and corresponding calls to increase legal aid funding beyond previous levels may well overlook the potential to self-consciously cultivate and grow a different ethos in law schools that would eventually bear fruit within legal aid practice. To be sure, this set of issues has been discussed elsewhere, most notably in the cause lawyering literature (e.g., Scheingold & Sarat, 2004; Shdaimah, 2006, p. 236), but pastoral rationality and related governmentality concepts are distinct in assuming this ethos and desire to give are non-essential, partially discursive, and historically contingent. More broadly, efforts to change legal aid along progressive lines should consider that discovering the historical logics that shape legal aid can be a useful first step before the alleviation of inequality based on gender, class, race/ethnicity, or other dimensions are sought. Such a mapping

> counters the tendency to subsume government under on ascendant rationality; creates
> spaces in which alternative governmental forms maybe identified and contests facilitated;
> opens up the possibilities for recognising hybridization, adaptation and change; in short,
> returns to political analysis the fluidity and contingency of relational politics without
> abandoning the characteristic analysis of governmentality. (O'Malley, 2001, p. 25)

Recognition of at least the possibility of two or more rationalities operating is necessary if progressive responses to inequitable programs are to seriously confront complex arrangements of government and to render legal aid truly accessible where it cannot be made unnecessary.

NOTES

1. While the present model of LAO is organized around a mixed-model system – a combination of certificate and clinic services – we focus on the certificate system. Community legal clinics and Student Legal Aid Services Societies are currently funded by LAO, but remain separate from certificates and have their own histories that may well be permeated with discourses in varied configurations as a consequence.

2. Other rationalities may be present in a given set of programmatic texts, as O'Malley et al. (1997, p. 505) note. One of these is neo-conservativism (see O'Malley, 2001) for which we found evidence of its presence, particularly in relation to family law and how family was conceived in legal aid eligibility. Neo-liberal discourses in legal aid texts construct the family as a provider economic support and management outside the state but in, for example, the *Area Legal Aid Manual* (LAO, 2006a), justification for merit to receive legal aid in family law transcends economic responsibility and is based on protecting the obligation of parents toward a child and the familial bond and therefore is consistent with neo-conservatism's focus on tradition.

3. These texts included: *Area Office Policy Manual* (Legal Aid Ontario – hereinafter LAO, 2006a), *Financial Eligibility Criteria for Certificate Policies and Procedures Manual* (LAO, 1999), *A Guide to Legal Aid Ontario for Area Committee Members* (LAO, 2001), *Complaints Policy* (LAO, 2002a), *Quality Service Principles* (LAO, n.d.k), *Panel Standards* (LAO, n.d.l), *Duty Counsel Manual* (LAO, 2002b), *Tariff and Billing Handbook* (LAO, 2002c), *Practice Manual: Representing Claimants Before the Refugee Protection Division* (LAO, 2003), *Post-Payment Examination Policies* (LAO, n.d.f; LAO, n.d.g; LAO, n.d.h; LAO, n.d.i; and LAO, n.d.j), brochure for new lawyers: *Legal Aid and You Partners in Justice* (LAO, n.d.e), and client brochures (LAO, n.d.a; LAO, n.d.m). In addition, *About Legal Aid, Historical Overview, Business Plan 2006/2007* (LAO, 2006b), *2005 Annual Report* (LAO, 2005), and the *Quality Service Office: Annual Report 2005–2006* (LAO, 2006c) that illustrate LAO's organizational goals were examined.

4. The interviews facilitated with LAO personnel in particular provided a familiarity with legal aid services and interviewee referrals. Due to ethical considerations no legal aid clients were interviewed.

5. Other services include Duty Counsel and legal advice programs. LAO also staffs Family Law, Criminal Law and Refugee Law Offices and specialty clinics in some jurisdictions (LAO, 2002b).

6. The notion that legal aid work can enhance a lawyer's career has been discussed in the cause lawyering literature (e.g., Sarat & Scheingold, 1998, p. 5).

ACKNOWLEDGMENTS

The authors contributed equally to the theoretical and substantive development of the chapter. We sincerely thank Glynis George, Brian Mazur, and two anonymous reviewers for thoughtful comments on earlier drafts of this chapter.

REFERENCES

Addario, L. (1998). *Getting a foot in the door: Women, civil legal aid and access to justice.* Ottawa: National Association of Women and the Law.

Beaman, L. (2002). Legal discourse and domestic legal aid: The problem of fitting in. In: G. MacDonald (Ed.), *Social context and social location in the sociology of law* (pp. 69–89). Peterborough: Broadview Press.

Bell, E., & Taylor, S. (2003). The elevation of work: Pastoral power and the new age work ethic. *Organization, 10,* 329–349.

Berg, B. (2001). *Qualitative research methods: For the social sciences.* Boston: Allyn and Bacon.

Brook, R. (1977). Legal services in Canada. *Modern Law Review, 40,* 533–552.

Chouinard, V. (1985). Transformations in the capitalist state: The development of legal aid and legal clinics in Canada. *Transactions of the Institute of British Geographers, 14,* 329–349.

Chouinard, V. (1989). Challenging law's empire: Rebellion, incorporation, and changing geographies of power in Ontario's legal clinic system. *Studies in Political Economy, 55,* 65–92.

Cruikshank, B. (Ed.). (1999). The will to empower: Technologies of citizenship and the war on poverty. In: *The will to empower: Democratic citizens and others* (pp. 67–103). Ithaca: Cornell University Press.

Currie, A. (1999). *Legal aid delivery models in Canada: Past experience and future directions.* Ottawa: Department of Justice Canada.

Dean, M. (1999). *Governmentality, power and rule in modern society.* London: Sage.

Foucault, M. (1982). The subject and power. *Critical Inquiry, 8,* 777–795.

Gavigan, S. A. M. (1999). Poverty law, theory, and practice: The place of class and gender in access to justice. In: E. Comack (Ed.), *Locating law: Race/class/gender connections* (pp. 208–230). Halifax: Fernwood Publishing.

Hoehne, D. (1989). *Legal aid in Canada.* Queenston: The Edwin Mellen Press.

Holstein, J. A., & Gubrium, J. (1995). *The active interview.* Thousand Oaks, CA: Sage Publications.

Jorgensen, M., & Phillips, L. (Eds). (2002). Critical discourse analysis. In: *Discourse analysis as theory and method* (pp. 60–95). London: Sage Publications.

Kesby, M. (2005). Re-theorizing empowerment-through-participation as a performance in space: Beyond tyranny to transformation. *Signs: Journal of Women in Culture and Society, 30*, 2037–2065.

Larner, W. (2000a). Neo-liberalism: Policy, ideology, governmentality. *Studies in Political Economy, 63*, 5–25.

Larner, W. (2000b). Post-welfare state governance: Towards a code of social and family responsibility. *Social Politics, 2*, 243–265.

Lawson, R. (1998). The Ontario legal aid plan in the 90's. *Windsor yearbook of access to justice, 16*, 252–260.

Legal Aid Ontario (LAO). (1999). *Financial eligibility criteria for certificates policies and practices manual*. Toronto: Author.

Legal Aid Ontario (LAO). (2001). *A guide to legal aid ontario for area committee members*. Toronto: Author.

Legal Aid Ontario (LAO). (2002a). *Complaints policy*. Toronto: Author.

Legal Aid Ontario (LAO). (2002b). *Duty counsel manual*. Toronto: Author.

Legal Aid Ontario (LAO). (2002c). *Tariff and billing handbook*. Toronto: Author.

Legal Aid Ontario (LAO). (2003). *Practice manual: Representing claimants before the refugee protection division*. Toronto: Author.

Legal Aid Ontario (LAO). (2005). *2005 annual report*. Toronto: Author.

Legal Aid Ontario (LAO). (2006a). *Area office policy manual*. Toronto: Author.

Legal Aid Ontario (LAO). (2006b). *Business plan 2006–2007*. Toronto: Author.

Legal Aid Ontario (LAO). (2006c). *Quality service office: Annual report 2005–2006*. Toronto: Author.

Legal Aid Ontario (LAO). (n.d.a). Can I get a legal aid certificate? Retrieved April 5, 2006, from http://www.lao.on.ca/en/info/PDF/General_Brochure.pdf

Legal Aid Ontario (LAO). (n.d.b). Criminal law panel standards. Retrieved April 5, 2006, from http://www.lao.on.ca/en/info/panel_standards-criminal_law.asp

Legal Aid Ontario (LAO). (n.d.c). Duty counsel panel standards. Retrieved April 5, 2006, from http://www.lao.on.ca/en/info/panel_standards-duty_counsel.asp

Legal Aid Ontario (LAO). (n.d.d). Family law panel standards. Retrieved April 5, 2006, from http://www.lao.on.ca/en/info/panel_standards-family_law.asp

Legal Aid Ontario (LAO). (n.d.e). Legal aid and you partners in justice. Retrieved April 5, 2006, from http://www.lao.on.ca/en/info/PDF/lao_and_you.pdf

Legal Aid Ontario (LAO). (n.d.f). Notice to lawyers: Post-payment examination. Retrieved on April 5, 2006, from http://www.legalaid.on.ca/en/info/post_payment_examination_notice.asp

Legal Aid Ontario (LAO). (n.d.g). Post-payment examination summary of policies: Failure to respond policy – Random and targeted examinations. Retrieved April 5, 2006, from http://www.lao.on.ca/en/info/post_payment_examination_policies2.asp

Legal Aid Ontario (LAO). (n.d.h). Post-payment examination summary of policies: Post-payment random and targeted examination policy. Retrieved April 5, 2006, from http://www.lao.on.ca/en/info/post_payment_examination_policies1.asp

Legal Aid Ontario (LAO). (n.d.i). Post-payment examination summary of policies: Recovery of over-payment policy. Retrieved April 5, 2006, from http://www.lao.on.ca/en/info/post_payment_examination_policies3.asp

Legal Aid Ontario (LAO). (n.d.j). Post-payment examination summary of policies: Reconsideration/appeal policy. Retrieved April 5, 2006, from http://www.lao.on.ca/en/info/post_payment_examination_policies5.asp

Legal Aid Ontario (LAO). (n.d.k). Quality service principles. Retrieved April 5, 2006, from http://www.legalaid.on.ca/en/about/principles.asp

Legal Aid Ontario (LAO). (n.d.l). Refugee panel standards. Retrieved April 5, 2006, from http://www.lao.on.ca/en/info/panel_standards-refugee.asp

Legal Aid Ontario (LAO). (n.d.m). You and your lawyer. Retrieved April 5, 2006, from http://www.lao.on.ca/en/info/PDF/YYL.pdf

Lightman, E. S., & Riches, G. (2000). From modest rights to commodification in Canada's welfare state. *European Journal of Social Work, 3*, 179–190.

Lippert, R. (1998). Rationalities and refugee resettlement. *Economy and Society, 27*, 380–406.

Lippert, R. (2005). *Sanctuary, sovereignty sacrifice: Canadian sanctuary incidents, power, and law*. Vancouver: UBC Press.

Makin, K. (September 12, 1997). Overhaul legal aid, Ontario told Committee proposes superagency to become an agent for changing the system. *The Globe and Mail*, p. A1.

Ministry of the Attorney General. (1996). *Ontario legal aid review: A blueprint for publicly funded legal services*. Toronto: Queen's Printer for Ontario.

Mittelstaedt, M. (September 15, 1995). Lawyers "reeling" over Tory reversal; "failure to communicate" with law society led to legal-aid crisis, government source says. *The Globe and Mail*, p. A9.

Mossman, M. J. (1993). Gender equality and legal aid services: A research agenda for institutional change. *Sydney Law Review, 15*, 30–58.

Mossman, M. J. (1998). From crisis to reform: Legal aid policy-making in the 1990s. *Windsor yearbook of access to justice, 16*, 261–270.

O'Malley, P. (2001). Genealogy, systematisation and resistance in "advanced liberalism". In: G. Wickham & G. Pavlich (Eds), *Rethinking law, society, and governance: Foucault's bequest* (pp. 13–25). Portland: Hart Publishing.

O'Malley, P. (2002). Globalizing risk? Distinguishing styles of "neo-liberal" criminal justice in Australia and the USA. *Criminal Justice, 2*, 205–222.

O'Malley, P., Weir, L., & Shearing, C. (1997). Governmentality, criticism, politics. *Economy and Society, 26*, 501–517.

Reilly, M. (1988). The origins and development of legal aid in Ontario. *Windsor yearbook of access to justice, 8*, 81–104.

Rose, N. (1999). *Powers of freedom: Reframing political thought*. Cambridge: Cambridge University Press.

Rose, N., & Miller, P. (1992). Political power beyond the state: Problematics of government. *British Journal of Sociology, 43*, 173–205.

Rose, N., O'Malley, P., & Valverde, M. (2006). Governmentality. *Annual Review of Law and Social Sciences, 2*, 1–22.

Sarat, A., & Scheingold, S. (Eds). (1998). Cause lawyering and the reproduction of professional authority: An introduction. In: *Cause lawyering: Political commitments and professional responsibilities* (pp. 3–28). New York: Oxford University Press.

Scheingold, S., & Sarat, A. (2004). *Something to believe in: Politics, professionalism, and cause lawyering*. Stanford: Stanford University Press.

Shdaimah, C. (2006). Intersecting identities: Cause lawyers as legal professionals and social movement actors. In: A. Sarat & S. Scheingold (Eds), *Cause lawyers and social movements* (pp. 220–245). Stanford: Stanford University Press.

Stenson, K. (1999). Crime control, governmentality and sovereignty. In: R. Smandych (Ed.), *Governable places: Readings on governmentality and crime control* (pp. 45–73). Aldershot: Ashgate.

Taman, L. (1976). Legal aid in Ontario: More of the same? *McGill Law Journal, 22,* 369–379.

Thornley, D. (1983). Legal aid Ontario: From rights to charity?. *Social Planning Council of Metropolitan Toronto, 2,* 1–10.

Tsoukalas, S., & Roberts, P. (2002). *Legal aid eligibility and coverage in Canada.* Ottawa: Department of Justice Canada.

Valverde, M. (1998). *Diseases of the will: Alcohol and the dilemmas of freedom.* Cambridge: Cambridge University Press.

Zemans, F. (1978). Legal aid and legal advice in Canada. *Osgoode Hall Law Journal, 16,* 663–693.

Zemans, F., & Monahan, P. (1997). *From crisis to reform: A new legal aid plan for Ontario.* North York: York University Centre for Public Law and Public Policy.

Legal Cases

R. v. Askov [1990] 2 S.C.R. 1199.

CAUSE LAWYERS AS LEGAL INNOVATORS WITH AND AGAINST THE STATE: SYMBIOSIS OR OPPOSITION?

Patricia J. Woods and Scott W. Barclay

ABSTRACT

The traditional and most common conception of cause lawyers has viewed them as necessarily oppositional to the state, leftist, and, at best, transgressive. This conception is significant to our analysis because of its tendency to treat "the state" as a rather singular arena of power – an "it" – rather than a multi-dimensional entity made up of competing institutions and personnel. Following work on the disaggregated and embedded state, we suggest that conflict and competition among state institutions and state personnel allow cause lawyers and state actors to engage in mutually-beneficial action in service of their agendas. Litigation has important benefits for both cause lawyers and state actors: within the arena of law, processes that usually require the backing of large constituencies in the context of majoritarian institutions require, instead, convincing legal arguments. We briefly present evidence from two highly disparate cases of similar processes of interaction among cause lawyers and state actors in Vermont and Israel, which we believe indicates that this type of interaction is far from idiosyncratic.

Studies in Law, Politics, and Society, Volume 45, 203–231
ISSN: 1059-4337/doi:10.1016/S1059-4337(08)45006-8

At its core, the late modern nation-state has sought to portray itself as infinitely powerful: the single legitimate locus of decision-making on a host of issues relating to its society, a unitary, mysterious entity that no individual can know and understand fully (Mitchell, 1988). The nation-state has used both ideological and practical tools in continuing attempts to make itself, in practice as well as image, the most salient rule-maker. These attempts have never been entirely successful; contest, dissent, and opposition have been present to varying degrees (McAdam, Tarrow, & Tilly, 2001; Skocpol, 1979). Nonetheless, nation-states have claimed to be the appropriate decision-making representative for the people, or "the nation," in matters of internal and external security, and a broad array of social and cultural practices, including education, official language, official religions or official secularism (Anderson, 1991; Gellner, 1983; Rhoodie, 1984; Robert, 2003), as well as far more specific practices at work at the local and individual levels, such as marriage and family law (Durkheim in Simpson, 1965, p. 530; Bourdieu, 1987, pp. 846–847; Woods, 2004; Diamant, 2004).

Some of the most powerful ideological claims placing the state at the center of decision-making for society include the claim to the legitimate monopoly of violence (Weber, 1965). This ideological and theoretical support for a state-centered political system has been so successful that it has become naturalized not only in many scholars' understanding of modern politics, but in the popular sphere as well.

> Today the relationship between violence and the state is an especially intimate one. In the past, the most varied institutions … have known the use of physical force to be quite normal. Today, however, we have to say that the state is the human community that (successfully) claims the *monopoloy of the legitimate use of force* within a given territory … . Specifically, at the present time, the right to use force is ascribed to other institutions or to individuals only to the extent to which the state permits it. Hence, "politics" for us means striving to share power or striving to influence the distribution of power, either among states or among groups within a state. (Weber, 1965, p. 1; emphasis in original)

In addition to such ideological efforts, late-modern states have gone to great ends to extend the knowledge and institutional reach of the state through enforced practices. James Scott has eloquently elaborated many of these new practices aimed at culling information to make it easier for a central state to rule (and extract) from afar. A few important examples include requiring the entire population to adopt surnames, systematizing weights and measures, and enforcing new rules of land tenure that would be comprehensible (or legible) to state officials not privy to local knowledge

(Scott, 1998; see also Geertz, 1983). While work in comparative politics for many years drew upon one particular reading of Weber's characterization of the state as gaining its power through the monopoly of violence, work on the state over the past twenty years has challenged that reading. This more recent conceptualization of the state has criticized a neo-Weberian naturalizing of the monopoly of violence as contributing to nothing less than the continued mystification of the state on the part of scholars (Migdal, 1988, 2001; Mitchell, 1988). By contrast, this school of thought, emphasizing the state–society interaction, has conceptualized the state as necessarily embedded in its society for what many would consider proper functioning (Evans, 1995); as made up of multiple actors each with his or her own social ties, personal connections, and interests (Vitalis, 1995); as made up of multiple, often competing institutions with their own agendas, interests, and constraints (Kohli, 1990); and as engaged in an on-going interaction with members of society (Jones Luong, 2003; Woods, 2003). Through inter-actions among institutions, state personnel, and social actors, some have argued that all parties are changed – mutually transformed – both at the institutional and individual levels.

While recent state theorists and others, including those working in the areas of bureaucracy and social movements, have treated the state as made up of many parts and/or individuals, work on cause lawyers has tended to take the state as a given rather than as an object of inquiry in itself. Cause lawyers have been defined as lawyers who work, first and foremost, in support of a cause rather than the client (Dotan, 1998; Scheingold & Bloom, 1998). In so doing, cause lawyers transgress professional norms in most democratic contexts across the world by which lawyers are expected to serve the client without regard to the lawyer's own ideological concerns (Krishnan, 2005; Scheingold & Bloom, 1998). Early understandings of cause lawyers viewed them as inherently oppositional and, at their best, transgressive in their presumably leftist opposition to the state (Abel, 1998; Menkel-Meadow, 1998; Sarat & Scheingold, 1998; Scheingold & Bloom, 1998). These works share a skepticism of state power visible in other works on law and courts, particularly those emphasizing the tendency of courts to entrench existing social and political power relations (Thompson, 1975; Scheingold, 1974), the interests of existing regimes (Ginsburg, 2003; Hirschl, 2004; Shamir, 1990), or the institutional and economic interests of the court as an organization (Blumberg, 1967; Eisenstein, Flemming, & Nardulli, 1999; Nardulli, 1986). While acknowledging these power issues, we argue that cause lawyers and state actors may engage in mutually beneficial interactions in service of their overlapping or complementary agendas. It is precisely conflict and competition among state institutions and individual personnel that create openings for this type of interaction. That is, attention to the disaggregated state allows an opening for scholars to investigate a wider range of possible relations between cause lawyers and state actors than assumed by the oppositional/transgressive model at work in early research on cause lawyering.

A small number of works have begun to address the relationship between cause lawyers and the state as more complex than the traditional view of cause lawyers as inherently oppositional to the state, transgressive, and leftist. Dotan (1998) provides one of the earliest arguments that cause lawyers should not be viewed as inherently oppositional to the state. He presents compelling evidence that cause lawyers and government lawyers in Israel regularly "cross lines" to work for what has usually been understood in the literature as the other side. He argues, based on interviews and observation, that government and cause lawyers share a common normative commitment to a sometimes extravagant notion of the rule of law and a strong judiciary (Dotan, 1998, p. 201), giving them more in common with one another than with their non-lawyering compatriots. Others have argued that right wing cause lawyers should, indeed, be defined as cause lawyers. Southworth has made this argument against a strong tradition of work contenting that they should not (for a discussion of this literature, see Southworth, 2005, p. 85; see also Heinz, Paik, & Southworth, 2003). Hatcher (2005) demonstrates that right wing cause lawyers have held important positions within the Reagan and Bush Sr. administrations as well as within the Federalist Society, complicating the notion that cause lawyers must be separate from or oppositional to the state. These right wing cause lawyers have used what they saw as effective strategies of "progressive lawyering" developed in the civil rights movement and beyond in order to serve conservative causes (Hatcher, 2005, pp. 116–117). Moreover, Hatcher's right wing cause lawyers have sought to draw upon as well as influence the direction of state power in service of their cause: neo-liberal economic reforms. As we discuss in Part III, left wing cause lawyers outside the state in Vermont and Israel have made similar decisions to interact with state officials in service of their agendas. The discussion of the cases in Part III is brief and is taken from more developed case studies published elsewhere (Barclay & Marshall, 2005; Woods, 2005; Woods, 2008). We find similar processes of interaction in these two highly disparate cases, indicating that cause lawyer interactions with state actors in service of common agendas or overlapping interests is far from idiosyncratic. We believe the existence of these similar interactions in extremely different contexts across demographic, cultural, and institutional lines is suggestive of the need for more work in this area.

These works on cause lawyers as working with the state have convincingly suggested important correctives to the more common understanding of cause lawyers discussed above. These works have not, however, attempted to theorize the relationship between cause lawyers and the state with the state at the center of inquiry. Drawing upon work on the state as disaggregated and embedded in society (Migdal, 2001; Evans, 1995), this article begins to address that lacuna with attention to two highly disparate cases of cause lawyer interaction with actors within the state. Because we develop our theory based upon two primary cases, this article is not a conclusive but rather an introductory inquiry suggesting a new and necessary avenue of research on the relationship(s) between lawyers – particularly cause lawyers – and the state.

The traditional conception of cause lawyer–state relations as necessarily oppositional, leftist, and, for some, transgressive is significant to our analysis because of its tendency to treat "the state" as a rather singular arena of power – an "it" – instead of a multi-dimensional entity made up of competing institutions and personnel. The possibility that some institutions and particularly some personnel within the state might ally with cause lawyers and even use state resources to support their causes has been overlooked until recently, we contend, at least in part because of the emphasis on transgressive opposition against "the state." In this approach, "the" (singular, unified) state is almost necessarily assumed to be wielding power in what, by the traditional cause lawyer definition, must be a rightist direction. In particular, lawyer interactions with the state have, at times, been assumed to imply or at least run a great risk of state appropriation (Blumberg, 1967; Cover, 1984; Scheingold, 1974; Shapiro, 1981). While we share the concerns with state power brought to light by a rich critical legal tradition, our goal is to bolster our ability to observe and recognize relationships between cause lawyers and state actors un-clouded by our uneasiness with various manifestations of state power.

SOCIAL MOVEMENT CAUSE LAWYERS AND STATE BUREAUCRATS

Some of the great examples of cause lawyers include lawyers for the NAACP and the ACLU (Sarat & Scheingold, 1998). Indeed, cause lawyers may or may not work for social movements (Barclay & Marshall, 2005; Shamir & Chinski, 1998). In one case that we outline herein, Israel, cause lawyers not only worked for social movements, they were at the forefront of the battles in which the social movement was engaged and appeared to be a significant factor driving the agenda of the movement in that direction. They were also critical in the decision to move to a strategy of litigation or legal mobilization (McCann, 1994; McCann & Silverstein, 1998). In the other case, Vermont, the cause lawyers in question did not initially work for social movements, although their work was conducted in some ways on behalf of social movements (Barclay & Marshall, 2005). Their legal work became a fulcrum around which other work on gay and lesbian rights in Vermont revolved, and they helped to catalyze organizations working in this area. While the social movements in question existed prior to the legal mobilization, in many ways the movements crystallized around litigation, moving in a new direction either in terms of substantive issue areas, methods (e.g., lobbying or litigation), or both. The theory of cause lawyer interaction with the state discussed herein has implications for our understanding of social movements, state bureaucracies, and the intersection between the two. This intersection, we suggest, is one important aspect of state–society relations and one that provides particularly useful opportunities to social movements, via cause lawyers, and to state bureaucrats.

Because social movements are apt to address the state in making demands for policy and other changes, many have linked opportunity structures to changing conditions within the state (Amenta, Dunleav, & Bernstein, 1994; Tarrow, 1994, 1998). For some, these changing conditions center on changing institutional configurations (Amenta & Young, 1999). Tarrow and others have suggested increased attention to the relationship between social movements and the state (Tarrow, 1998; McAdam et al., 2001). Following this literature, we suggest that conditions within the state – such as the centrality of legal argument within the legal arena (Conley & O'Barr, 2005; Epstein & Kobylka, 1991) – provide important opportunities both for social movement and for state actors. However, within the state, rather than majoritarian politics, we focus on state actors in their capacity as bureaucrats, and on the arena of law. The arena of law, we suggest, provides critical opportunities both to social movement cause lawyers and to state actors: in the arena of law, reputation, visibility, and framing of issues are all achieved through convincing legal arguments. Membership numbers and even mobilization of membership to collective action – two factors receiving great, sustained analysis in work on social movements over the last 15 to 20 years – are less important in the legal arena than in the context of majoritarian politics. Convincing legal arguments, in turn, require the legal innovation that cause lawyers are able to provide to interested state actors.

Much work on social movements has focused on mobilization issues with some focusing on mobilization of membership to the organization or movement, and some on mobilization within the membership to collective action (Gamson, 1997; McAdam, McCarthy, & Zald, 1996). This attention is critical given concerns with mass mobilization in the context of electoral and/ or wider majoritarian political processes. Work on social movements has emphasized opportunity structures as critical to social movements' ability to engage in collective action, frame issues, mobilize membership, and sustain themselves over time (Tarrow, 1994). Through collective action, social movements may succeed in framing issues (from Goffman's (1974) concept,) in a way "that will resonate with a population's cultural predispositions and communicate a uniform message to powerholders and others" (Tarrow, 1994, p. 122). This framing is important for mobilization and retention of members, in turn allowing organizations to coordinate capabilities so that they can exist beyond initial protest cycles (Tarrow, 1994, p. 136). The focus on opportunity structures for mobilizing collective action, membership, framing, and movement longevity hinges on concerns with the ability of social movements to attract and retain large enough numbers of members to have legitimacy in the context of majoritarian politics, and to overcome free-rider problems within the movement (Gamson, 1997).

In drawing upon the arena of law, social movement cause lawyers are able to circumvent the need that state actors – both bureaucrats and elected officials alike – usually have to develop broad-based coalitions in support of their agendas. By providing state actors with legal knowledge and legal innovation, social movement cause lawyers provide an opportunity for state actors to move more quickly toward their agendas without the longer process of broad-based coalition building. Popularity and coalitions are less salient in the legal arena than in the arena of majoritarian politics. For social movements engaging in legal mobilization, mobilization of membership numbers and collective action may work in tandem with legal mobilization, or may even become secondary to legal mobilization. While there is reason for caution in choosing the latter route (Scheingold, 1974), many social movements choose to engage in multiple strategies of legal, majoritarian, and grassroots mobilization (McCann & Silverstein, 1998). Nonetheless, legal mobilization is one important strategy that social movements use, making the role of social movement cause lawyers and the legal arena important to our understanding of social movements more broadly.

Framing remains important in the legal arena (see, e.g., Haltom & McCann, 2004). However, within the legal arena, framing of issues, visibility, and legitimacy are, like the politics of legitimacy and issues of reputation addressed in work on bureaucracy (Carpenter, 2001a, 2001b), all produced through convincing legal arguments rather than a movement's membership numbers. It is true that for higher courts, a greater number of cases addressing a similar issue will be important to the court's decision to hear a case (Lawrence, 1991; Rosenberg, 1991). However, it is the salience of an issue in the case law and the convincing nature of legal arguments that are most significant to high court decisions to hear a case rather than membership numbers of a social movement bringing the case (Epstein & Kobylka, 1991). Indeed, long-standing movements may be increasingly successful as repeat players in court not by representing increasing numbers of members over time but, more simply, by their long-standing presence in court (Galanter, 1974).

Thus, for social movements, the decision to move into the legal arena rather than (only) the "majoritarian" arenas of legislative or bureaucratic (executive) politics changes the nature of the game. As social movements enter the legal arena, rather than the issue being numbers and collective action, as are often critical in legislative politics, it becomes convincing and innovative legal arguments (Conley & O'Barr, 2005; Epstein & Kobylka, 1991). As social movements challenge bureaucratic agencies through the arena of law, rather than legitimacy and reputation resting on broad coalitions, as they normally would in bureaucratic politics (Carpenter, 2001, 2001b), again, the key is convincing and innovative legal arguments. The legal arena allows social movement cause lawyers and state actors to circumvent the need for numbers or coalitions by drawing upon the language of the law to develop convincing, innovative legal arguments in service of their agendas. For better or for worse (Bickel, 1986), we suggest that the emphasis on convincing legal arguments within the legal arena in itself provides an important opportunity to both state actors and social movements.

CAUSE LAWYERS AND THE LEGAL ARENA IN STATE THEORY

We integrate the emphasis on institutional configurations and opportunity structures at the heart of much work on social movements with Migdal's analysis of the multiple, and particularly *competing* institutions, practices, and personnel within the state (Migdal, 2001). The institutional emphasis within the legal arena on legal argument, as we have suggested above, provides critical opportunities for social movements and state actors – particularly bureaucrats – alike. Equally important, conflict among institutions, personnel, and the implementation of rules and configurations into conflicting practices is, we suggest, a primary source of opportunities for social movement cause lawyers and state bureaucrats to develop ties aimed at common interests and goals. Cause lawyers, by providing legal innovation and an avenue into the arena of law, give state actors opportunities to pursue their agendas more quickly and directly than would usually be feasible otherwise. The arena of law may allow cause lawyers to enter into relations with state actors without being captured or appropriated, although we note that cause lawyers would be wise to remember the power differential between themselves and bureaucrats working within state institutions.

The notion of the state as relational, embedded, engaged in mutually transformative interaction with members of society suggests an analysis of two important factors that allow a better understanding of cause lawyer interactions with state actors. First, it requires that we disaggregate the state and attend to both its multiple institutions and its personnel. Second, it invites an analysis of the competition, conflict, cooperation, or coexistence among state institutions, as well as the roles of individual personnel, themselves tied to various segments of society. Competition or cooperation among state institutions and personnel may have a significant impact on the opportunities available to cause lawyers to work with (or against) different parts of the state. In short, disaggregating the state and focusing on conflict and competition within it fundamentally changes our understanding of when, how, and against what or whom cause lawyers have acted in opposition, as well as the conditions under which they have fruitfully, symbiotically collaborated with (other) parts of the state.

These conflicting practices among state institutions are important in the current context because the same social and political conflicts that culminate in legal battles and court decisions (Zemans, 1983) can also be the primary catalyst transforming variance in the goals of state institutions into a clash of interests. This crystallization of inter-institutional differences may be compelled as a consequence of the ability of cause lawyers and social movements to exploit existing institutional characteristics. For example, as in the case of civil unions in Vermont and the conflict over religious law in Israel, the institutional characteristics of courts, including their association with the idea of justice and fairness, make them a key site for any social and political conflict that can be expressed in terms of rights claims (e.g., McCann, 1994; Scheingold, 1974; Zemans, 1983). Moreover, cause lawyers in both cases were able to capitalize on fissures either across judicial and executive (religious) agencies (Israel), or among and across executive agencies and other parts of the state (Vermont).

This crystallization of inter-institutional differences may also occur because the demand for increased social status by marginalized groups or the introduction of a new social good may represent a new constituency that can be utilized by current state actors attempting to increase their own power within the competitive state apparatus. The ascendancy of a new social group represents an opportunity by an existing state actor or – via a state actor, an existing state institution – to alter the existing arrangement of social forces in a manner advantageous to his or her own agenda.[1]

Based on this approach to the state, the examples of Vermont and Israel outlined in brief in Part III demonstrate that the space occupied by cause lawyers in relation to state actors must be defined in terms of the specific institutions and state actors with which one is in opposition, *and* those with which one might (at least temporarily) be engaged in joint action. In such cases, rather than being appropriated or captured, cause lawyers act both (symbiotically) with and (oppositionally) against certain state institutions.

PART II: THE VALUE OF CAUSE LAWYERS FOR STATE ACTORS: LEGAL INNOVATION, COMPETING STATE INSTITUTIONS, AND POLITICAL RE-CONFIGURATION

Cause Lawyers as Legal Innovators

As discussed above, the decision to move to the legal arena provides cause lawyers and state actors with important opportunities, particularly the ability to circumvent the need for large social movement numbers or for large coalitions in support of bureaucratic policies. Indeed, it is this ability to provide critical legal innovation in the form of convincing legal arguments that is the primary motivator for state actors to join forces with cause lawyers. Work on cause lawyers has pointed out that certain laws and legal norms may allow state institutions to oppress selected groups for their characteristics or their behavior in ways that institute or perpetuate social inequality and the marginalization of these groups (Abel, 1998; Sarat &

Scheingold, 1998). Such laws, highlighted by cause lawyers as oppressive, contribute to the consolidation of state power and social control. More importantly, some of this work has emphasized that the nature of law facilitates state institutions in justifying the unequal treatment meted out to such groups in a manner that allows their diminished status to become, over a relatively short period of time, unquestioned by the larger society (and often to many of the members of the marginalized group). Social movements develop as the members of these marginalized groups and their supporters challenge the social status accorded to them as either individuals or groups. The explicitly normatively driven job of cause lawyers is, thus, to bring these inequities to light and to change them (Kilwein, 1998).

In order to achieve this goal, cause lawyers engage in a campaign of legal innovation that attempts socially and legally to re-invent the members of the marginalized group in ways that improve their social and legal status. Cause lawyers do so, in part, by directly questioning the fairness of the application of existing laws to individual members of the marginalized group. Yet, many ordinary lawyers, in response to client requests and the prospect of a fee, are willing to bring cases in relation to the unequal application of existing laws.

One factor that distinguishes cause lawyers from most other lawyers is that they go beyond simply challenging the application of existing laws in individual cases. They take existing legal issues faced by the group and theorize them into an abstract legal form to highlight commonalities between the current laws as applied to the marginalized group and historical examples of discrimination and/or injury. They draw upon both concrete historical examples and abstract theoretical notions of fairness and justice, which they assert are compatible with their societies' accepted norms. They do so in order to develop an expansive new framework, both *legal* and *social*, with the goal of empowering the members of the marginalized group. It is this aspect that we define as legal innovation.

Legal innovation has three components. First, cause lawyers exploit contradictions in the existing law to develop new legal definitions or re-define existing legal definitions that can be applied by analogy to the aspects of the law that constrain the members of the marginalized group. These new legal definitions seek to extend accepted legal definitions to incorporate the behavior or activities that underlie that social rejection of this marginalized group. These new legal definitions allow cause lawyers to define the existing laws applied to the members of these groups as discriminatory and as an injury.

Second, as a positive extension of these new legal definitions, cause lawyers conceptualize new rights and create a legal framework explaining how those rights are derived from existing legal principles, statutes, or precedents.

Inherent in these new rights is the implicit drive to rectify the existing inequality suffered by these groups. But, more importantly, the development of new rights entails the construction of a comprehensive legal and social framework that would eventually act to re-assign a marginalized group to a higher social and legal status. As part of constructing this framework, cause lawyers are required to: (1) re-imagine the future legal world in a less discriminatory fashion for the marginalized group; (2) construct the legal and social arguments to justify the creation of that imagined world; and (3) lay out a clear plan for the activity required of the state to move from the current position to the eventual achievement of this goal.

Third, cause lawyers assert these rights in courts, allowing for a reinvention of the community in question in the public eye. This public form of announcement serves several purposes. It signals to the court that the previously unquestioned status of the marginalized group is now identified as a social and legal problem (see, e.g., Zemans, 1983). It does so by highlighting their plight as defined by the new legal definitions and by challenging the categorization of those behaviors and activities that the state has previously sought to demonize by criminalization. It allows the cause lawyers to test the acceptance of their newly developed rights in a judicial, legislative, or sometimes administrative forum. Further, it permits them to construct, over time, the finer points of this framework in a dynamic exchange with the judges and other state actors.

The assertion of rights and a sociological re-conceptualization of the community in question allow cause lawyers to begin the process of re-inventing *publicly* the nature of the activities or behavior of the members of the marginalized group in a way that seeks to increase their social status. The public airing of their new legal and social frameworks is part of the process of creating conditions that will support the changes they seek. The plight of the community in question is highlighted in terms of the legal definitions developed by the cause lawyer. And, ideally, for the cause lawyer, the new social framework will render acceptable those behaviors and activities that the state has previously held as illegitimate (e.g., same-sex marriage, male-only prayer rituals conducted by women at a national holy place, etc.).

Law as the Shared Language

In all of these interactions between cause lawyers and state actors, the law is central – it is the shared language that allows such exchanges to occur.

Cause lawyers speak the same language as the state in a way that social movements related to the cause may not choose to speak (e.g., Smart, 1989). The use of legal language in re-conceptualizing the legal and social status of groups allows the state to engage the ideas associated with the cause without extensive "translation." If cause lawyers can "speak law to power" (Abel, 1998), it is because the state, in exercising power, understands the language of law.

The law exists as both ideas and as rules. As ideas, law allows for debate of principles in the abstract. As rules, it allows cause lawyers and state actors to begin with a common understanding of the rules of interaction and debate. The common language of the law permits the lawyers and the state actors to engage one another using a common language for defining wrongs, understanding social status, and proposing future action. This idea explains why we find cause lawyers interacting with state actors as members of a shared intellectual community as they enter into a dynamic exchange on the legal assumptions and ideas encapsulated in the rights and legal status sought by the newly emerging group.

As part of legal innovation, cause lawyers frame the logical steps necessary to adoption of the new status of formerly marginalized groups in a language that state actors can use to their advantage. Through case analogies drawing on existing groups and appeals to wider social norms embedded in the law, cause lawyers demonstrate how the proposed re-formulation of social relations for the current marginalized group compares to the status of similar social groups already comfortably situated within the existing political configuration. This framing in legal terms with analogies to other groups provides state actors with a simpler justification to offer other state institutions and other power holders (including economic elites) to explain the newly restructured power relations they face in the future after the re-introduction of the newly empowered group.

State actors may engage with cause lawyers to fulfill their own interests and agendas in competition with other state institutions and personnel. Thus, the particular state actors who join forces with cause lawyers may be wholly supportive of the normative agenda of the social movement at least vis-à-vis the specific issue at hand. It is in this sense that cause lawyers and state actors may engage in mutually beneficial interactions that serve one another's goals (those goals may or may not be served entirely equally in each case). At the more abstract, theoretical level, however, cause lawyer interactions with state actors may serve to reinforce precisely the image of the all-powerful, seemingly unitary state that we, following many others, warned against at the onset of this article. Thus, what are in fact mutually beneficial interactions in terms of the specific item on which the cause lawyer and state actor have joined forces, may, through the use of the language of law, serve to perpetuate a myth of (singular, unified, hegemonic) state power and control.

In the abstract, whether consciously or not, the adoption of this framing through legal argument allows state actors to perpetuate the *myth* of hegemonic social control while simultaneously introducing new groups into a re-configured set of power relations. The use of the language of law allows some state actors to advance the notion (which we claim is a myth) that any subsequent changes in social relations is not truly transformative but is rather a natural extension of the application of existing law. Outside of the judicial arena, this idea explains why we find some state actors drawing upon cause lawyers as "experts" at the very moment those state actors are in the process of publicly justifying the transition in the social status of groups.

PART III: CAUSE LAWYER–STATE INTERACTIONS IN THE DISAGGREGATED, EMBEDDED STATE

We draw from two cases of cause lawyer interactions with state actors. The cases, that of the legal debates over gay and lesbian marriage rights in Vermont, and conflict between the secular High Court of Justice and state religious institutions in Israel beginning in 1988, emerge from two highly disparate contexts. We have discussed these cases in detail elsewhere (Barclay & Marshall, 2005; Woods, 2005; Woods, 2008). The fact that similar processes of interaction among cause lawyers and state actors are found in such disparate cases suggests that cause lawyer interactions with state actors is an important area of inquiry worthy of increased attention in work on cause lawyers, state actors (especially bureaucrats), social movements, and state–society relations more broadly.

Vermont is a sub-national state within a federal system with a population of approximately 600,000 at the time of the legal cases in question. Vermont is a highly homogenous state with approximately 75% of the population self-identifying as "white," 12.3% as "black," and 10% falling in other categories (American Indian, Asian, Hawaiian or Pacific Islander, and Other). More than 82% of the population in Vermont speaks only English at home (U.S. Census, 2000). At the state level, Vermont maintains elections at the municipal, county (for county officials as well as state senators), district (for state legislators), and state-wide levels (for governor and several other executive branch officials). It has a single district for national elections. Two to three parties have been predominant in Vermont elections for many years.

By contrast, Israel is a small national state with a heterogeneous population of approximately 4,500,000 in the late 1980s, the time of the cases in question, approximately 82% of whom were Jewish, 16% Arab (Muslim or Christian), and 1.7% other (Druze, etc.) (Israel Central Bureau of Statistics, 1987). The Jewish population was roughly evenly split between Jews of European descent on the one hand, and Jews of Middle Eastern, African, and Asian descent, on the other hand. A highly immigrant population, in the first group, maternal languages included a range of languages from across Eastern and Western Europe. In the second group, the slightly larger group by this time, the most common maternal language for adult immigrants was Arabic. Today, the state's population is approximately 6,300,000 and remains highly heterogeneous with a third distinct segment of population among Jews along cultural and institutional lines, those from the Soviet bloc (Russian, East European, and other Soviet) (Israel Central Bureau of Statistics, 2005). Israel maintains a single district proportional representation electoral system at the national level with municipal elections at the local level but no district executive or legislative offices (there are district courts). From 1977 until the mid-2000s, it was common for up to 33 parties to be represented in the Israeli Knesset, the national parliament, with small religious parties often acting as veto players.

Vermont maintains a clear, legal separation between religion and state whereas Israel includes religious institutions from fourteen officially designated religions as part of the state apparatus (including 14 separate systems of courts, one for each official religion). This factor is salient to both legal issue areas under discussion, gay and lesbian rights in Vermont, and religious freedom and "freedom from religion" in Israel. Both Vermont and Israel had active social movements entrenched and working on the issues in question at the time of the cause lawyer–state interactions that we outline below.

The Vermont Supreme Court is the highest court of appeal within that sub-national state. Under limited conditions, cases may be moved from the state Supreme Court to the federal courts, or to the U.S. Supreme Court. The highest court in Israel has two separate functions with two separate names pertaining; the same justices sit on both courts. The Israel Supreme Court is the highest court of appeal for regular cases that come through the "civil" lower court system. The secular civil court system refers to what we in the U.S. would usually call civil and criminal courts. The Israel High

Court of Justice is the court of first resort for cases involving claims of administrative oversight or abuses of rights against citizens or residents. The High Court also acts as a court of last resort for the three additional subsystems of courts within the judicial system: military, labor, and religious courts. It may be used as court of last resort for the civil court system under certain conditions (particularly involving problems with jurisdiction or rights) (Moaz, 1991). Legal education in Vermont is highly dispersed, with many lawyers attaining their educations out of state. Legal education in Israel is fairly concentrated in two primary law schools. Legal work in large law firms is common in Vermont; it is less common, although growing, in Israel.

These two highly disparate cases share a few factors in common that we believe are significant to cause lawyer interactions with state actors. These include a strong tradition of the rule of law, a functioning democratic electoral system, and state bureaucrats working under conditions that would be expected from the works of Migdal (2001) and Carpenter (2001a). That is, state bureaucrats functioned under conditions of conflict and competition within and among state institutions, as well as among state personnel, and within their offices they worked with a certain degree of freedom from direct oversight of legislative branch or central executive authorities.

The Cases

After a long struggle in the courts, in December 1999, the Vermont Supreme Court decided in *Baker v. State* (170 Vt. 194 (1999)) that depriving same sex couples of the benefits of marriage violated the Common Benefits Clause of the Vermont Constitution. In May 1988 in *Shakdiel v. the Minister of Religion et al.* (H.C. 153/87 P.D. 42(2) 309 (1988) [original in Hebrew]) the Israel High Court of Justice upheld the right of women to be part of local religious councils, which are important administrative agencies overseeing key religious issues within the Israeli state. The legal claims in both cases were initiated by cause lawyers, and their framing of the issues were critical to the courts' subsequent decisions. Cause lawyers in both of these cases used their legal arguments in the courts to bring to the forefront of the public agenda issues over which the society was deeply divided: in Vermont, a battle with national repercussions over the meaning and nature of committed, romantic relationships and marriage; in Israel, a conflict over the role of religion in the state, which has been nothing less than a culture war within both state and society since the late 1980s. At first glance, these cases appear to fit the traditional model of cause lawyers using the access to the state inherent in the legal system and the social influence embodied in the law "to undertake controversial and politically charged activities" (Sarat & Scheingold, 1998, p. 7) on behalf of a socially marginalized group.

Yet, in each of these cases, some of the influence that the cause lawyers exercised occurred outside of the oral arguments and legal briefs offered directly to the court. In both cases, cause lawyers engaged in important interactions with state actors in strategizing regarding their cases. Cause lawyers litigating in favor of marriage rights for gays and lesbians in Vermont, for example, worked in communication with key actors within the administrative and legislative arms of the state for several years in determining the most effective moment to bring the case to the Vermont Supreme Court. In addition, they had ties within the wider legal community in Vermont. As lawyers and repeat players (Galanter, 1974) before Vermont's highest court, they were in a prime position to follow trends on the court, a critical skill in determining when best to bring a case on civil unions. By maintaining contact with a few state actors, these lawyers were able to keep abreast of developments in the relevant administrative offices as well as the legislature.

The cause lawyers in the *Baker* case identified their ties and standing in the Vermont legal community as one key to their ability to achieve legal and political success in relation to same sex marriage in Vermont (Barclay & Marshall, 2005). Further, they had informal ties to the Vermont Supreme Court. Susan Murray, one of the three cause lawyers in the *Baker* case, had clerked in 1983/1984 for an influential justice then on the court before moving into private practice at a major Vermont law firm. These informal ties, along with their involvement in an earlier lesbian and gay rights' case before the court (Adoption of B.L.V.B. and E.L.V.B. 160 Vt. 368 (1993), allowed the cause lawyers to predict a very high likelihood of a positive result[2] in the Vermont Supreme Court long before they initiated the claim in *Baker*.

This expectation of a positive result in the courts altered the cause lawyers' strategy and the timing of their litigation in the *Baker* case. As early as 1995 they were approached to take on a same sex marriage case by clients, but rejected the case on the grounds that did not believe that the political and social environment was ripe for the successful endorsement *by the legislature* of such a case when they were to win the legal case in the courts (Robinson, 2001, p. 241). "Murray and Robinson believed that even before initiating the litigation, they needed to commit resources to an active public relations campaign targeted at both legislators and the public at large to protect any victories in the courts from legislative reversal." (Barclay & Marshall, 2005, p. 180).

In addition, the *ideas* of the cause lawyers in each of the cases were solicited and utilized by state actors beyond the formal setting of the court room and the immediate legal case at hand. Within fewer than two years of the announcement of the *Baker* decision and the introduction of Vermont Civil Union Law (15 V.S.A. § 1204), one of the same cause lawyers who initiated the *Baker* case, Mary Bonauto, was used by a state commission to assess the reception of the Civil Union Law and the related Vermont Supreme Court decision in other states and locations. More interestingly, Mary Bonauto was presented as a *neutral* legal expert on the progress of other same sex marriage litigation occurring outside Vermont that might have impact on Vermont (according to the Minutes of August 7, 2001 meeting of the Vermont Civil Union Review Commission). Her discussion with the State's commission included, among other cases, consideration of the case of *Goodridge v. Public Health* (440 Mass. 309 [2003]). That case was, at that time, progressing though the Massachusetts court system. Her legal expertise on this particular case was assured since Bonauto herself had initiated the case on behalf of seven Massachusetts lesbian and gay couples shortly after her victory in *Baker* and using lessons learned in the Vermont case. Bonauto's claim in *Goodridge* was ultimately successful, subsequent to her remarks to the Vermont state commission. On November 18, 2003, the Massachusetts Supreme Judicial Court held that Massachusetts had violated the state constitution by not issuing marriage licenses to lesbian and gay couples who met all the other criteria of marriage in the state and ordered the state to begin marrying interested same sex couples as of May 17, 2004.

In Vermont, interactions relevant to the issue of the original legal case – gay and lesbian partnership rights in Vermont – continued before, during, and after *Baker* with increasing numbers of Vermont state actors. These varied from informal interactions of long duration with a few supportive state actors to presentations before a wider state commission, which is to say, short-term interactions with larger groups of state politicians and bureaucrats. Interactions before *Baker* centered on the timing and legal strategies best suited to winning the case in Vermont. Subsequent interactions on the same sex marriage included a wider set of issues, including regional legal developments. The history of this case, and the lawyers' involvement in it, has been elaborated in more detail elsewhere (Barclay & Marshall, 2005). The important point for our purposes is the extent of interactions outside of the formal legal sphere, between cause lawyers and state actors, culminating in a (successful) legal case, and continuing cause lawyer input regarding appropriate means to implement the decision at the level of state policy.

Turning to the legal sphere allowed both cause lawyers and state actors interested in some form of legal partnership rights for gay and lesbian couples to circumvent the need for a broad coalition of political support – in the form of mass politics, interest groups, or otherwise cultivated legislative support. In December 1999, the Vermont Supreme Court declared the refusal to allow marriage benefits to gay and lesbian couples was against the Vermont constitution. The legislative solution to that impasse was the establishment of civil unions for gay and lesbian couples, an alternative that surprised many advocates of *Baker* as well as its detractors. (For some detractors, it was seen as a better alternative than full marriage rights.) Thus, while few people were entirely satisfied with the end result, it is clear that a new right was entrenched as a result of cause lawyer legal mobilization, which was assisted greatly by interaction – especially informal interaction – with a few key state actors (Barclay & Marshall, 2005).

In Israel, a different type of interaction – in degree if not in kind – was important. Israel is an excellent illustration of long-term, highly informal contacts, with a socio-professional community that includes justices, legal scholars, government lawyers, clerks, interns, and many cause lawyers. It is through such associations over time that we found one of the most interesting interactions between cause lawyers and state actors. In this shared intellectual community, cause lawyers and state actors engaged in discussions and debates regarding pressing legal issues of the day. Left-wing legal scholars and cause lawyer became part of this intellectual community with justices themselves through mutual social movement activity, particularly regarding civil rights and religious freedom, as early as the 1970s. The debates persisted over decades in the context of social movement activities and workshops, academic conferences, as well as through formal court cases themselves. These interactions were characterized by close physical or communal contact (most living in the same city), and diffuse ties (intellectual and professional acquaintances), not close ties. As Woods has argued elsewhere, new legal norms developed through these debates; some of these new legal norms became binding principles through judicial decisions (Woods, 2005). One key legal norm ("women's equality" joined with administrative legality) first became the basis of cause lawyer briefs and then, ultimately, High Court decisions attacking the institutional autonomy of state religious institutions beginning in the late 1980s.

The mechanism changing a legal norm debated within the judicial community to a binding legal principle within the judiciary typically developed as follows. Because of their involvement in this "judicial community,"[3] cause lawyers knew about trends on the High Court, following judicial signals in formal cases as well as informal, extra-judicial writings, speeches, conference discussions, debates and addresses at social movement events, and the like. Equally as important, due to their participation in the judicial community, justices knew the cause lawyers by reputation. This knowledge of cause lawyer reputation had an important impact, as discussed below, on their initial reception by the justices in court.[4] In addition to informal interactions at conferences and the like, cause lawyers helped to form new legal norms by pushing justices to the logical ends of their own positions on rights through social movement legal mobilization in the form of legal claims formulated by cause lawyers. Some of these were in turn followed by changing legal language on the High Court. At each of these steps, informal as well as formal legal processes were crucial (Woods, 2003). It is important to note that we are not suggesting that cause lawyers are the only lawyers to bring important litigation seeking social and political change. However, they have had an important role in some critical landmark cases and on-going politicized issues that have played out at least in part within the judiciary in both Israel and Vermont.

As a result of judicial signals in both informal and formal contexts, cause lawyers like Frances Raday began a drive of legal mobilization, pushing the High Court, sometimes faster than it would or could move, on issues such as sexual harassment and women's rights in the spheres of labor (beginning in the late 1970s) and religious institutions. By 1986, Raday opened the Legal Department of the Israel Women's Network, which, under her tutelage, developed:

> A policy linking litigation and legislation, using the cases to promote legislation, and ... using the legislation to promote cases. It was actually a good strategy ... . We did have to work hard on it, but things went through fairly easily on all the economic issues. On labor and on the family, and on amending the rape laws, on a whole series of issues [both cases and legislation were successful]. The reforms went through quite easily. We got very good decisions on the High Court on equality for women ... . *It was clear that we had a court that was open to these arguments on rights.* And it was: we got very favorable decisions on issues of rape and violence against women and pay." (emphasis added)[5]

Having achieved success on women's economic rights, cause lawyers attacked an issue even closer to the hearts of many Israelis, the status of religion in the state, an issue the court had studiously avoided for 19 years even while it supported other rights issues. Cause lawyers drew upon new rights' precedents, and used new, innovative legal arguments in the hopes that the court, sensitive to rights issues, would not be able to ignore their arguments. Indeed, in the challenge of religious authorities, the High Court ultimately drew upon the new language of women's equality and used it to undermine the institutional autonomy of state religious authorities in Israel.

Informal membership in the judicial community, as much as formal legal activities, was critical in the process of defining the reputation of cause lawyers with the High Court justices. Cause lawyers' reputations were created through both formal legal activities and their informal membership in the judicial community. A cause lawyer's reputation was likely to influence his or her initial reception from justices in the petition process. As noted by one former clerk for President of the High Court, Aharon Barak:

A: Some groups he [President of the High Court since 1995, Aharon Barak] has a lot of respect for and some groups he has no respect for. So it depends on which groups and individuals bring the case ... . Frances Raday is one [social movement lawyer] he would have respect for because she's a professor at the Hebrew University. She's known to be intelligent, and she brings in [relatively] few cases. So, I certainly think it is relevant who brings the case.

Q: More so than the issue itself?

A: No, both. I think it depends. I mean, I think if there's a movement – for example, the Association for Civil Rights in Israel. It's a very highly regarded body. It's also highly regarded by him [Barak]. So, if the Association for Civil Rights in Israel brings in a petition, it's taken more seriously than if some loony, a left-wing loony brings in a petition.

Q: Like the *X* [I name a group that is considered by many leftist groups in Israel to be a left-wing fringe group]?

A: Yes, exactly. If *X* would go and hang themselves from the trees in the cause of something, so he's [Barak's] not going to take it very seriously. Or if it's a foreign movement or observer, he couldn't care less. But if I it's a serious matter ... I mean ... no, I take back what I said about a foreigner. For example, if there were a serious lobby from the States on religious issues under the umbrella of Yale or Harvard University, some place that matters to him, he would take it a lot more seriously than if there were some lobby from, you know, some group he's never heard of that call themselves – I don't know – Action Freedom, or something. It really does matter.

Q: Do you think that is true of other justices as well?

A: I think it's true of every justice in every country in the world, to a certain extent.[6]

The informal ties through which these new legal norms emerged were cultivated by both justices and cause lawyers. For example, Chaim Cohn, a former President of the High Court, co-founded Council for Freedom of Science, Religion, and Culture in Israel (HEMDAT) in 1983, an organization advocating religious pluralism in a state with a formal state religious bureaucracy. On the other hand, cause lawyers welcomed the opportunity to engage in debates with and around justices at academic and legal conferences, public fora, etc. Deeply committed cause lawyers, as well as deeply committed and consummately independent, intellectual justices, did not direct one another in these debates. No individual was able to control the norms that emerged over years of debate in, for example, crowded conference rooms. While clearly in the less powerful position, cause lawyers were active agents in the creation of these norms, which developed through conflict and debate, rather than predominantly through consensus. These norms were then reinforced in High Court case decisions, in some of which cause lawyers tested the justices on principles justices may have supported, but the legal application of which to specific cases they were often uncomfortable. Thus, the development of these norms, while clearly emerging through a community of un-equals, included the input of cause lawyers, who, with the justices, then became subject to them (Woods, 2008).

As in Vermont, in Israel, interactions between cause lawyers and state actors regarding issues of freedom of and freedom from religion took place before, during, and after the landmark legal cases of 1988 in which the High Court of Justice first successfully undermined the institutional autonomy of state religious institutions. The primary interactions we have discussed here were, by contrast to the Vermont case, within the judiciary itself, although cause lawyers in these and other religion-related cases have also spoken before various Knesset committees throughout the 1990s. In Israel, the most critical interactions with state officials took place in the geographically condensed, socially diffuse, changing normative environment of the judicial community. These interactions took place over very long periods of time – in this case, decades. They involved the development of new legal ideas, which were subsequently translated into legal principles through convincing legal arguments ultimately accepted as such by the High Court. The most important interactions in this case took place informally, outside of the formal legal context. They decidedly did not involve influence peddling or coercion of any kind but rather an organic process of legal norms development within a close-knit (in the sense of seeing one another on a regular basis), diffuse (as acquaintances) community. Key cause lawyers were critical in developing innovative new legal arguments that could be used effectively to curb the power of state religious institutions, in this case, curbing their ability to bar women from religious offices because those offices were "administrative" posts rather than requiring religious training, per se. (For more discussion of these cases and of the judicial community, see Woods, 2005; Woods, 2008.)

Because cause lawyers in Israel turned to the legal sphere, rights-oriented cause lawyers were able to thwart the domination of veto players that had made the Knesset extremely inefficient on any controversial subject since 1977. Thus, they were able to avoid the broad coalition-building needs inherent in the sphere or majoritarian institutions. Since the most effective veto players after 1977 were religious parties (Barzilai, 1998), the ability to get around their influence on issues of religion and state was particularly useful to cause lawyers on the liberal rights side of the battle. Cause lawyers, together with judicial elites who already leaned toward the "freedom from religion," were able to address an issue that had been at impasse because of an inefficient electoral institution. The case of religious-secular conflict in the Israeli legal sphere highlights the extent of inter-institutional conflict that may be present in a state, and the extent to which those conflicts may allow cause lawyers and state actors a fruitful space for interaction on common goals or overlapping interests.

CONCLUSIONS

While all cause lawyers can be identified by their use of the law to compel reluctant parts of the state apparatus to change their current policy toward a marginalized group (e.g., Abel, 1998; Jones, 2005; Menkel-Meadow, 1998; Sarat & Scheingold, 1998; Scheingold, 1998), some cause lawyers may engage in interactions with state actors that occur outside of the traditional boundaries of litigation but are directly related to advancing their cause as cause lawyers. Under girding arguments regarding cause lawyers as inherently at odds with the state there is, at times, an assumption of the state as something of a singular entity of power. We argue, following work on the state, that states are made up of multiple institutions and personnel that exist in frequent conflict and competition with one another. Such moments of conflict or competition provide a space for fruitful (often informal) interaction among cause lawyers and state actors in service of their agendas and/or overlapping interests. The highly disparate cases of Vermont and Israel demonstrate that this type of cause lawyer interaction with state actors is far from an aberration. These cases highlight the importance of further study of this dynamic for work on cause lawyers, state actors (especially bureaucrats), social movements, and state–society relations.

We suggest that cause lawyers and other state actors occasionally work in a symbiotic relationship. By turning to the legal arena, cause lawyers (often working for social movements) and state actors are able to circumvent the needs within the context of majoritarian politics for large coalitions. Within the legal arena, reputation, legitimacy, visibility, and framing are all built through convincing legal arguments. Cause lawyers provide state actors with a path to the legal arena as well as with the innovative legal arguments necessary to frame issues in such a way that courts – and subsequently other state institutions – can present the legal change as having always existed in the law (for a theoretical discussion of this tendency within positive law, see Fitzpatrick, 2001). As such, while cause lawyers and state actors may actually each benefit from interaction with the other without the cause lawyers being "captured," the legal arena may also serve to uphold the very image of the unchanging, powerful, singular state that we have suggested masks significant interactions among cause lawyers and state actors.

NOTES

1. For example, the New York Attorney General's public release of the New York Solicitor General' opinion on the legality of same sex marriages in the state (Halligan, 2004) acted to differentiate the state Attorney General from the other state personnel and garner the support for the actions of his office from the increasingly influential lesbian, gay, bisexual, and transgendered social movement in New York (*New York Times*, March 4, 2004, p. 1, Section A, Column 6). The New York State Comptroller has followed this example with similar recognition of same sex marriages from other states and foreign jurisdictions in direct conflict with other state personnel (*Gay City News,* October 14, 2004).

2. However, while the cause lawyers might have expected a positive result, they certainly never expected to have civil unions rather than same sex marriage as that result (Murray & Robinson Interview, 2002).

3. The interactions within this "judicial community" (Woods, 2003, 2005, 2008) – a select intellectual and legal community centered on the justices of the High Court – were high in frequency, meaning that members see one another on a regular basis. However, they were diffuse in manner, reflecting the "weak ties" (Granovetter, 1983) of acquaintances interacting at proceedings such as academic conferences or social movement events. The judicial community is similar to the court communities discussed in the context of the United States (Nardulli, 1986). The primary differences between the "court community" and the judicial community is that, in the former, norms regarding personal and professional behavior, judicial procedure, and the like, are usually treated as an outgrowth of organizational interests (especially economic interests). These interests are treated as fairly constant. Judicial communities, by contrast, are intellectual communities of legal norms generation in which legal norms develop and continually change through conflict and debate. Thus, judicial communities center on changing ideas, developed through informal interactions among individuals, rather than individual interests and norms being largely determined by organizational interests and incentives.

4. Author personal interview with Israel High Court of Justice Clerk A (April 2000) (clerk in early 1990s); and Israel High Court of Justice Clerk B (clerk in 2000) February 2000. Both requested anonymity.

5. Personal interview, Frances Raday (June 1997), Jerusalem.

6. Interview, CA, April 2000, Israel. It is important to note that the international influences on the Israeli justices became far more important in the 1990s than during the period during which the judicial community was developing, namely, the 1970s and 1980s. The judicial community remains central to judicial processes and especially norms-generation in Israel, even as international influences have become increasingly important in certain legal areas, such as, for example, torture.

ACKNOWLEDGEMENTS

The authors would like to thank the following people who offered substantive feedback on drafts of this article: Herbert Kritzer, Anna-Maria Marshall, Michael W. McCann, Joel S. Migdal, Austin Sarat, Stuart Scheingold, and Benjamin B. Smith.

REFERENCES

Abel, R. (1998). Speaking law to power: Occasions for cause lawyering. In: A. Sarat & S. Scheingold (Eds), *Cause lawyering: Political commitments and professional responsibilities*. New York: Oxford University Press.

Amenta, E., Dunleav, K., & Bernstein, M. (1994). Stolen thunder? Huey Long's share our wealth, political mediation, and the second new deal. *American Sociological Review, 59*, 678–702.

Amenta, E, & Young, P. M. (1999). Democratic states and social movements: Theoretical arguments and hypotheses. *Social Problems, 46*(2), 153–168.

Anderson, B. (1991). *Imagined communities*. New York: Verso.

Barclay, S., & Marshall, A. M. (2005). Supporting a cause, developing a movement, and consolidating a practice: Cause lawyers and sexual orientation litigation in Vermont. In: A. Sarat & S. Scheingold (Eds), *The worlds cause lawyers make*. Palo Alto: Stanford University Press.

Barzilai, G. (1998). Judicial hegemony, polarization of parties, and social change. *Politika, 3*(1998), 31–51.

Bickel, A. (1986). *The least dangerous branch: The supreme court at the bar of politics*. New Haven: Yale University Press.

Blumberg, A. S. (1967). The practice of law as a confidence game: Organizational cooptation of a profession. *Law and Society Review, 1*, 15–39.

Carpenter, D. (2001a). *The forging of bureaucratic autonomy: Reputation, networks, and policy innovation in executive agencies, 1862–1928*. Princeton: Princeton University Press.

Carpenter, D. (2001b). The political foundations of bureaucractic autonomy: A response to kernell. *Studies in American Political Development, 15*(Spring 2001), 113–122.

Conley, J. M., & O'Barr, M. W. (2005). *Just words: Law, language, and power*. Chicago: University of Chicago Press.

Cover, R. (1984). Violence and the word. *Yale Law Journal, 95*(8), 1601–1629.

Diamant, N. J. (2004). Making love 'legible' in China: Politics and society during the enforcement of civil marriage. *Politics and Society, 2004*, 447–480.

Dotan, Y. (1998). Cause lawyers crossing the lines: Patterns of fragmentation and cooperation between state and civil rights lawyers in Israel. *International Journal of the Legal Profession, 5*(2/3), 193–208.

Eisenstein, J., Flemming, R. B., & Nardulli, P. F. (1999). *The contours of justice: Communities and their courts*. New York: University Press of America.

Epstein, L., & Kobylka, J. F. (1991). *The supreme court and legal change: Abortion and the death penalty*. Chapel Hill: University of North Carolina Press.

Evans, P. B. (1995). *Embedded autonomy: States and industrial transformation*. Princeton, NJ: Princeton University Press.

Fitzpatrick, P. (2001). *Modernism and the grounds of law*. Cambridge: Cambridge University Press.

Galanter, M. (1974). Why the "haves" come out ahead: Speculations on the limits of legal change. *Law and Society Review, 9*, 950–997.

Gamson, W. A. (1997). Constructing social protest. In: S. M. Buechler & F. Kurk Cylke, Jr. (Eds), *Social Movements: Perspectives and Issues*. London: Mayfield Publishing Company.

Geertz, C. (1983). *Local knowledge: Further essays in interpretive anthropology*. New York: Basic Books.

Gellner, E. (1983). *Nations and nationalism*. Oxford: Blackwell.

Ginsburg, T. (2003). *Judicial review in new democracies: Constitutional courts in Asian cases*. Cambridge: Cambridge University Press.

Goffman, E. (1974). *Framing analysis: An essay on the organization of experience*. New York: Harper and Row.

Granovetter, M. (1983). The strength of weak ties: A network theory revisited. *Sociological Theory, 1f*, 201–233.

Halligan, C. (March 3, 2004). Opinion of the New York state solicitor general on the legality of same sex marriages in New York state. Issued by the New York State Attorney General's Office.

Haltom, W., & McCann, M. W. (2004). *Distorting the law: Politics, media, and the litigation crisis*. Chicago: University of Chicago Press.

Hatcher, L. (2005). Economic libertarians, property, and institutions: Linking activism, ideas, and identities among property rights advocates. In: A. Sarat & S. Scheingold (Eds), *The worlds cause lawyers make*. Palo Alto: Stanford University Press.

Heinz, J. P., Paik, A., & Southworth, A. (2003). Lawyers for conservative causes: Clients, ideology, and social distance. *Law and Society Review, 37*, 5–50.

Hirschl, R. (2004). *Toward Juristocracy: The Origins and Consequences of the New Institutionalism*. Boston: Harvard University.

Jones, L. C. (2005). Exploring the sources of cause and career correspondence among cause lawyers. In: A. Sarat & S. Scheingold (Eds), *The worlds cause lawyers make*. Palo Alto: Stanford University Press.

Jones Luong, P. (2003). *The transformation of Central Asia: States and societies from Soviet rule to independence.* Ithaca: Cornell University Press.

Kilwein, J. (1998). Still trying: Cause lawyering for the poor and disadvantaged in Pittsburgh, Pennsylvania. In: A. Sarat & S. Scheingold (Eds), *Cause lawyering: Political commitments and professional responsibilities.* New York: Oxford University Press.

Kohli, A. (1990). *Democracy and discontent: India's growing crisis of governability.* New York: Cambridge University Press.

Krishnan, J. (2005). Transgressive cause lawyering in the developing world: The case of India. In: A. Sarat & S. Scheingold (Eds), *The worlds cause lawyers make.* Palo Alto: Stanford University Press.

Lawrence, S. E. (1991). Justice, democracy, litigation, and political participation. *Social Science Quarterly, 72,* 464–477.

McAdam, D., McCarthy, J. D., & Zald, M. N. (Eds). (1996). *Comparative perspectives on social movements: Political opportunities, mobilizing structures, and cultural framings.* New York: Cambridge University Press.

McAdam, D., Tarrow, S., & Tilly, C. (2001). *Dynamics of contention.* New York: Cambridge University Press.

McCann, M. W. (1994). *Rights at work: Pay equity reform and the politics of legal mobilization.* Chicago: University of Chicago Press.

McCann, M. W., & Silverstein, H. (1998). Rethinking laws' allurements': A relational analysis of social movement lawyers in the United States. In: A. Sarat & S. Scheingold (Eds), *Cause lawyering: Political commitments and professional responsibilities.* New York: Oxford University Press.

Menkel-Meadow, C. (1998). The causes of cause lawyering: Toward an understanding of the motivation and commitment of social justice lawyers. In: A. Sarat & S. Scheingold (Eds), *Cause lawyering: Political commitments and professional responsibilities.* New York: Oxford University Press.

Migdal, J. S. (1988). *Strong societies and weak states: State-society relations and state capabilities in the third world.* Princeton, NJ: Princeton University Press.

Migdal, J. S. (2001). *State in society: Studying how states and societies transform and constitute one another.* Cambridge: Cambridge University Press.

Mitchell, T. (1988). The limits of the state: Beyond statist approaches and their critics. *American Political Science Review, 85,* 77–96.

Moaz, A. (1991). Enforcement of religious courts' judgments under Israeli law. *Journal of Church and State, 33*(3), 473–494.

Nardulli, P. F. (1986). "Insider" justice: Defense attorneys and the handling of felony cases. *Journal of Criminal Law and Criminology, 77*(2), 379–417.

Rhoodie, E. (1984). *Discrimination in the constitutions of the world.* Columbus, GA: Brentwood.

Robert, J. (2003). Religious liberty and French secularism. *2003 Brigham Young University Law Review, 637.*

Rosenberg, G. (1991). *The hollow hope.* Chicago: University of Chicago Press.

Sarat, A., & Scheingold, S. (1998). Cause lawyering and the reproduction of professional authority: An introduction. In: A. Sarat & S. Scheingold (Eds), *Cause lawyering: Political commitments and professional responsibilities.* New York: Oxford University Press.

Scheingold, S. (1974). *The politics of rights: Lawyers, public policy and political change.* New Haven: Yale University Press.

Scheingold, S. (1998). The struggle to politicize legal practice: A case study of left-activist lawyering in Seattle. In: A. Sarat & S. Scheingold (Eds), *Cause lawyering: Political commitments and professional responsibilities.* New York: Oxford University Press.

Scheingold, S., & Bloom, A. (1998). Transgressive cause lawyering: Practice sites and the politicization of the professional. *International Journal of the Legal Profession, 5,* 209–253.

Scott, J. C. (1998). *Seeing like a state: How certain schemes to improve the human condition have failed.* New Haven: Yale University Press.

Shamir, R. (1990). "Landmark cases" and the reproduction of legitimacy: The case of Israel's high court of justice. *Law and Society Review, 24,* 781–805.

Shamir, R., & Chinski, S. (1998). Destruction of houses and construction of a cause: Lawyers and bedouins in the Israeli courts. In: A. Sarat & S. Scheingold (Eds), *Cause lawyering: Political commitments and professional responsibilities.* New York: Oxford University Press.

Shapiro, M. (1981). *Courts: A comparative political analysis.* Chicago: University of Chicago Press.

Simpson, G. (1965). A Durkheim fragment. *The American Journal of Sociology, 70*(5), 527–536.

Skocpol, T. (1979). *States and social revolutions: A comparative analysis of France, Russia, and China.* New York: Cambridge University Press.

Smart, C. (1989). *Feminism and the power of the law.* London: Routledge.

Southworth, A. (2005). Professional identities and political commitment among lawyers for conservative causes. In: A. Sarat & S. Scheingold (Eds), *The worlds cause lawyers make.* Palo Alto: Stanford University Press.

Tarrow, S. (1994). *Power in movement: Social movements, collective action and politics.* New York: Cambridge University Press.

Tarrow, S. (1998). *Power in movement: Social movements and contentious politics.* New York: Cambridge University Press.

Thompson, E. P. (1975). Whigs and hunters: The origins of the Black Act. London: Peregrine Books.

Vitalis, R. (1995). *When capitalists collide: Business conflict and the end of empire in Egypt.* Berkeley, CA: University of California Press.

Weber, M. (1965). *Politics as vocation.* Philadelphia, PA: Fortress Press.

Woods, P. J. (2003). Legal norms and political change in Israel. *Droit et Société, 55,* 3.

Woods, P. J. (2004). Gender and the reproduction and maintenance of group boundaries: Why the "secular" state matters to religious authorities in Israel. In: J. S. Migdal (Ed.), *Boundaries and belonging: States and societies in the struggle to shape identities and local practices.* Cambridge: Cambridge University Press.

Woods, P. J. (2005). Cause lawyers and judicial community in Israel: Legal change in a diffuse, normative community. In: A. Sarat & S. Scheingold (Eds), *The worlds cause lawyers make.* Palo Alto: Stanford University Press.

Woods, P. J. (2008). Judicial power and national politics: Courts, gender, and the religious-secular conflict in Israel. Albany, NY: SUNY Press.

Zemans, F. Z. (1983). Legal mobilization: The neglected role of the law in the political system. *American Political Science Review, 77,* 690–702.

Court Cases Cited:

H.C. 153/87 *Shakdiel v. the Minister of Religion* et al. P.D. 42(2) 309 (1988) (Hebrew).
Adoption of B.L.V.B. and E.L.V.B. 160 Vt. 368 (1993).
Baker v. State 170 Vt. 194 (1999).

Israel Personal Interviews:

Frances Raday, June 1997, Jerusalem.
High Court Clerk A (anonymous), April 2000, Israel.

PART III:
NEW PERSPECTIVES IN LEGAL DOCTRINE

IGNORED NO LONGER: CONTRIBUTIONS OF THE LAW OF AGENCY TO PRINCIPAL-AGENCY THEORY AND CONGRESSIONAL LEADERSHIP

William J. Phelan, IV[1]

ABSTRACT

Principal-agency theory was adapted from business and economics to explain the behavior of various government actors. Yet the idea of an agent and a principal is only depicted in a limited fashion when discussed in light of the realm of business and economics. Legal studies has grappled with the idea of agency well before political science or economics. I lay out the basic principles of both agency law and Congressional principal-agent theory. I then establish the groundwork for drawing important connections between agency law and principal-agency theory. I also analyze and attempt to ameliorate differences between these two theoretical approaches.

As seen throughout history, particularly that of western civilization, a frequent cloak dictators and depots dress themselves in is that they are

Studies in Law, Politics, and Society, Volume 45, 235–254
Copyright © 2008 by Emerald Group Publishing Limited
All rights of reproduction in any form reserved
ISSN: 1059-4337/doi:10.1016/S1059-4337(08)45007-X

operating for such intangibles as "the crown" or a deity. All along, most of these leaders probably knew they were acting on their own behalf; claiming to act for some common good was simply an attempt at pacifying the masses. This tactic had some merit: revolutions aside, people were usually hesitant to topple a leader who was supposedly put in place and acting on behalf of, for example, God. Yet it was not till after the Enlightenment and the creation of the democratic republic known as the United States of America that a leader could truly understand and claim to be working on behalf of the people. The representational government found in the U.S. Congress is an excellent case in point. The members of Congress are proportionally elected by their constituents to become leaders in Washington, DC and represent them in a collective, deliberative body. Further, within this legislative body, there are the leaders of these leaders. Over the years, both the United States Senate (2007) and the United States House of Representatives (2007) have developed unique leadership structures that enabled the chambers to carry out business.

The manner in which the leadership structure of Congress has developed was, in part, controlled by the attitudes of those who filled the leadership positions. Speaker Joe Cannon, for example, made sure to advance rules that helped keep his tight grip on the speakership and Rules Committee. Such a course of action was a result of a desire to use the speakership as a source of power to dominate the House. Yet early in the development of Congressional leadership, Henry Clay had a different view on being elected Speaker.

> Gentlemen. In coming to the station which you have done me the honor to assign me – an honor for which you will be pleased to accept my thanks – I obey rather your commands than my own inclinations ... Should the rare and delicate occasion present itself when your speaker should be called upon to check or control the wanderings or intemperance in debate, your justice will, I hope, ascribe to his interposition the motives only of public good and a regard of the dignity of the house. (Shepsle & Bonchek, 1997, p. 382)

Whether Clay actually was an agent for his House is not important; Clay raises an early attitude found in Congressional leadership that can also be seen today: the leader is an agent of the body that selected him. Clay wanted the members to know that they were the ones principally in charge. He was merely an agent/leader present to carry out their will.

The idea of being one's agent is not novel. In fact, concepts of the agency/principal relationship predate Clay's notion by millennia. Currently, several in the academic community have taken Clay's sentiments and attempted to formalize this principal-agent theory (P-A theory) in the field of political theory. Yet long before political scientists and economists focused on P-A theory as a method to explain leadership, the idea of agency was utilized by, inter alia, religion, the Roman Empire and the courts of chancery in England. The best discipline to look for these early uses of agency is the law. The field of agency law is the best path to follow the development of the interaction between principals and their agents because this topic was integral in the formation and sustainment of both ancient and modern civilizations. Simply put, people, in any society, can never personally carryout every act necessary to exist. Whether it was a Roman son to make sure his father's villa and slaves were properly handled upon his death or a Benedictine monk overseeing the acres of land for his order, agency law was frequently present in the daily operations of the history of the world.

Thus, with this history of agency law, this author was curious as to why the political scientists who wrote on the topic of P-A theory never made reference to the common law notion of agency in their discussions. Such an occurrence is particularly unusual considering how P-A theory is used not only in the field discussed here, Congressional leadership, but also other aspects of political science (Magleb, Patterson, & Thurber, 2002; Rush, 1993). To date, the existence of any published material on the relevance, differences, or similarities of agency law to P-A theory is not present, despite (as shall be shown) the obvious correlations between the two areas of study. This chapter gives groundwork for such a discussion, specifically in the context of P-A theory and Congressional leadership. First, the basic concepts and history of agency law are explained. This explanation will include the ancient roots of agency law up until its use in modern-day corporation law. Then there is discussion about the concepts of agency law as it stands today in the American legal system. Section 2 discusses the tenants of P-A theory. First, the origins of P-A theory, vis–à-vis economic theory, is put forth. A restatement of P-A theory is given, specifically as it is applied to the leadership of the U.S. Congress. Section 3 takes up the similarities between P-A theory and agency law. It is shown that there are aspects of agency law that can easily be imported into P-A theory. These similarities can actually help further explain P-A theory. Section 4 handles the differences between P-A theory and agency law. The impact of these differences on P-A theory, as a method to explain Congressional leadership, is analyzed. Finally, Section 5, the conclusion, shows that the likenesses between agency law and P-A theory are beneficial to political science and should be promptly incorporated into this field of theory.

1. THE LAW OF AGENCY

1.1. Historical Development of Agency Law

It is important to have an understanding of the historical development of agency/trust law in order to put P-A theory into context; because P-A theory comes from agency law, it is only proper to fully discover the theory's true roots. Those, specifically Terry Moe (1984), who have written on P-A theory do correctly trace its initial roots to economic literature and the way economists characterize business organizations, however, more of a history is necessary. As will be seen below, the organizational structures concerning the business fiduciary relationship draw their concepts from the development of the law and the legal system. Corporations could not exist if it were not for agency law. By explaining the historical development of agency law, the applicable concepts of agency law to P-A theory can be understood better. It is one thing to note that P-A theory comes from the neo-classical view of business structures, but more justice is done to P-A theory when the deeper roots are exposed and an awareness of the relevant history is developed. Professor of Law, Mary Szto (2004), provides an excellent summation of the history of agency and trust law that will be used here.

Going back to the beginning of the Judeo-Christian religion, we can find evidence of a relationship between the principal and the agent. When looking at the Genesis story, it is quite clear that Adam and Eve were agents of God; Yahweh created the world and then entrusted its care to the first man and woman. Additionally, Jesus Christ is seen as an agent by those of the Christian faith. In fact, he is the perfect agent because he sacrificed himself in order to serve the purpose of his principal (God): to bring life everlasting to the human race (Szto, 2004). These examples show how the agency relationship is older than some may think. These observations on the Old and New Testaments were certainly not made by those at the time but are rather reflections made by those living after agency/trust law's initial formal development. Such reflections may merely be a noble attempt to apply agency theory to important historical and religious events post hoc.

Moving away from the creation story and into more concrete history, the Roman Empire contributed much to the idea of agency law. The idea of an agent came about through property law: when a Roman citizen died, he left a *fideicommissio*, or trust, to a *fiduciarius*, or heir. The testator typically gave his trust to a legal beneficiary who then made sure the heir received the trust, or legacy. This temporary legal beneficiary was an agent acting on behalf of the recently deceased. The *fideicommissio*, and these related entities were "the seeds of agency, partnership and corporate law" (Szto, 2004).

The Roman Catholic Church, after the decline of the Roman Empire, adopted concepts of the *fideicommissio*. Due to the fact that the religious of the Church were not allowed to own property, because of their vows of poverty and the like, Church law needed to create a legal fiction that would enable these clerics to have legal authority over the increasing amount of land owned by the Church. The fiction that was created was the *utilitas ecclesiae*, or the ecclesiastical use. Basically, the *utilitas ecclesiae* allowed the religious to have stewardship over Church land, not actual ownership. It was believed that physical goods, such as buildings, cattle, or wagons, were to be used "spiritually" by those who watched over them for the Church. In the 12th century, the Franciscan order began to popularize the *utilitas ecclesiae*. Due to their extreme and well-known vow of poverty, the religious concept of a use was combined with the secular and legal concept of the use. This spiritual concept of agency law was also paralleled at the time by Frank Salic law which had a Salman or Treuhand act as an agent "to receive property from a grantor on behalf of beneficiaries" (Szto, 2004, pp. 93–94).

In the 15th century, the Catholic Church in England began to hand over its control of the development of uses and trusts to the courts of chancery. The chancery courts developed the idea of the use into the trust. This idea of a trust is similar to the modern concept of a trust whereby the trustee has legal control over trust property while having a fiduciary relationship with the beneficiary. The idea of a trust, therefore, has a theological origin and only highlights the sacredness of a fiduciary relationship. The framework for agency law, partnership law, and corporate law was rooted in the sacrality of fiduciary duties found in the English common law concepts of uses and trusts (Szto, 2004, p. 98).

In the present day, it is agency law that defines a vast portion of corporate law. Therefore, any theories dealing with corporations and their organization can be directly traced back to agency law and the fiduciary relationship. Even though agency is typically viewed today as a relatively small topic in the field of corporate law, its earlier non-commercial roots must be acknowledged. Agency law does not have to be confined to discussions of corporations law. For instance, the point has been made that the Necessary and Proper Clause of the U.S. Constitution would not have come about if it were not for the concepts developed in agency law (Natelson, 2004).

1.2. Basic Principles of Agency Law

After all of this historical development, agency law in America has several commonly acknowledged tenants. A guiding work on agency law is The Restatement of Agency (Third) (2005) that is published by the American Law Institute (2006).[2] In that restatement, agency is defined as

> the fiduciary relationship that arises when one person (a "principal") manifests assent to another person (an "agent") that the agent shall act on the principal's behalf and subject to the principal's control, and the agent manifests assent or otherwise consents so to act. (§ 1.01)

There are a few aspects of this definition that are important to note. First, there needs to be consent between the principal and the agent. Both parties must be aware of the fact that they are entering into this legal relationship; one party can not fool the other into thinking there is no agency relationship when there really is, and vice versa. Additionally, omission is not allowed. One can not assume, for example, that silence after a request to have an agency relationship is a construction of the actual relationship. Second, there must be control by the principal over the agent. For the most part, the principal must have ultimate authority over what the agent does. It must appear that the principal is always in charge. Further, just because someone can control another does not mean that there is an agency situation. The principal needs to have a *right* to control the agent. Simply because Joseph Stalin controlled the peasant's action through fear of being sent to the gulag, does not mean that the peasant was an agent of Stalin when he stole the loaf of bread. This is especially true considering that Stalin did not care (much less know) whether a peasant stole some bread. Third, the agent is to act on *behalf of* the principal. Simply put, an agent, when acting as an agent, can not act for his own interests; he must act *primarily* in order to advance the interests of his principal (Hynes, 2001). The Stalin example just given is applicable here too: the peasant, when stealing the bread, was certainly not doing it for Stalin. He stole the bread for himself so he would not starve to death; therefore, the peasant is not an agent of Stalin because he was primarily acting on behalf of himself, not Stalin. Finally, it is important to point out that the agent, through the Restatement definition, is specifically considered a fiduciary. The relationship as a whole is considered fiduciary (adjective), or to have the qualities of a relationship based on trust; but only the agent can be the fiduciary (noun), or the "one who acts primarily for the benefit of another" (Gregory, 2001, p. 13). With this tag, the agent has certain responsibilities that have been developed under common law which will be discussed below.

Before moving on to the rights and duties of the agent and the principal, the law has created a specific type of agent that is relevant to the topic at hand: a gratuitous agent. Unlike a relationship established by a contract, an agency relationship does not need something of value for both parties to receive (commonly known as consideration in contract law). An agent can be considered a gratuitous agent and does not have to receive anything in return from the principal (Gregory, 2001). For the most part, a gratuitous agent is treated like an agent who does not receive consideration.

1.3. Duties among the Agent and Principal

According to common law, the most important duty of the agent to the principal is probably that of loyalty. This duty is drawn from the role of the agent as a fiduciary. An agent, because he has the ability to affect the legal rights and decisions of his principal by acting on his behalf, must give his allegiance only to that principal. No other entity or person can interfere with this loyalty. The agent must also be sure to keep "the principal's interest foremost in mind when acting on the matter entrusted to him" (Hynes, 2001). Loyalty is often referred to as the hallmark of one's agent status (Kleinberger, 2002, p. 117). Such an importance on loyalty is present due to the development of agency law as a sacred trust. From this duty of loyalty stem other obligations. An agent must conform to ideas of good conduct and obedience. When the agent is acting on behalf of the principal, he can also reflect the principal. He must therefore present a reputable image of his principal. Related to this is the duty of the agent to obey instructions. Obviously, an agent can not be controlled by the principal if he does not listen to the principal's orders. To be faithful, an agent must also fully disclose all relevant facts to the matter at hand.

There is also an important duty that the courts have implied in the agent–principal relationship. The agent must act with skill and diligence when attempting to attain the goals of the principal. It is believed that because the agency relationship exists, both parties must expect that the actions taken are to be done with care, and perhaps even zeal. If an agent is accused of violating this implied expectation, then the court will hold the agent to a standard of ordinary care. This standard holds that the agent should have performed at a level on par with most others in that particular field.[3] Yet a gratuitous agent is held to a significantly lower standard, that of gross negligence. Basically, a gratuitous agent is culpable for gross negligence if his actions amounted to an almost intentional disregard for performing properly.

On the other end, the principal is also assigned various duties, a few of which will be discussed here. When an agent performs, it is expected that the principal compensate (i.e., pay) and/or indemnify (i.e., reimburse) the agent for his work. The law usually talks of monetary reimbursement; however, especially if the agent is gratuitous, compensation/indemnification can be given in other forms. The principal also has his own implied duty to deal fairly and in good faith with the agent. This duty is quite broad, yet is similar to an agent's duty not to harm the reputation of the principal (Hynes, 2001).

A final and important aspect of agency law concerns the interaction between both the agent and the principal. It is somewhat related to the idea of control-in-fact versus the right to control discussed earlier. As already mentioned, authority needs to be established as something the principal has as a *right* to use over the agent. Furthermore, it is this authority/right that is necessary for actual *power* to be exerted over the agent. The law has distinguished several types of authority which then give the agent the power to act for the principal. Several relevant forms will be discussed here.

The first type of authority given to the agent is express authority (also referred to as real or actual authority). This is the bluntest manner in which to create an agency relationship: the principal clearly manifests his will that the agent is to act on his behalf. In turn, the agent is to be able to reasonably interpret that manifestation so that he believes he is able to act on behalf of the principal.

There is also implied authority which can arise from the circumstances. Sometimes the situation will create authority for an agent by implication. Custom and past conduct of the parties involved are relevant factors in the determination of implied authority. This authority is not explicitly mentioned by the principal when giving an assignment, but the agent requires such authority to complete the task.

Finally, authority can retroactively be granted from the principal to the agent. This type of authority is known in the law as ratification. If the agent did not have power at the time he bound the principal, the principal can later condone such an action, thus giving it full legal binding force. The principal can ratify an unauthorized action either implicitly, through his conduct, or by failing to object. These various classifications of an agency relationship are not an exhaustive listing; there are other types of power in agency law that are not relevant to our discussion here.

2. BASICS OF PRINCIPAL-AGENT THEORY

With the historical and basic concepts of agency law now before us, it is evident that the origins of economic theory regarding business partnerships and organization come from the field of agency law. If it were not for the developments outlined above, P-A theory may not have been created.

2.1. Principals and Agents: From Economic Theory to Political Science

Professor Terry Moe of Stanford University is credited with importing P-A theory into the realm of political science. Until his piece, "The New Economics of Organization" in 1984, no political scientist had looked at P-A theory. Although Moe did not directly apply P-A theory to Congressional leadership, his effort was a broad analysis of P-A theory in connection with any type of organizational relationship in the field of government. He gives an excellent synopsis of the development of economic theory, which will now be briefly covered.

As discussed by Moe (1984), in the early 1970s, the economic academic community was beginning to move away from the rational individual and group based decision making process of neoclassical economics into the "new economics of organization." Such a view related to the operation of the corporate firm. The British economist Ronald Coase helped this diversion by looking at the internal operations of the firm. He claimed that a business has a fiduciary relationship between the entrepreneur (or leader) and the agent. The American, Herbert Simon, along similar lines, analyzed Coase's idea of a one-on-one interaction between the entrepreneur and agent. Simon believed that business decisions are made not via the neoclassical rational choice paradigm, but rather what one individual thinks is best. When dealing with agents, the leader can program them to better serve the organization. From the ideas of Coase and Simon, it was stated that business decisions were not made by rational group calculi, but instead through the behavior of a coalition. Organizational members utilize these coalitions to change the goals, which in turn change the behavior of the leadership. Moe points out that all of this new theory can apply to other organizations besides corporations.

Conveniently, Moe (1984) applies this theory to the field of political science. He outlines various problems and advantages of P-A theory, in general, which will not be covered here. Moe also applies P-A theory to the public bureaucracy. He makes the claim that the people are the principal, and the politicians are the agents of the people. He points out that the politicians then create bureaucracies. It is only logical for politicians to create these bureaus so that they may carry out the will of their principal, the people. Moe (1984) concludes by saying that the key to integrating P-A theory into political theory is to focus on P-A theory's ideas on hierarchical control. This focus on hierarchical control is stressed by Moe when talking about "both the bureaucratic and the political dimensions of administrative performance". It was not until 1987 that the concepts incorporated by Moe were applied to Congress and its leaders (Rohde & Shepsle, 1987) and it was from that point forward that the political science community began to advance a theory that Congressional leaders are agents of the party which they lead.

2.2. Principal-Agent Theory and Congressional Leadership

The Congressional slant of P-A theory begins on an important premise: "that leaders must secure the support, if not the cooperation, of their followers" (Shepsle & Bonchek, 1997). An agent/leader can not properly guide the flock if that flock does not support him. Although this point may seem moot, because in the case of Congress the principal actually elects the agent, a leader can fall out of grace with the membership just as easy as he rose to power.[4] This light P-A theory placed on the image of a leader may actually buck preconceived notions as to how a leader should operate. Typically, a leader is seen as one who is "above the fray" with a sizable amount of power that can be utilized to keep people below him in line. Yet when it is understood that a leader is simply an agent, it can be observed that the power is actually used to appease those followers who put him in that position. Whether a Congressional leader is the Speaker of the House or just a regional whip, the principal-membership must support him if they are going to follow, let alone select him as a leader in the first place.

In order to be selected as a leader, there are some qualifications. First, the candidate must have a good reputation. A respected reputation serves as a bond the membership can identify with in order to trust the leader. Also, the intentions of the candidate must be proper. The actual intentions of a potential agent must be aligned with what a majority of the body wants so the agent, when later given authority to act on behalf of the principal, does not override or ignore the will of the principal. Contrary to ordinary opinion, the actual capabilities of the leader are secondary to the intentions of the candidate-agent (Shepsle & Bonchek, 1997).

Once elected, a Congressional leader must satisfy the expectations of the party (his applicable section of the membership) to remain in power. Generally, the main expectation is that the leader is to set and control the agenda for the party (Shepsle & Bonchek, 1997). The agenda may change as the party-principal alters its viewpoints, as a collective. The reason why expectations of the party-principal are so important to the leader-agent is because the party, as a whole with many individuals, proposes a collective action dilemma for the leader. Due to the fact that a party is made up of numerous members, all with their unique demands, it is difficult for a party to act with one voice; yet when a general consensus is reached, although not rare, a leader needs to take advantage of that consensus and make sure it is enacted upon (Sinclair, 1999). When the agent-leader is put in place, the consensus' decision must not be derailed by any political entity.[5] Some political scientists have noted that the agent-leader of the majority party is like a "senior partner" who makes sure the party's collective agenda does not get rolled (Cox & McCubbins, 1993).

3. CONTRIBUTIONS FROM AGENCY LAW TO PRINCIPAL-AGENCY THEORY

Due to the roots of P-A theory in agency law, it is perplexing why political scientists have never turned towards agency law to help support P-A theory; the roots of P-A theory have only been traced to economic theory from the mid-20th century. More can be taken from agency law to show that P-A theory is well-grounded and applicable to the way leadership in Congress works.

The first major area that can apply to P-A theory is the creation of the agency relationship. Once an agent-leader is elected or appointed to his position, it must first be noted who actually controls him. Especially in the House, there are large populations in each party. To whom does the agent listen? A majority? A plurality? The base of the party? Agency law states that an agent is under the control of the majority of those who make up the principal; or if there is disagreement among the principal, the agent may also listen to those who favor the status quo (Gregory, 2001). The first option is applicable to P-A theory. Under P-A theory, an agent needs to follow the majority to help solve the collective action dilemma. It is in the interest of the agent-leader to listen to the majority if he wishes to attain enough votes for reelection or not run the risk of being removed from office. The second option for listening to the principal may be applicable. A recent example is the Democratic position to the war in Iraq. The Democratic Party is obviously not in agreement as to how to practically approach the issue. There are those within the Democratic Party who want immediate troop withdrawal from Iraq while most others who want a structured redeployment/withdrawal. The latter position, as seen in the results of the 2006 mid-term elections, is more in line with the American people. It appears that the leadership of the party is reaming with the status quo: the party stance is that immediate troop withdrawal is not currently an option, but rather there should be a redeployment timeline (Office of Steny Hoyer, 2007). In politics, it would make sense for an agent-leader to stay with the status quo, barring any strong and abrupt mood change in the American public. Parties typically like to pick a position based on their ideals and not waiver, for any change in a party position may, for example, put themselves in line with the opposing party's viewpoints or portray them as "flip-flopping" on the issue.

The rationale for the creation of the agency relationship is the same as the rationale found in P-A theory. P-A theory posits that there is much work to be done by Congress. Due to this fact, the members need one of their own to organize the party and the chamber in order to complete the various tasks entrusted to Congress (Sinclair, 1999). The rationale for one to attain an agent is the same. Taking the business world as an example, there is much a board of directors needs to accomplish for the company to function. By hiring a CEO or CFO, the board delegates authority to the officers in order to carry out the operational and financial duties of the organization. Expertise is also another reason for the creation of an agency relationship. The majority of Americans do not know how to create a will that can be legally executable. Therefore, a lawyer is hired as an agent to translate the principal's wishes into a legally recognizable document. Agent-leaders in Congress are also chosen for their unique ability to move bills through the legislative process both effectively and efficiently. These striking similarities not only further solidify the contention that P-A theory comes from concepts of agency law, but also illuminates the reality of the modern world: sometimes tasks (whether in the halls of Congress or the boardroom) require delegation in order to have them completed more thoroughly and efficiently.

Agency law provides an excellent label that can be used for most Congressional agent-leaders. There are a few classifications of agents, namely a general agent and a specialized agent. A general agent is used

> to conduct a series of transactions involving continuity of service ... [and] has authority to transact all of the business of the principal. (Gregory, 2001, p. 17)

Conversely, a special agent is used for a single instance that does not involve continuity of service. Most Congressional leaders can be seen as general agents: they are elected to make sure that the basic purpose for which members are in Congress (passing legislation) is completed. Entrepreneurial leaders, on the other hand, may be best described as special agents. Senator John McCain was not elected as a Senate leader, but his expertise on campaign finance reform certainly allowed the Republicans to create a sort of fiduciary relationship with him, thus giving Senator McCain authority to form the basis of a campaign finance reform bill with Senator Russ Feingold.

After a relationship is created, there are issues concerning the authority given to the agent. Out of the types of authority outlined above, it appears that implied authority is derived by the agent-leader from the leader's position and Congressional norms. An agent can have implied authority that is not explicitly granted to him if custom dictates that the authority for certain tasks are required for completion. This type of authority is quite evident with Congress. After a leader is elected, the members do not contact the leader and tell him exactly what needs to be done and in what fashion; rather, the coalition typically tells the leader what the goals are and the agent-leader is to make sure those goals are met. It would be quite absurd, for instance, to have the leader go to the principal and ask them for permission each time he wishes to hold a press conference on a bill. Instead, it is implied that the leader can hold a press conference and speak for his party in order to push through legislation. Actual authority, however, may be required by the principal-membership for certain important actions, such as temporarily taking a position that is contrary to the party platform because such an action is not customary.

It can also be argued that power through ratification is a mode by which the membership gives power to the leader. A leader may bring a bill to the floor that the membership does not see as in their interests, or in the legal sense, a bill the leader had no authority to bring to the floor; yet if this bill passes and becomes popular with the constituents, the membership may ratify the disputed action taken by the leader. In fact, the floor vote on this once unpopular bill can actually be seen as a later ratification by the principal of the leader's unauthorized action.[6]

From the concept of implicit authority, it would also be worth while to note how it impacts the liability of the agent to the principal. In agency law, the agent's liability will depend upon the degree of his capacity (Gregory, 2001). If an agent has implicit authority, as just posited, then his range of authority is quite broad; therefore, a leader can be held more accountable than an agent who is given actual or express authority.[7] Most leaders are held to a great deal of accountability by their political party. It is only natural for a party to point the finger of blame at the whip or party leader, especially if it is the majority that was rolled. The leaders were given the trust and ability to speak for the party in order to get the agenda through. It is therefore only natural for such broad responsibility to translate into broad culpability on the Hill.

Aside from the authority that is given, there are duties outlined in agency law that may help explain P-A theory. The most obvious duty that agency law can give to P-A theory is that of obedience or loyalty. The political nature of Congress easily enables the importation of the idea of a duty of obedience. An elected leader, as mentioned above, must have the correct intentions to take on that position. The intentions of a leader can easily be defined in his allegiance for the party. Members will not elect a leader who may fail to tow the party line. Additionally, a leader will not remain in power if he is not obedient to the collective will of the party. This same type of allegiance is almost identical to the fiduciary duty of loyalty. Congressional relationships within the party inherently assume a duty of loyalty because the two-party system requires a party member to "support the team." Congressional scholars have even discussed how loyalty from the rank and file is necessary to make sure an agenda is passed (Cox & McCubbins, 2005). Such a claim assumes that the party gives a substantial amount of power, through its authority, to the leader so that he may set the agenda. This assumption only goes to show that the fiduciary relationship between the principal-membership and the agent-leader is a fiduciary one that is based on assurances; the power to set an entire legislative agenda requires much trust between the two entities. Ultimately, it must also be recognized that from this sense of loyalty and trust the principal is assuming that the agent will carry forth the work with an adequate duty of care, another element of the agency relationship discussed earlier.

Further, much like the reality on Capitol Hill, agency law recognizes that "[h]aving a standard set of loyalty rules ... reduces transaction costs" (Kleinberger, 2002, p. 118). Just as a CFO is entrusted in keeping the books for the board of directors, a whip keeps note of who votes on certain issues; both examples show how the trust between the agent and the principal help the efficiency of the operation. Part of this duty of loyalty is for the agent to respect the confidences of the principal. Such a duty is typically understood in Congress.

An important duty of the principal to the agent, that is usually assumed, is that the principal must provide the agent the opportunity to serve. It is counter-intuitive to claim an agency relationship exists when there is never anything for the agent to do on behalf of the principal. Such a duty is even more important if the agent enters the relationship believing that he is to "derive some benefit from the work itself" (Gregory, 2001, p. 156). In the world of politics, these parallels from agency law are applicable. More often than not, a Congressional leader takes his position to receive the benefits of the notoriety of the office (i.e., then utilized to advance to a higher political office) and the ability to control the agenda so as to help his constituents. Thus, the membership is expected to give the agent-leader work (i.e., an agenda to promote). There is always work to be done in Washington, DC, therefore, it is safe to say that a party should never have to worry about violating this duty. Such a duty may seem to rely on common sense too much to be considered noteworthy, however, it is another perfect compliment from agency law to P-A theory. In fact, P-A theorists have taken note that leaders must be given the opportunity to work for the body (Shepsle & Bonchek, 1997).

Unless the agent is a gratuitous one, a principal has the duty to indemnify the agent for any losses sustained.[8] In agency law, these expenses are usually financial in nature; they are either directly accrued by the agent in attempting to act on behalf of the principal or for tort liability if the agent was acting within his relegated scope of authority. It would be beneficial, nonetheless, to adapt the idea of a duty to indemnify to P-A theory. As discussed earlier, a Congressional leader receives a form of political capital when acting as a leader. He can alter the agenda to benefit his constituents or use the leadership post as a platform to run for a higher office. This type of political situating can actually be seen as the party's way of paying the agent-leader for all of his hard work and the intangible troubles accrued on its behalf.

Once the relationship is created and the duties understood, there are two issues that agency law covers that would be beneficial to the development of P-A theory. First, agency law has a portion dedicated to how third parties interact with either the principal or the agent. A key principle is that when the agent says that there will be performance on a certain issue, he is not guaranteeing that he will be the one doing the performing, but rather the principal. Just because the agent is acting *on behalf* of the principal does not mean he is acting *for* the principal. When a Congressional party leader says that his party will vote for a certain measure, he is not guaranteeing that he will necessarily vote for the bill, but rather the party (on a whole) will vote for the bill. It is important to note that in agency law, the agent can legally bind performance on the principal but a party leader can not legally bind his party to vote a certain way. This difference is attributable to the inherent nature of the American political system.[9] Another analogous concept is that when the agent, for whatever reason, breeches his duty to the principal, that does not mean that he breeches a duty (and thus creates a damage claim) to an associated third party. For example, if a party leader allows his party to get rolled, there is no breech of duty to the constituents associated with the representatives of that party. There is another benefit of brining in this valid idea of third parties to P-A theory: there are numerous entities to analyze as third parties. For instance, is the third party the American public? A constituent group? The president? An administrative agency? The national party? The areas of analysis here are plentiful.

A second issue that arises when the relationship is created is when the agent or principal delegates authority/power to a third entity. In agency law, the agent does not have to be the sole actor for the principal; a principal can have co-agents or subagents. With the principal's permission, an agent can bring in a sub-agent to do the job. The original agent is then treated as both an agent (to the original principal) and a second principal (to the subagent). A subagent, therefore, can act on behalf of and bind an agent (and thus the principal) just as the first agent can the original principal. For efficiency's sake, the subagent usually reports to the agent, not the principal. It can be argued that subagents are a commonly utilized entity in Congress and their use has even been mentioned in P-A theory literature, for example Barbra Sinclair (1999): "The party set the agenda; party leaders held the committees to a tight schedule and exerted a strong influence on the substance of legislation" (p. 435). Party leaders use other leadership positions to carry out the work of the membership such as whips and committee chairs.[10] In the end, these positions can bind the party leader to a certain position, thus binding the party. A whip or committee chair also reports first to the party leader, who in turn addresses the party. Just like agency law, politics usually dictates that delegation by the leader does not relieve him his responsibilities. A party leader, the superior agent, is not discharged of the responsibility of getting a bill to the floor simply because he gave that responsibility to the chairman of the committee, the subordinate agent.

In a different context, bureaucracies, as seen through Moe's (1984) initial handling of P-A theory, can also be seen as a subagent. Agencies were created by Congress, not the American people. Thus, there is a principal–agent relationship between the electorate and Congress, but a removed subagency relationship is present between Congress and the bureaucracies. Moe does not go into such a mode of analysis during his discussion, however, he is describing relationships already defined in agency law.

Yet the inherent nature of a subagent allows the agent to select him. In Congress, these proposed subagent positions of whip and chairman are not, in fact, selected by the party leader; instead, they are elected by the party caucus or the entire chamber. It is the principal-membership who always selects these agent-leaders. Therefore, this occurrence in Congress requires these agents to instead be described as co-agents. Co-agents are employed by, not necessarily hired by, the principal only. A co-agent works on behalf of the principal directly while the subagent works on behalf of the original agent. Furthermore, the already-existing agent assumes no liability for the co-agent (Hynes, 2001). An example of a co-agent would be a secretary and a CFO who are both employed by the board of directors of a corporation. The secretary is a co-agent of the board, just like the CFO. Although the secretary may do tasks for the CFO, she works on behalf of the board of directors (again, like the CFO). Similarly, a chairman has to answer to the party leader, but in the end, the chairman has to answer to the party caucus along with the party leader.

The only problem in importing the idea of a co-agent into Congress is that the party leader, especially in the media, is often held accountable to the party if the chairman does not perform. Nonetheless, the idea of a co-agent (and even a subagent) has potential to contribute to P-A theory.

4. DIFFICULTIES AND DISCONTINUITY BROUGHT BY AGENCY LAW

Of course, when attempting to meld two theories from two different academic worlds, there are going to be some holes left behind or some inconsistencies. In all, the differences outlined below are not insurmountable; on the contrary, I believe that these differences can help fortify P-A theory. Agency law has been in development for over two millennia – well before P-A theory. The tenants of agency law have been tweaked and rebuilt in response to numerous variables such as human nature, forms of government, and ideological trends. If anything, it is urged that the discrepancies that agency law points out in P-A theory be utilized to modify the latter. One of the reasons an agent-leader takes his position, as already mentioned several times before, is to either further aid his constituents or to catapult himself to a higher leadership position. Yet agency law is clear on this subject: "those who hold powers for their own benefit ... are not agents" (Gregory, 2001, p. 26). This conflict, however, can be easily reconciled when looking at the true nature of the agent-leader/principal-membership relationship. The relationship is a fiduciary one: the party trusts the leader to push the agenda and therefore gives the leader the ability to set the chamber's schedule. True, the leader does receive some benefit from this relationship, but, as seen above, the relationship is truly fiduciary in nature. Moreover, the leader is held accountable to his principal – he must answer to the party membership at the end of the day. Such accountability further accents the agency relationship found in Congress. It is also recognized in agency law that both parties can agree that the agent will receive benefits from his efforts on behalf of the principal.

Another difficult area is the duty of loyalty from the agent to the principal. It is proposed in political science, and rightly so, that leaders are very ambitious (Rohde & Shepsle, 1987, p. 117). Additionally, there are other factors a Congressional leader must keep in mind when allocating his time and resources, such as keeping his leadership post and being reelected in his district. One could suggest that the duty of loyalty would be placed in jeopardy when the political process works itself out on Capitol Hill, especially if a morally lacking character assumes the leadership position. This line of argument would state that the duty of loyalty is simply a chivalrous and lofty sentiment outsiders like to place on Congress. Ultimately, however, it is P-A theory which answers this concern, not agency law. P-A theory literature assumes a duty of loyalty that is necessary to explain why a leader must satisfy the needs of the membership (Sinclair, 1999, pp. 421–422). Political scientists have already shown that leaders are not so ruthless and self-serving that they ignore the principal; for if they did ignore the party, they would not remain in power.

5. CONCLUDING THOUGHTS

Some in the legal community have attempted to summarize agency law into a simplified two-part test: for an agency relationship to exist, (1) the principal must have the right to control at least the goals of the relationship and (2) the agent must act on behalf of the principal (Kleinberger, 2002, p. 170). As seen in the discussion above, both elements of this test are, if not already assumed, integral to P-A theory. Such congruency only goes to show how the common law notions of agency are worth studying in light of P-A theory. The historical roots of P-A theory – going back through corporate economic theory – are additional evidence of how agency law and P-A theory are closely related.

For whatever reason, political scientists have only, at best, mentioned notions of agency law when discussing P-A theory. This piece is meant to serve as an introduction of some of the ideas of agency law and how they can be injected into portions of P-A theory. Not all concepts advanced in agency law are applicable to P-A theory, however, this does not mean that the other issues are useless. Concepts such as the duty of loyalty, the duty to provide work, co-agency, etc. were cultivated in the English and American common law; in the realm of political theory they can serve as a bolster for the principal-agent theory. Even the variations found between agency law and P-A theory serve as grounds to better the latter. Agency law has more of a history and has survived the trial by fire; it would be to the benefit of P-A theory to entertain and import the similar aspects and contemplate the aspects of agency law that are contrary.

NOTES

1. The views expressed herein are solely those of the author and not of the American Bar Association.
2. The American Law Institute is a well-respected organization of lawyer-academics whose restatements on various topics of law are utilized by the entire legal community, including lawyers, judges, and law professors.
3. For example, a patent lawyer may be sued by his client for not telling him about a defect in the patent process if such a disclosure is customary among the patent lawyer community.
4. One would find it hard to say that U.S. Representative Tom Delay, a darling of the 1994 Republican Revolution, would have found cooperation with the Republican Party in the House if he remained in power.
5. For example, the minority party, the executive branch, interest groups, etc.
6. Assuming, of course, that the required majority of the party participates in the floor vote.
7. The synonymous legal term utilized here for "accountability" is "liability;" however, the latter term carries too much weight when talking about a Congressional setting (e.g., liability can have a connotation of criminal conduct).
8. For example, repair expenses, litigation expenses, interest on borrowed funds, etc.
9. That is, no one can (legally) force another to vote a certain way.
10. It is assumed that these positions meet all the qualifications of the agency relationship discussed above.

ACKNOWLEDGMENTS

In addition to expressing my gratitude for the time and effort of my Politics Department supervisor, Dr. Matthew Green, I would like to thank Raymond Wyrsch, Esq., Distinguished Lecturer (Full-Time) at the Columbus School of Law, for his assistance and comments on the legal aspects of this chapter.

REFERENCES

American Law Institute. (2006). *Restatement of the law, agency: As adopted and promulgated by the American Law Institute at Philadelphia, Pennsylvania, May 17, 2005.* St. Paul, MN: American Law Institute Publishers.

Cox, G. W., & McCubbins, M. D. (1993). *Legislative Leviathan.* Berkley, CA: University of California Press.

Cox, G. W., & McCubbins, M. D. (2005). *Setting the Agenda: Responsible Party Government in the U.S. House of Representatives.* New York: Cambridge University Press.

Gregory, W. A. (2001). *The Law of Agency and Partnership.* St. Paul, MN: West Group.

Hynes, J. D. (2001). *Agency, Partnership and the LLC in a Nutshell.* St. Paul, MN: West Group.

Kleinberger, D. S. (2002). *Agency, Partnerships, and LLCs: Examples and Explanations.* New York: Aspen Law and Business.

Magleb, D. B., Patterson, K. D., & Thurber, J. A. (2002). Campaign consultants and responsible party government. In: J. C. Green & P. S. Hernson (Eds), *Responsible Partisanship?* (pp. 101–119). Lawrence, KS: University Press of Kansas.

Moe, T. M. (1984). The new economics of organization. *American Journal of Political Science, 28,* 739–777.

Natelson, R. G. (2004). The agency law origins of the necessary and proper clause. *Case Western Law Review, 55,* 243–322.

Office of Steny Hoyer. (March 9, 2007). America agrees with Democrats' Iraq goals. Office of Steny Hoyer, House Majority Leader Press Release. Retrieved April 20, 2007, from the World Wide Web: http://majorityleader.house.gov/docUploads/Redeployment-Benchmarks.pdf

Rohde, D. W., & Shepsle, K. A. (1987). Leaders and followers in the House of Representatives: Reflections on Woodrow Wilson's congressional government. *Congress and the Presidency, 14,* 111–133.

Rush, M. E. (1993). *Does Redistricting make a Difference?* Baltimore: The John Hopkins University Press.

Shepsle, K. A., & Bonchek, M. S. (1997). *Analyzing Politics: Rationality, Behavior, and Institutions.* New York: W. W. Norton & Company.

Sinclair, B. (1999). Transformational leader or faithful agent? Principal-agent theory and house majority party leadership. *Legislative Studies Quarterly, 24,* 421–449.

Szto, M. (2004). Limited liability company morality: Fiduciary duties in historical context. *Quinnipiac Law Review, 23,* 61–113.

United States House of Representatives; Committee on Rules. (2007). Rules of the House of Representatives. Retrieved April 27, 2007, from the World Wide Web: http://www.rules.house.gov/ruleprec/110th.pdf

United States Senate; Committee on Rules and Administration. (2007). Standing rules of the Senate. Retrieved April 27, 2007, from the World Wide Web: http://rules.senate.gov/senaterules

REFORMING LABOR LAW IN THE CZECH REPUBLIC: INTERNATIONAL SOURCES OF CHANGE

Gabriela Wasileski and Gerald Turkel

ABSTRACT

In the aftermath of the Communist Era, Czechs and Slovaks sought to enter the European Union (EU) in order to participate in Western European markets and polities. To gain entry, they had to reform their labor laws based on EU protocols. This study analyzes changes in labor law in the Czech Republic by focusing on differences between statutes and regulations in the Communist and Post-Communist Eras. The study is framed by international approaches to law that locate sources of legal change in international organizations and protocols. In reforming Czech labor law, EU labor law standards were established through internal political processes that were themselves shaped by EU requirements rooted in pluralism and the rule of law.

Studies in Law, Politics, and Society, Volume 45, 255–280
ISSN: 1059-4337/doi:10.1016/S1059-4337(08)45008-1

INTRODUCTION

In the aftermath of the Communist era, Czechs and Slovaks sought to participate in the international community as independent economic actors and nation states. Most particularly, they sought to strengthen their ties with Western European markets and polities, primarily through membership in the European Union (Vaughan-Whitehead, 2003). As part of this effort, new labor law statutes were established that were in keeping with European Union principles and requirements (Cazes & Nešporová, 2003).

The new labor law statutes were part of a broader process of change in which rule of law principles, including individualism, equality, freedom of contract, the relative autonomy of political and legal institutions, and neutrality of rule enforcement, were becoming features of public life in the post-communist era. To some degree, this process reflected internal social, cultural, and political dynamics that were unleashed with the collapse of communism. Yet legal and policy approaches in the new regimes, including those regulating labor, were shaped by legal discourses codified in protocols and international standards required for membership in the European Union.

This chapter focuses on sources of change in labor law in the Czech Republic. It analyzes sources of change in policy requirements established by the European Council and by international treaties, principles and regulations in light of the social, economic and legal conditions prevailing in the Czech Republic. Efforts to meet European Union and international standards created new tensions that reverberated through society and its newly established legal and political institutions.

The abstract and universal requirements stipulated by the European Union and related international codes and guidelines contributed to new patterns of political and legal discourse into Czech public life which had been severely limited by Communist Party dominance through state organized collectivism. The new labor codes, while reflecting particular conditions in the Czech Republic, established forms of legal discourse more consistent with political and market activity, social welfare standards, and bureaucratic rationality based on criteria for accountability to the European Union. In this light, rule of law principles had to be adapted to particular historical circumstances and contexts. The rule of law was incorporated relative to Czech conditions in the post-communist era in conformity with market rationality, formal democracy, and societal corporatist discourses that facilitated broader patterns of participation at the national and international levels.

THEORETICAL FRAMEWORK

This study of Czech labor law is rooted in analytic approaches and empirical studies that focus on international contexts and forces that shape law in both regions of the world and in individual nation states (Boyle & Preves, 2000; Boyle & Thompson, 2001; Dezalay & Garth, 1996; Vachudova, 2005). "Rather than viewing each law as an end point in a national political struggle" (Boyle & Preves, 2000, p. 794), law creation is analyzed as part of a broader international process. Law creation in nation states is affected by regional multi-state institutions, international treaties, and international conventions. This international approach provides for both a more expansive framework of analysis and explanation and a more adequate interpretive context for locating legal action and discourse.

Focusing on international sources of law creation provides grounds for rethinking established frameworks. Typologies that have been primarily concerned with the nation-state as a locus for law creation and for comparative inquiry can be given new analytic scope. In particular, Roberto Unger's (1976) approach, which focuses on the internal tensions in law and the social forces surrounding legal institutions and discourses, has not attended sufficiently to the international forces that shape law and policy. While Unger's typology stresses comparative study, it emphasizes the individuality and autonomy of cultures and nation states. This typology gains analytic scope by infusing it with international as well as internal sources of law creation.

Most significantly, Unger's typology can be enhanced by combining it with Sabino Cassese's (2006) framework for studying globalization of law. Cassese focuses on sources of legal change in global and international processes. Yet he also maintains that law is increasingly affected by relations among national cultures, nation states, and nongovernmental institutions. By combining aspects of Unger's typology with Cassese's processual approach to global changes in policy and law, an analytic framework for studying the combined effects of global forces and internal conditions can be more fully articulated.

Customary law, bureaucratic law, and legal order are the major types of law formulated by Unger (1976). Customary law is rooted in the everyday interactions that people routinely have with one another. As a result of these repeated interactions, normative expectations are developed as well as a sense of social reality. These expectations constitute a normative order that is informal, particularistic, not codified, and coterminous with everyday beliefs. By contrast, bureaucratic law is codified and universal.

Most typically, it is imposed by distant elites, such as imperial rulers or centralized state agencies, on a range of disparate communities. Bureaucratic law is enforced through administrative power, extrinsically legitimated, and takes an abstract form. Finally, legal order results from patterns of group conflict in which no one group or combination of groups has power to dominate society as a whole. Legal order, or the rule of law, is limited and claims neutrality in the application of legal norms through procedures and institutions that have autonomy from surrounding social forces. It enables ordered and nonviolent conflict under normative and institutional constraints.

While locating the tensions and conflicts of each of these types of law in their sociopolitical relations provides important directions for inquiry, their full potential can be realized by enhancing their international content. In this light Cassese's analysis of legal globalization is valuable. Locating law in global and international relations, Cassese provides five forms of legal change (2006, p. 978): (1) direct transfer from one nation to another; (2) imposition of a "global legal principle upon a national public administration"; (3) imposition by a global legal body; (4) the "transplant-ing" of a national legal system to the global level; and (5) the "spillover' of law to the global level from interactions among nations and institutional actors.

By analyzing changes in Czech labor law, concepts formulated by Unger and Cassese are specified empirically through a case study of legal change in a nation state seeking membership in an international body. Labor law under communism was bureaucratically imposed administratively through highly centralized and coordinated processes. European Union (EU) labor law stipulations, while also bureaucratic in form, have a general character and are adopted by states seeking voluntary membership. In this sense, they constitute a more consensual form of voluntary bureaucratism in which international principles are transplanted rather than imposed. In addition, the rule of law established to govern the Czech Republic that emerged with the end of communism was an EU demand that facilitated this transplant through pluralism and a range of public debate to arrive at agreement about the labor law provisions. In this light, the case study demonstrates how types of law are related to one another through a historically located process with both internal and international dimensions. This study contributes to the analysis of the international forces affecting law creation by expanding Unger's typology through the processual features developed by Cassese. It demonstrates the value of making international sources of law central to the study of law creation.

The study proceeds by analyzing labor law under communism as a form of bureaucratic imposition. It then presents EU labor law principles as bureaucratic legal requirements for voluntary membership. Within this historical and global context, the study analyzes the transition in Czech labor law, as internally realized through rule of law procedures that were also qualifications for EU membership. In effect, both substantive and procedural requirements established by an international body were sources of Czech labor law. The study focuses on collective bargaining and contractualism in the politics of labor law transformation as two key differences between labor law during the era of communist era and membership in the European Union.

BUREAUCRATIC IMPOSITION: CZECH COMMUNISM AND LABOR LAW

During the communist era, Czechoslovakia was composed of two republics, each sharing responsibility with the federal government. The highest legislative body, the Federal Assembly, was recognized as "the supreme organ of state power and the sole statewide legislative body" (Ústava Československé socialistické republiky 100/1960 Sb). The Federal Assembly was divided into two equal chambers, the Chamber of the People and the Chamber of the Nations. The Chamber of the People reflected a system of proportional representation: in 1986 it included 134 deputies from the Czech Socialist Republic and 66 deputies from the Slovak Socialist Republic. The Chamber of Nations had 150 members, 75 from each republic. Deputies were selected through popular elections and served five-year terms of office. All 350 members served concurrently. After an election each chamber met to select its own presidium consisting of three to six members.

The formal state framework enabled the Communist Party to impose its policies by dominating governmental and social institutions. The party determined legislative priorities and presented them to Federal Assembly for its unanimous approval. In addition, the Federal Assembly elected the President for a five-year term of office. The president was first selected by the KSČ leadership and then "officially" voted into office by the Federal Assembly. Legislation presented to the assembly had to be approved by both chambers. The parliamentary bodies typically approved 100 percent of the bills created by the Communist Party (Carey, Formanek, & Karpowicz, 1999). In addition, judges on the Supreme Court of Czechoslovakia were elected by the Federal Assembly to serve 10-year terms of office (Malý & Sivák, 1993).

The Communist regime in Czechoslovakia formulated its bureaucratic dominance through an ideology focusing on work: Every person must work and do the job that they are assigned. From the work they do, they will earn the money and property that they need. If everyone is expected to work under the same conditions with no strict managers, workers will be freed from their lives of poverty and domination by the bourgeoisie.

Based on institutional monopoly by and an ideology centering on work, Communist labor codes focused on eight major policy areas that blended party control of the state with codified institutional regulation of employees and their conditions of employment: (1) the politicizing of the state bureaucracy through the policy of lustration; (2) policies delineating the obligation to work; (3) compulsory labor; (4) regulation of work time; (5) social benefits; (6) equality between men and women; (7) the role of the trade union; and (8) child labor.

Lustration

According to Krygier (1990), communist legality is "the one among an array of instruments for translating the government's – or party's wishes into action and maintaining social order" (p. 641). For the Czechs, this was realized through state dominated employment. Everyone was an employee of the state, and the state was an extension of communist party and its political goals.

The key qualification for promotion of senior bureaucrats was their political and ideological reliability. The Communist Party selected, or at least approved, these senior bureaucrats (Konig, 1992). For senior bureaucrats, this meant that young administrators would enter at the bottom ranks of a ministry and seek promotion to the lowest managing ranks. Bureaucrats were aware that their career depended on their commitments to the party. The state bureaucracy was comprehensively politicized, as personnel policy emphasized political loyalty and reliability. In policy terms, state administration was "under-politicized," in personnel terms "over-politicized" (Goetz & Wollmann, 2001).

In pre-1989 Czechoslovakia, lustration was a policy usually conducted by the police to determine whether a person was registered in the secret police records (Žáček, 2000). It was used by the secret police (ŠtB) to conduct checks on citizens' loyalty to the Communist Party during its 40-year rule.

The most extensive acts of lustration took place after the Soviet invasion in 1968. At the same time, between 70,000 and 100,000 people were expelled from the Czechoslovak Communist Party and lost their jobs (Žáček, 2000).

The Obligation to Work

Codes regulating work articulated the principle that each individual had the obligation to work for the collective. The "right to work" was established in the Constitution of Czechoslovak Socialist Republic (Ústava Československé Socialistické Republiky 100/1960 Sb. čast' 19). Nevertheless, Czechoslovaks did not have the right to desist from that work. Violation of that rule was punishable by law. Stating that those rights serve not only the "full assertion of the justified interests of individual citizens," but also "the common interest of society" put the limits on rights and freedoms. Consequently, individuals had an obligation to work for the greatest good of society. "The foremost duty" of all is to work for the "benefit of the whole" (Ústava Československé Socialistické Republiky 100/1960 Sb. čast' 19). The right to work is "the foremost right of every citizen," but to desist from work was viewed as sabotage against society and people.

Compulsory Labor

The *right* to work was an implicit *obligation* to work. Those who did not supply their own means of life through "honest work" were in danger of being accused of the criminal activity of "social parasitism." Czechoslovakia had statutes concerning so-called "social parasites" or "spongers" (i.e., people out of school and unemployed). Such persons were obliged to produce evidence of their means of support and to report to certain agencies (usually police departments), as they were believed to be living at the expense of others.

The criminal legal code, including the Forced Labor Camps Act No. 247/ 1948 (Zákon o táboroch nútenej práce 25 č. 247/1948 Zb. októbra 1948, Part 8), was directed against political opponents of the regime. It was aimed at four groups: (1) people who were willfully idle; (2) political saboteurs; (3) saboteur of the national economy; and (4) those who sought to disrupt the socialist community (Vrabcová, 2001). Labor camps sought to re-educate political and socially non-conformist people. The core of reeducation process was to destroy the capitalist principles in cultural and individual spheres (Forced Labor Camps Act No. 247/1948, Part 8).

In 1950, forced and compulsory labor took a different form as the National Assembly adopted four new acts of legislation: the Criminal Code (Act No. 86/1950 Coll.), the Criminal Procedure Code (Act No. 87/1950 Coll.), the Criminal Administrative Code (Act No. 88/1950 Coll.) and the Criminal Administrative Procedure Code (Act No. 89/1950 Coll.). The new statutes ended labor camps and, at the same time, criminalized activities that ran counter to the stated goal: "Protect the People's Democratic Republic, build its socialist structure, uphold the interests of working people and individuals, and provide education concerning the observance of the rule of socialist co-existence." The age of criminal liability was set at 15 years and over. The definitions of types of crimes allowed for broad discretion and criminal sanctions of all actions considered to be against the interests of the state, particularly political and economic interests.

Compulsory work was required of the prison population. Part-time, volunteer labor of students and white-collar workers were drafted in massive numbers to work without pay under the slogan, "Working for the building of socialism." These "volunteers" served not only after World War II, but also through the entire communist era. Prisoners usually filled up the dangerous jobs and had very high productions quotas, and the failure to fulfill quotas was penalized. Work was the primary activity for prisoners (Turnock, 1995).

Codifying Work Time

Following the Soviet model, Czechoslovakia emphasized the rapid development of heavy industry, the small business sector was neglected, and private sector was partially tolerated in agriculture field (Boeri & Terrell, 2002). Growth in the heavy industry sector required additional labor. Czechoslovaks were subjected to a six-day workweek with a maximum of 46 hours in order to meet production quotas (Labor Code No. 65/1965 Part 84-87Coll.). The amendment No. 188/1988 Part 83(1) Coll. of pre-1989 Labor Code 65/1965 Coll., regulated the organization of working time in detail, ensuring a maximum 43-hour week, 3 weeks paid holiday, and a 12-hour rest between shifts. The Labor Code recognized "over time work" (Part 96). The agreement of trade unions was required for overtime work (Part 98). Ordered overtime work could not exceed 8 hours/ week and 150 hours/calendar year (Part 97 (2, 3)). For performing overtime work, the employee was given the opportunity for extra leave (Labor Code

65/1965 Part 116(1) Coll.) or for additional earnings if time off could not be scheduled (Labor Code 65/1965 Part 116(2) Coll.).

The Labor Code ensured the right to rest after work through legal regulation of working time and paid holidays. The state organized the use of workers' free time for recreation and cultural activities. The Czechoslovak Constitution 1960 Part 23 also established the right to the protection of health and to healthcare. Party and government officials set wage scales and work norms.

Neither the Labor Code nor other related legislation in Czechoslovakia established or recognized part-time jobs or special work conditions for employees who worked part-time. The Labor Code stated that earnings should be provided in proportion to hours worked and importance of each job classification (Labor Code 65/1965 Part 111 Coll.). Employers could arrange shorter than established weekly hours in work contracts for operational reasons, on the employee's request, or due to health or other serious reasons on the part of the employee if it would not cause economic harm (Labor Code 65/1965 Part 86 Coll.).

Social Benefits

The communist "system was held together with police terror, the threat of invasion, ideology, job security, and social benefits" (Vachudova, 2005). Labor Code Act No. 65/1965 Coll. and social benefits such as full time employment, free health care, and free education was applicable to all employees without consideration of race, gender, and ethnicity. The Communist political system provided broad social welfare assistance in order to balance women's work and family responsibilities (Bretherton, 2001). On the other hand, however, it repressed any political expression and individual freedom, including the right to assert ethnic identity. Women workers had a full complement of maternity and childcare benefits. Maternity leave was 26 weeks in the 1980s (Labor Code 65/1965 Coll. Part 157 (1)). Employers could not deny a woman's request for an additional year of unpaid leave for child rearing without loss of job security (Labor Code 65/1965 Coll. Part 157 (2)). In Czechoslovakia the communist government established sick leave and pension insurance for all workers without discrimination and recognized the social benefits to those who needed it and were not entitled to pension. The government also provided the payment of family allowances according to the number of children in a family. A wide range of benefits were provided to families with children to maintain household income, and to encourage parents to work and have children. The main programs included monthly allowances for families (such as those with many children); lump-sum birth grants; maternity benefits; parental and child care benefits; paid leave for care of a sick child; and funeral benefits; and health care.

Gender Equality

Equality between men and women in Czechoslovakia, codified in the Czechoslovak Constitution, was implemented by the Communist Party. Full time employment, equal rights for free education and health care, long maternity leave with a guaranteed job, and extended social rights in case of sickness of a family member were taken for granted by the majority of women (Czechoslovakia National Census, 1980). The labor code entitled every employee, regardless of gender, to equal remuneration for work of equal value and obliged the employer to facilitate the improvement of employees' professional qualifications.

Protecting women's work also meant that women were obligated to work and would be channeled into proper occupations. They could not choose between working and staying at home and childcare. Consequently what communism called equality between men and women actually violated a provision of the Constitution for Europe (Treaty establishing a Constitution for Europe, 2004) that guarantees the right of individuals to choose an occupation and the right to engage in work. The Labor Code 65/1965 Part 150 Coll. also banned numerous jobs that were supposed to be inappropriate for women, primarily pregnant women and women who had recently given birth. These included jobs in mines and other jobs that required hard physical labor. There were special conditions for women working night shifts (Labor Code 65/1965 Part 152 Coll.). In addition, an employer was obliged to give a pregnant woman different work with the same salary if her health or her pregnancy was likely to be jeopardized (Labor Code 65/1965 Part 153 Coll.). Pregnant women or mothers looking after children younger than 15 years of age were entitled to flexible or shorter working hours. Mothers could take breaks to breastfeed, which were included in the number of hours worked. Pregnant women and mothers with a child younger than one year could not be sent on business trips without their agreement, work on night-shifts, work overtime, or to be fired. Finally, maternity leave was guaranteed for women. Financial assistance based on their previous salaries for 28 weeks. Assistance was 90 percent of the mother's net earnings (Mother's Earning Act No. 154/1969 Coll.). However, Pollert (2003) pointed out that state social benefits policies were enforced insufficiently, women health care was inadequate and of law standard, and public child care was overcrowded. In addition as a result of segregation and discrimination, women earned between 70 and 80 percent of men's earnings and were excluded from political power (Pollert, 2003).

Communist labor codes prohibited child labor and provided protections for young workers. School policies supported the prohibition of child labor and compulsory school attendance began for children at the age of six. Obligatory school attendance was for ten years and School enrollment was high. Higher education, however, did not necessary lead to higher incomes. Wages were set according to a centrally determined wage grid which was used to maintain low education-related wage differentials (Munich, Svejnar, & Terrell, 2005). Although women received more higher education then men and entered qualified professions in higher numbers than in the West, men with only ten years of compulsory education earned almost as much as women with collage degrees (Pollert, 2003).

The Subordinate Role of Trade Unions

While trade unions were the largest of all Czechoslovak organizations and represented most wage earners (Czechoslovakia National Census, 1980), they played a highly subordinate role. Trade unions disseminated socialist thought in order to mobilize workers for imposed production goals. Unions operated as an arm of the state and followed bureaucratically determined goals rather than as independent representatives of workers (Flanagan, 1998).

The Czech Labor Code 65/1965 Coll. provided wide powers for trade unions. These included changes and termination of the work contract, determination of working time, overtime work and night-work, determination of holidays, approving working conditions in the enterprise in compliance with the Labor Code and ensuring that they were applied in a meaningful way in the enterprise, employees participation in the management of the enterprise, work protection, especially safety and health protection at work and compensation for employment related accidents and diseases. These powers of the trade unions were arranged into four categories:

(1) Decision-making rights of the trade unions. Unions, for example, were able to forbid overtime or night work in cases of risk to the health or to the life of the employees (Labor Code 65/1965 Part 136 (3g) Coll.).

(2) Making joint decisions. A decision made by the employer was valid only after reaching agreement with the trade unions. According to Labor Code 65/1965 Part 59 (1) the employer cannot fire the employee without agreement of union.

(3) Trade union cooperation with the employers. Employers were obliged to negotiate their decision before it became effective. The bargaining agreement or any changes in it must be approved by trade union to have validity (Labor Code 65/1965 Part 20(3) Coll.)

(4) Controlling competence. This included the right to monitor compliance of the collective agreements (Part 20), compliance with the conditions of health, safety and protection at work (Part 136 (2)), observation of the wages and compliance with all regulations provided by the Labor Code 65/1965 Coll. Wages were not defined as the price of labor negotiated in the process of bargaining between social actors. Wages were payments for labor provided by the central authorities according to their ideological and production values.

EU REQUIREMENTS: BUREAUCRATIC VOLUNTARISM AND CZECH LABOR LAW

European Union requirements provided a voluntary legal context for ordering of labor relations and labor unions in the Czech Republic. European Union membership for post-communist societies was linked to procedural democracy and economic and political stability. In addition, the prospect of EU membership enhanced the likelihood that post-communist countries could catch up economically with Western Europe countries (Vachudova, 2005).

Labor statutes formulated on the basis European Union requirements have provided a framework rooted in market principles and civil liberties that recognize both individual and collective rights of workers in their relationships with employers especially in terms of rights of association, bargaining, and speech. In addition, corporatist features of interest representation in decision-making at the levels of the individual firm and the industrial sector were introduced.

Since Europe unification was largely economically inspired (Elman, 2001), frameworks for formulating a new labor code were accompanied by substantive concerns about Czech economic and social conditions and its consequences for EU western states after Czech accession. The 2003 Employment

Guidelines provide a framework for the national labor law for each member state (Council Decision (2003/57 8/EC) of 22 July 2003 on guidelines for the employment policies of the Member States). The specific guidelines seek to prevent unemployment and to enhance skills of the unemployed for labor market participation. Those measures should include training, retraining, and work practice for long-term unemployed individuals. Member states must have effective employment services and labor market programs. They must encourage the creation of a job market and provide opportunities for entrepreneurship. Yet there is also a consensual dimension to these recommendations. Labor statutes, predicated on democracy and pluralism, should support the development of a social dialogue around economic and employment issues involving limiting working time, equal treatment for all individuals, access to training, and better working conditions at the place of employment.

Specific Czech Conditions

The EU had specific concerns about conditions in the Czech Republic and how they would affect realizing the membership requirements. First, the EU criticized slow economic development and insufficient public administration reform, low employment levels, especially among women, youth, elderly people, and low skill levels of the work force in the Czech Republic. Secondly, there was concern about regional differences in the employment and unemployment level and patterns. Third, the relatively high poverty rate among the Roma population was troubling (European Commission Progress report Summary, 1999).

Impact of EU Requirements: Free Association and the Right to Strike

European Union requirements have significantly shaped codes regulating trade unions and labor markets. Both trade unions and employer associations in the Czech Republic are "free" in the sense that they can be established without state intervention (Casale, Kubínková, & Rýchly, 2001). In particular, the right to organize and establish trade unions is protected in article 27 of the Charter of fundamental rights and freedoms, which is an integral part of the Constitution of the Czech Republic (The Constitution of Czech Republic No. 1/1993 Coll. of the Czech National Council of December 16, 1992 as amended).

The law provides workers with the right to form and join unions of their own choice without prior authorization. Most workers are members of unions affiliated with the Czech-Moravian Chamber of Trade Unions (ČMKOS). The ČMKOS is democratically oriented and, as the biggest union confederation with 35 affiliated unions, provides republic-wide organization and representation for branch unions. It is not affiliated with any political party and carefully maintains its independence (Casale et al., 2001).

To conform to European Union demands and in the face of internal pressures, the role of unions in the workplace and principles of collective bargaining were changed several times through amendments in Czech's Labor Code No. 65/1965 Coll. Under Czech law, trade unions and trade union bodies are the only legitimate representative bodies of employees in labor relations. Only unions have the right of collective bargaining. Trade unions represent all employees in labor relations, including those who are not union members.

An amendment to Labor Code No. 65/1965 Coll. from 2001 introduced a new type of employee representation. In companies with at least 25 employees that do not have unions, employees can elect work councils. However, trade unions and employee councils are not allowed to exist side by side in the same company. Employee councils are conceived as an alternative solution (Casale et al., 2001).

Since January 2001, the labor code guarantees of the right to organize and affords protection from anti-union discrimination. The law does not restrict international cooperation and affiliation by Czech unions. Moreover, foreigners and migrant workers also have the right to organize. In addition, employee councils, like trade unions, provide all workers with the right to information and consultation regarding major company decisions. Employee councils prohibit discrimination based o membership in employee councils or any activity resulting from membership.

Workers have the right to strike, with the exception of those who play a crucial role in maintaining public order or public safety. These include military personnel, police, and workers in nuclear energy, oil, and on natural gas pipelines. Some other public sector occupations are forbidden by law to go on strike. These include firefighters, prison guards, customs officers, and mining inspectors. The labor law requires that labor disputes be subject first to mediation and that strikes may take place only after mediation efforts fail. Trade unions must provide employers with a list of the names of strikers at least one day before the strike (Act of collective bargaining No. 2/1991 part 17 Coll.).

Labor law for public employees has been evolving since prohibitions against collective bargaining for wages may violate International Labor

Office (ILO) Convention No. 98 from 1949. The Act on Salaries and Readiness to Work in Budget-Funded Institutions No.143/1992 Coll. and the Government Order on Salary Conditions for State Administration Employees No. 253/1992 Coll., as amended several times applies and regulates wages for government employees, employees' organizations financed by the state budget, state foundations and employees of administrative subdivisions. It established a unified remuneration scheme for public employees. There have been ongoing efforts to have these codes conform to ILO standards in the face of budgetary pressures.

BOUNDARIES TO CONTRACTUALISM

The central importance of voluntary association and contractual obligations constrained by social and labor market standards was heightened by compliance with EU mandates. Participation in labor markets is contractual, intended primarily for socially and legally competent adults within a labor policy framework that aims at full employment, upgrading labor force skills, and representation. In keeping with EU requirements, the minimum age is established in Section 11 of the Labor Code No. 65/1965 Coll. The exception to the minimum age law applies to special schools for children with disabilities, whose graduates may be employed at age 14. Additional protections for children are established under Sections 165, 166, and 167 of the Labor Code No. 65/1965 Coll. Employment conditions for children aged 15–18 are subject to strict safety standard and Czech government sets minimum wage standards as well. These prohibitions are enforced through workplace inspections and monitored jointly by the Ministry of Health and the Ministry of Labor and Social Affairs. The law requires labor offices throughout the country to carry out inspections and investigations.

Labor regulations limit the workweek and the workday. Act 85/2001 Coll. reduced the standard workweek to 40 hours from 42 and 1/2 and to 37.5 hours per week for mine workers effective from January 1, 2001. Act 85/2001 Col. also requires paid rest of at least 30 minutes during the standard 8-hour workday, as well as annual leave of 4 to 8 weeks, depending on the profession. Teachers and college professors, for example, have 8 weeks in year. Overtime ordered by the employer may not exceed 150 hours per year of 8 hours per week as a standard practice (Section 95-98 of Act 85/2001 Coll.), although the local employment office may permit overtime above this limit. The Labor Ministry enforces standards for working hours, rest periods, and annual leave. Government, unions, and employers promote worker safety and health and the Office of Labor Safety is responsible for enforcement of health and safety standards. Workers have the right to refuse work endangering their life or health without risk of loss of employment.

Labor statutes structure the labor market and contractualism by imposing limitations on temporary and part-time work. In 2004, a new employment law, Act no. 435/2004, took effect. It includes provisions on employment through temporary employment agencies, which is also covered by an amendment of the Labor Code adopted in 2004; No. 436/2004 Coll. (which came into force on January 1, 2005). The amendment specifies the conditions under which employees may be hired out to companies on a temporary basis. Under this legislation, and in contrast to the previous legal position, only licensed employment agencies may hire out their employees to another employer.

The amendment of the Labor Code no. 46/2004 Coll. is intended to prevent repeated signing of fixed-term contracts with the same employee as well. The maximum total duration of successive fixed-term employment contracts is two years. The relationship between the state's social policy and new work forms is defined in the National Action Plan for Employment for 2004–2006. The plan seeks recognition of forms of flexible work by union, councils and employers. It states that social partners should strive to incorporate all legally admissible forms of flexible work into collective agreements.

Non-standard forms of employment are not at all widely used in the Czech Republic. Employees have not been interested in anything other than full-time employment for an indefinite term. Indeed, the proportion of persons working part-time has been actually falling. In 1993, part-time work accounted for 6%, in 2002 just 4.8%. The main reasons for the low popularity of flexible forms of employment are the low level of wages they offer and the reduced job security during a time when enterprises are undergoing transformation. According to the Labor Force Survey for the second quarter of 2004, 9.7% of the total workforce is engaged in fixed-term employment and 4.9% of the workforce works part time. Most part-time workers are women (76.4%). The number of employees with a fixed-term employment contract or working part-time is rising slightly year-on-year (ČSU: Český statistický úřad, www.czso.cz/csu/csu.nsf/kalendar/2004-zam). The Labor Code defines only two forms of work performed outside an employment relationship. Both are expected to be exceptional and limited to cases when the employer cannot ensure the work tasks by its permanent staff or if it would be unjustified or inefficient to so do. The two forms are *Agreement on the performance of work task* (used mainly for individual work tasks) and the *Agreement on working activity* (used mainly for long-term activities).

Conditions for termination of employment by the employer are regulated by the labor code. Termination by notice of firing is a common basis for labor disputes. Notices can be found to be invalid and dismissals are very often challenged, which could cause serious difficulties for employers (ČTK, 2005). Consequently, many employers prefer to use termination by mutual agreement, in spite of the requirement for severance pay. The new Czech Labor Code brings only minor changes to this area of the law. The old and new Czech labor codes are based on the rule that an employee may be dismissed only for a reason listed in the Labor Code. The dismissal "for organizational reasons" as an example, the wording in the new Czech code was taken word for word from the old code. In the 1965 labor code the required notice period was three months, the employee was entitled to severance pay equal to two months' wages, and the employer was obliged to "effectively help" him/her in looking for a new job. The new Czech code stipulates a two-month notice period and three months' worth of severance pay.

The new labor legislation canceled the 1965 limitations on terminating a single parent of a child under 15 years of age, while the ban on terminating employees who are pregnant or on parental leave remains. Under the Czech code, protection of pregnant employee is absolute. Table 1 summarizes both the labor code under communism and the labor code adopted by the Czech Republic made by the Czech government based on European Union requirements.

THE POLITICS OF LABOR LAW TRANSFORMATION

The internal political process through which changes in labor law have been accomplished has been characterized by conflicts typical of pluralistic societies with multiparty systems governed by the rule of law. EU bureaucratic requirements were not imposed but, rather, negotiated and realized through a political process structured largely through procedures claiming neutrality from particular interests and parties. As exemplified by the most recent changes in labor law, political parties and the interest groups they represent have been divided over specific legislative proposals in order

Table 1. Comparison of Major Differences in Labor Code Through Diverse Period of Time in Czech Republic.

Labor Code No. 65/1965 Coll. as Amended During Communism Until 1989	New Labor Code No. 262/2006 Coll.
The employer should, in cooperation with the competent state administrative authority, actively assist him/her in obtaining another suitable job because of re-organizational changes made by the employer (Sec. 47(1) of Labor Code).	It does not contain such obligation.
In some cases, such as the case of a notice of termination given to a single female or single male employee who is raising a child under the age of 15 years or to a disabled employee who is not a recipient of a pension, the employer is obliged to ensure to such an employee other suitable work, and the notice period does not end until the employer fulfils this duty, unless the employer agrees otherwise with the employee (Sec. 47(2) of Labor Code).	It does not contain such obligation.
The Labor Code does not recognize a severance payment.	Enacted Labor Code No 262/2006 sec. 67 Coll. increased for these cases the amount of severance pay up to minimum of triple his/her average earnings. Sec. 67(1) of new Labor Code increased severance payment for the cases when an employee gives a notice of termination under grounds of (medical) prohibition to perform the existing work because of an accident at work or occupational disease (risk of this disease) the amount of severance pay up to minimum of twelve fold his/her average earnings.
Does not define and recognize the *dependent work*	It contains a definition of *dependent work* and specifies the documents governing labor relations. The basic documents governing dependent work are employment contracts and agreements for work performed outside the employment relationship (Sec. 4 and 5 of Labor Code).
The Labor Code does not provide or allow special arrangement. The "labor relationship" is arranged only in collective agreement and partially in employment contract.	The Labor Code provides for special arrangement between parties to a "labor relationship" in cases where parties may use an employment contract, collective agreement, or contract not defined in the Civic Code.

Table 1. (*Continued*)

Labor Code No. 65/1965 Coll. as Amended During Communism Until 1989	New Labor Code No. 262/2006 Coll.
	The health and safety requirements are no longer contained in the Labor Code but are detailed in the law No. 309/2006 that enters into force together with Labor Code No. 262/2006 on January 1, 2007. The Act on health and safety at work covers the minimum workplace requirements, safety of work equipment, organization of work, safety signs, and risks at work, health and safety experts, and other health and safety at work issues. The Act applies to employment relationships and relationships based on contracts which are similar to employment contracts.
Working time is maximum 43 hours weekly Labor Code provides opportunity of shortened working hours for employees with health reasons without their wage reduction (sec. 83(4))	Working time is maximum 40 hours weekly. The shorter working hours without wage reduction for employees with health problems are not enacted by Labor Code anymore
The Labor Code does not define the term *the account of the working hours*	Labor Code provides the possibility of the employers to flexibly react to the changing demand for work by introducing the account of the working hours (sec. 86), the pay when applying the account of the working hours (sec. 87). Thus, legislation on working time accounts in particular should help flexibility.
The Labor Code does not contain provision about employer's obligation of wage compensation for the first 14 days of employees' work incapacity	The new Labor Code defines the duty of the employer to provide its employees wit wage compensation for the first 14 days of work incapacity (as per the new Sickness Benefits Act No. 187/2006 Coll.).
	The Labor Code defines competences of the trade union organizations attached to the employers and new possibilities of the collective agreement, in particular of the extension of the employees' rights, the duty to enter into a collective agreement with the largest trade union. If the trade unions fail to reach consensus on procedures during collective bargaining, the employer is entitled to conclude a collective agreement with the organization that has the most members (sec. 24(2)).

Table 1. (*Continued*)

Labor Code No. 65/1965 Coll. as Amended During Communism Until 1989	New Labor Code No. 262/2006 Coll.
	The role of a collective bargaining agreement is not mentioned anymore
Area of compensation for business trips have been covered in separate legislative Acts	The new Labor Code introduces new regulations in respect of employees in the commercial/for profit and non-profit sectors and compensation for business trips.

to meet EU and international standards. While meeting EU requirements have been central to the legislative process, meeting them has generated political conflict, mobilization of discourses and constituencies, and efforts at reaching compromises and common ground. In contrast to communist regime, democracy in Czech Republic established that policy making processes go through political parties' competitions, parliamentary debates, and political parties are forced to reach a consensus about thrust of political and economic reform (Vachudova, 2005).

Legislating the Labor Code

Recent changes in labor legislation were proposed by the senior ruling coalition party, the Social Democratic Party (ČSSD) in 2005 and passed in the lower house in early 2006 (Parlament České Republiky (2006a), www.psp.cz/sqw/historie.sqw?o = 4&T = 1153). The Senate rejected the proposed of new labor act and returned it to the Chamber of Deputies. The Chamber of Deputies was expected to pass the new Labor Code because the Social Democrats had the support of the Communists (KSČM), the opposition party. Since the country's two left-of-center parties held a majority in the lower house, it was very likely that the proposal would be passed.

The proposal ran into trouble when Christian and Democratic Union-Czechoslovak People's Party (KDU-ČSL) refused to approve the bill sponsored by their coalition partner, the Social Democrats. Their disapproval centered on the extent of trade unions rights and power, which the KDU-ČSL believed was not related directly to the protection of all employees but, to ensure the institutional security of unions. Nevertheless, the Social Democrats, with the support of its Prime Minister Jiří Poroubek, stated that they would push for Labor Code in the Chamber of Deputies with or without help from their coalition partners (Zvěřina, 2006).

The Civic Democrats (ODS) and the two junior ruling coalition parties the Christian Democrats (KDU-ČSL) and the Freedom Union opposed the proposed changes because, in addition to enhancing union powers, it would be more difficult for employers to terminate and replace "unproductive" personnel (Dnes, 2005, http://www.zdenek-skromach.cz). The Civic Democrats (ODS), backed the employers, rejected the bill.

President Vaclav Klaus sent the new labor code back to the Chamber of Deputies. Vaclav Klaus, founder of the opposition political party Civic Democrats (ODS) and ODS's honorary chairman, exercised his veto of the labor legislation. After vetoing the bill, Klaus said it was not "modern" enough. He said the bill would increase power differences between employers and employees, giving preference to unions. He called the code inflexible, said it would destabilize the power balance between employers and unions, and increase unemployment. He also said parts of the bill were at odds with the Czech Constitution (Lidové noviny, May 3, 2006, http://lidovky.zprávy.cz).

Disputes Over Specific Policies: Minimum Wages and Union Powers

Another dispute involved an initiative by the Civic Democrats to abolish the minimum wage in favor of state-guaranteed minimum income. Finance Minister Bohuslav Sobotka, acting chairman of the Social Democrats, was very critical this proposal as well as other Civic Democrat proposals to allow employers to dismiss an employees without just cause, cutting short the notice period from two months to one, as well as the extending the trial period for secure employment from 3 to 12 months. Sobotka denounced these proposals as "asocial" (ČTK, November 29, 2005).

According to the Social Democrats, a new code labor was necessary because the core elements of the extant code dated back to the Communist code of 1965. Its numerous amendments, qualifications, and inconsistencies made it confusing and ambiguous with regard to fulfilling EU require-ments. The Social Democrats claimed that their proposal reflected the needs of the Czech market economy, and would overcome provisions in the 1965 code that restricted the autonomy and power of labor unions and would provide for rights of individual employees (Kučera, 2006). The proposal based on the principle of contractual freedom, enabled parties to define their mutual obligations toward one another as legally binding commitments.

Disagreements over the proposal centered on the power of unions and the relative power of employee rights. The ODS took a strong position against it, arguing that the proposal was as an obstacle to free market, would impede economic growth and employment, and, moreover, had unconstitutional features (Hovet, 2006).

Debates over the bill escalated conflicts between left and right wings in the coalition government. Yet the majority of Social Democrats and Communists in the Chamber of Deputies overrode the Senate, and the Presidential veto with total of 111 votes. Only 101 were needed (Parlament České Republiky (2006b), www. psp.cz/sqw/historie.sqw?o = 4&T = 1154). The new Labor Code took effect in January 1, 2007.

The parliamentary disputes over the new labor code reflected wider disagreements in Czech society, especially within the labor union movement and in the business community (Zvěřina, 2006, http://lidovky.zpravy.cz/zbuldozerovany-zakonik-0wt-/). Many union opponents disagreed with the proposed legislation because it enhanced the powers of the strongest unions in the bargaining process. The prior law required the consensus of all involved trade unions within companies to reach an agreement. However, the new statute, Labor Code No. 262/2006 sec. 24(2) specifies that, if the trade unions fail to reach consensus on procedures during collective bargaining, the employer may reach an agreement with the organization that has the most members. Some professional unions were of the opinion that such a practice would restrict the rights of smaller trade unions active within a company and, as a result, could lead to the demobilization of minority organizations. Another example is a statement of director of the Confederation of Industry of the Czech Republic (Svaz průmyslu a dopravy ČR0), stated in the "Lidové noviny" newspaper that ČSSD did not take on board more than 700 objections to the legislative intention of the act and 2,000 comments and employers considerations on the bill itself (Kadavá, 2005).

While business interests were critical of powers provided to unions and extended rights to employees, employer's associations approved of a new "working hours account" scheme that apply to all companies, including those without unions. This new provision will make it possible to regulate employees' weekly working hours when this is necessary to react to changing needs for labor depending on shifting demand, while keeping pay constant. So-called "partial-unemployment" permits employers to pay workers

60–80% of their usual salary instead of laying them off. Overtime pay would be voluntary and the draft also gives employers more flexibility in firing sick or handicapped workers (Mlčochová, 2005).

CONCLUSIONS

International approaches to law focus on relations among nation states and among nation states and regional and global organizations and protocols. These approaches entail a reworking of established frameworks that have emphasized comparative rather than international inquiry. This case study of labor law change in the Czech Republic is based on a reworking of Unger's typology (1976) in light of Cassese's (2006) processual approach to the globalization of law. It aims at demonstrating the value of this approach by analyzing labor law as changing from a bureaucratically imposed form under communism to a form established through the rule of law based, in part, on voluntary compliance with bureaucratic requirements for EU membership.

Labor law reform in the Czech Republic has been part of a broader process of political, economic, and legal transformation. With the collapse of the communist regime and the independence of the Czech Republic, a process of integration in the European Union and international political and economic relations took a greater importance in developing a new regime of labor law. In particular, EU principles were brought into the political institutions and discourses of the Czech Republic. In this way, international standards combined with internal social and legal conditions in Czech political life to raise both new patterns of conflict and new possibilities for law and social life. However, once the Czech Republic pursued its commitment to EU membership, it is also voluntarily subjected every domestic legislation process to the examination and evaluation of the EU community (Vachudova, 2005).

Communist trade unions and European Treaty requirements for union roles and rights in labor relations differed considerably in terms of the independence of unions and their powers. Most significantly, labor law under communism and in the period of entry in the EU differed on collective bargaining. The structure of the communist union depended on compulsory membership and unions acted as mediators between their members and the bureaucratic implementation of policies and decisions made by the state controlled by the Communist Party (Labor Code No.65/1965 Part 22 and 23 Coll.). Unions did not represent a voluntary membership nor did they have the right to bargain. Rather than a free association of workers engaged in bargaining with their employer counterparts, as was the case after EU membership, unions under communism organized workers primarily for the purpose of realizing production targets set by the Soviet styled centralized planning system.

While the rule of law was dominant in realizing labor law reform, it was framed through voluntarily accepted restraints in a historical context that had been shaped by Communist Party domination. In this light, Czech labor law reform exemplifies a form of "societal constitutionalism" in which action is voluntarily conducted on the basis of institutionally established values (Sciulli, 1992). The study demonstrates that types of law rooted in international sources may interact over time and across levels of political and legal action facilitating wider economic and political participation.

REFERENCES

Act on Salaries and Readiness to Work in Budget-Funded Institutions No. 143/1992 Coll.

Boeri, T., & Terrell, K. (2002). Institutional determinants of labor reallocation in transition. *Journal of Economic Perspectives, 16*(1), 51–76.

Boyle, E. H., & Preves, S. (2000). National legislating as an international process: The case of anti-female-genital-cutting laws. *Law and Society Review, 34*, 401–432.

Boyle, E. H., & Thompson, M. (2001). National politics and resort to the European commission on human rights. *Law and Society Review, 35*, 1001–1024.

Bretherton, C. (2001). Gender mainstreaming and EU enlargement: Swimming against the tide? *Journal of European Public Policy, 8*, 60–81.

Carey, J. M., Formanek, F., & Karpowicz, E. (1999). Legislative autonomy in new regimes: The Czech and polish cases. *Legislative Studies Quarterly, 24*(4), 569–603.

Casale, G., Kubínková, M., & Rýchly, L. (2001). Social dialogue – the Czech success story. International Labour Office, Geneva. Available at http://www-ilo-mirror.cornell.edu/public/english/dialogue/ifpdial/downloads/czech.pdf

Cassese, S. (2006). The globalization of law. *International Law and Politics, 37*, 973–993.

Cazes, S., & Nešporová, A. (2003). *Labour markets in transition: Balancing flexibility and security in Central and Eastern Europe.* Geneva: International Labour Organization.

Český Statistický Úřad (ČSU). (2004). Zaměstnanost a nezaměstnanost v ČR podle výsledku VŠPS. Available at www.czso.cz/csu/csu.nsf/kalendar/2004-zam

Council Decision 2003/57 8/EC of 22 July 2003 on guidelines for the employment policies of the Member State. *Official Journal of the European Union,* L 197/13, 5.8.2003.

Criminal Administrative Code No. 88/1950 Coll.

Criminal Administrative Procedure Code No. 89/1950 Coll.

Criminal Code No. 86/1950 Coll.

Criminal Procedure Code No. 87/1950 Coll.

Czechoslovakia, National Census. (1980). Census of population, houses and apartments Czechoslovakia 1.11.1980. Sčítanie l'udu, domov a bytov 1.11.1980. Obyvatel'stvo, domy, byty a domácnosti SSR. Edited by Federální statistický úřad. Praha 1982/Edited by Slovenský štatistický úřad. Bratislava 1982, 28.

ČTK. (2005). Middle class would pay for ODS plan – Kalousek in press. November 29. Available at http://www.prague.st/upload_ctk/articles/czech-ods-reforms-reactions-press_20051129F00801.php

Dezalay, Y., & Garth, B. G. (1996). *Dealing in virtue: International commercial arbitration and the construction of a transnational legal order*. Chicago: University of Chicago Press.

Dnes, M. F. (2005). Koalice jednala o zákoníku práce, shody nedosáhla. September 20. Available at http://www.zdenek-skromach.cz

Elman, R. A. (2001). Testing the limits of European citizenship: Ethnic hatred and male violence. *NWSA Journal*, *13*(3), 49–69.

European Commission Progress Report Summary. (1999). *Central Europe Review*, *1*(17), October 18.

Flanagan, R. J. (1998). Regional studies of comparative international industrial relations: Institutional reformation in Eastern Europe. *Industrial Relations*, *5*(3), 295–312.

Forced Labor Camps Act No. 247/1948 Coll. (Zákon o táboroch nútenej práce 25 č. 247/1948 Zb. október 1948).

Goetz, K. H., & Wollmann, H. (2001). Governmentalizing central executives in post communist Europe: A four country comparison. *Journal of European Public Policy*, *8*, 864–887.

Hovet, J. (2006). Labor Code may face early court challenge. *Czech Business Weekly*, May 22.

International Labour Office, Convention (No. 98) from 1949 Right to organize and collective bargaining. Available at http://www.ilo.org/ilolex/english/reportforms/pdf/22e098.pdf

Kadavá, Ch. (February 2, 2005). *Některé problémy transformace Českých drah. Research Institute for Labor and Social Affairs*. Praha: Czech Republic.

Konig, K. (1992). The transformation of a "Real Socialist" administrative system into a conventional West European system. *International Review of Administrative Sciences*, *58*, 147–161.

Krygier, M. (1990). Marxism and the rule of law: Reflections after the collapse of communism. *Law and Social Inquiry*, *15*(4), 633–663.

Kučera, P. (2006). MPs set to pass 'flawed' Labor Code. *Czech Business Weekly*, April 18. Available at http://www.cbw.cz/phprs/2006041831.html

Labor Code No. 65/1965 Coll. as amended.

Lidové noviny (May 3, 2006) Klaus vetoval 'nejhorší zákon roku'. Available at http://lidovky.zprávy.cz

Malý, K., & Sivák, F. (1993). *Dějiny státu a práva v českých zemích a na Slovensku do roku 1918*. Praha: H&H.

Mlčochová, J. (2005). Labor bill favors unions. *Czech Business Weekly*, February 7. Available at http://www.cbw.cz/phprs/2005020714.html

Mother's Earning Act No. 154/1969 Coll.

Munich, D., Svejnar, J., & Terrell, K. (2005). Returns to human capital under the communist wage grid during the transitions to a market economy. *Review of Economic and Statistics*, *83*(1), 100–123.

Parlament České Republiky. (2006a). Sněmovní tisk 1153 Vl. N. Zákoníku práce. Available at www.psp.cz/sqw/historie.sqw?o = 4&T = 1153

Parlament České Republiky. (2006b). Sněmovní tisk 1154 Novela zákoníku práce. Available at www. psp.cz/sqw/historie.sqw?o = 4&T = 1154

Pollert, A. (2003). Women, work and equal opportunities in post-communist transition. *Work, Employment and Society*, *17*(2), 331–357.

Sciulli, D. (1992). *Theory of societal constitutionalism*. Cambridge: Cambridge University Press.

The Constitution of Czech republic, Act No. 1/1993 Coll. of the Czech National Council of 16 December 1992 as amended.

Treaty establishing a Constitution for Europe. (2004). *Official Journal of the European Union* 310/C61 from December 16. Available at http://eur-lex.europa.eu/JOHtml.do? uri = OJ:C:2004:310:SOM:en:HTML

Turnock, D. (1995). Rural transition in Eastern Europe. *Geo Journal, 36*(4), 420–426.

Unger, R. (1976). *Law in modern society: Toward a criticism of social theory*. The New York: The Free Press.

Ústava Československe socialisticke republiky 100/1960 Sb. (The Constitutional of the Czechoslovak Socialist Republic No. 100/1060 Coll.) English version available at http://www.psp.cz/docs/

Vachudova, M. A. (2005). *Europe undivided: Democracy, leverage, and integration after communism*. Oxford: Oxford University Press.

Vaughan-Whitehead, D. C. (2003). *EU enlargement versus social Europe: The uncertain future of the European social model*. UK: Edward Elgar Publishing.

Vrabcová, E. (2001). Pracovné tábory a tábory nútenej práce. In: F. Mikloško, G. Smolíková & P. Smolík (Eds), *Zločiny komunizmu na Slovensku 1948–1989* (pp. 367–402). Slovakia: Prešov.

Zvěřina, M. (2006). Zbuldozerovaný zákonník. *Lidové noviny*, May 13. Available at http:// lidovky.zpravy.cz/zbuldozerovany-zakonik-0wt-/

Žáček, P. (2000). Boje o minulost (Struggles for the Past). Czech Republic, Brno, Barrister and Principal.